HOLISTIC CHRISTIANITY

HOLISTIC CHRISTIANITY

The Vision of Catholic Mysticism

by

Joseph Conti, Ph.D.

First Edition 2005

Published in the United States by
Paragon House
1925 Oakcrest Avenue, Suite 7
St. Paul, MN 55113

Library of Congress Cataloging-in-Publication Data

Conti, Joseph G.
Holistic Christianity : the vision of Catholic mysticism / by Joseph Conti.—1st ed.
p. cm.
Includes bibliographical references (p. 331) and index.
ISBN 1-55778-830-8 (pbk. : alk. paper) 1. Spirituality. 2. Christianity. 3. Holism. I. Title.
BV4501.3.C6624 2005
230—dc22

2005016532

The paper used in this publication meets the minimum requirements of American National Standard for Information Sciences—Permanence of Paper for Printed Library Materials, ANSIZ39.48-1984.

Manufactured in the United States of America
10 9 8 7 6 5 4 3 2 1

For current information about all releases from Paragon House, visit the web site at http://www.paragonhouse.com

Joseph Conti's website is http://www.catholicmysticism.com

This book is dedicated to a nameless Roman Catholic priest whom I telephoned when my mother, Adele, was on her deathbed in 2001.

This man was unknown to me, but I called him in my family's hour of need (at 1 AM in fact) and he came straightway to her bedside, prayed and comforted, and gave her Last Rites.

Although I don't remember his name, his devoted face is the face of the Church I love.

ACKNOWLEDGMENTS

I want to thank...

My father and mother, Mickey and Adele Conti, in whose gentleness I first experienced God's love in this world, and by whose faithfulness I was baptized into Life beyond this world.

Bernadette Roberts for her profound contribution to the literature of Christianity.

My editor at Paragon House, Rosemary Yokoi, for her very generous support, wise advice, and spiritual friendship.

Ben Stumpf for his many insightful manuscript suggestions over many months; Ric Williams, for suggesting that I develop certain motifs more fully, which proved fruitful; Keith Hansen, for his thoughtful comments on so many chapters; Brad Stetson, whose keen literary sensibility aided me throughout this project; and Stacy Shotsberger Russo, for comments that aesthetically enriched this book.

I would like to express my love and appreciation for those friends of God with whom I make a yearly retreat at the New Camaldoli Hermitage at Big Sur—and the monks who serve God on that mountain of contemplation.

My faithful prayer friends Lidia Sinde, Jack Mewes, Soledad Elizondo, Vera Termokish, Mitzi Bataglia, Celia Dascano, and Colleen Wildery.

Great thanks to a very talented artist, Lisa Ruiz, who created the book's illustrations.

And to all the others in whose souls I have beheld the beautiful, you have helped me understand that: "We live only to discover beauty. All else is a form of waiting" (Kahlil Gibran).

CONTENTS

INTRODUCTION

What is *Holistic* Christianity?

"A Christian who searches is, in his innermost efforts, searching with everyone for everything."
—Henri de Lubac, S.J.

In the mid-1960s, soon after the movie *The Sound of Music* had premiered in the United States, it was scheduled to play in a foreign theater as half of a double-feature. The manager realized he didn't have time to show the whole movie because of the twin bill. He would have to edit it.

Guess what he cut out?

He cut out all the songs in *The Sound of Music.*

Ridiculous? Yes, but really not so rare as may first appear. A moment's reflection reveals the strange truth that such absurd editing is very common in daily living.

Have you ever felt this? Have you felt that there exists a deep magic to life but that somehow this magic is being edited out?

Certainly you have had vivid glimpses of such enchanted dimensions. They come easily to you when you are relaxed and in contact with nature. The perfume of the jasmine flower in the night air. Ocean waves foaming on glinting grey beach rocks. A fall afternoon drive through pine-crested hills.

You feel in these moments ineffable beauty, nothing less than life beckoning to life. Such moments are episodes of high intuition. Of precious contact with life triumphant. They show that vital energies within us have not forgotten the true promise of life. These parts are ever in joyous revolt, in ecstatic rebellion against the superficial, the mechanical, the artificial. The French philosopher Blaise Pascal expresses the protest of the soul:

> We labor unceasingly
> to preserve an imaginary existence,
> and neglect the real.

Along these lines, a story is told about the very first performance of Beethoven's Ninth Symphony

At its conclusion, as the long applause from the awestruck, delirious audience reluctantly ended, a child was heard to wonder aloud, "What must we do *now?*"

A beautiful question, isn't it? The child is moved by beauty to ask how to live in the light of beauty. And you have wondered, too, in moments of deep enchantment, "What shall I do *now?*"

"How can I invite this overarching beauty into all aspects of my life?"

These are the questions that have moved you to open this book. That's good. These are our questions, too.

How shall we live in the light of the deep beauty of life we sense? How can our days and nights be made one with the overarching goodness of existence we feel?

We will be meditating on these questions under a phrase which acclaims the superlative generosity of Life: holistic Christianity.

The pairing of "holistic" and "Christianity" is, of course, provocative. To some, they are quite incongruous terms, irreconcilable visions. But as we shall see, they are not. Holistic Christianity is avid for all that is true, wholesome, and authentically superb in all areas of life.

> [W]hatever is true,
> whatever is noble,
> whatever is right,
> whatever is pure,
> whatever is lovely,
> whatever is admirable—
> if anything is excellent or praiseworthy—
> think about such things.
>
> —*Philippians 4:8*

An unforgettable expression of this principle occurs in the final pages of Kahlil Gibran's masterpiece, *The Prophet.* Almustapha—a seeker of truth—has lived for years abroad in quest of the luminous depths of life. On the morning of his sea-departure back home, he is asked by villagers to share what he has realized during his days among them.

They ask him questions relating to diverse elements of living—love, marriage, clothing, work, home, beauty, conversation—and he speaks on each. Finally, an old priest implores, "Speak to us of Religion." Almustapha says:

> Have I spoken this day of aught else?
>
> Is not religion all deeds and all reflection,
> And that which is neither deed nor reflection, but a wonder and a surprise springing in the soul, even while the hands hew the stone or tend the loom?[1]

Does this expansive vision match your own intuition of what religion and spirituality are really about?

You might be wondering if by the phrase "holistic Christianity" I am describing some new denomination of Christianity. I am not. Holistic Christianity is not a new denomination, but simply the flower of Catholic Christianity unfolding her own holistic depths.

Try These Experiments

By "holistic," many contemporary presentations mean a vital partnership of mind and body, unified to invite wellness and fulfillment. The mind-body connection is easy to demonstrate. Think of a lemon in your hand. See clearly its bright yellow. Feel its smooth, slightly oily texture. Now imagine biting into it. Think of its juicy pulp in your mouth—visualize it clearly. Is your mouth watering yet? If so, your thoughts have affected your body, proving the holistic unity of mind and body.

The powerful effects of thoughts on the body are well-documented. According to Herbert Benson, M.D., of the Harvard Medical School,

---

[1] Kahlil Gibran, *The Prophet,* (New York, NY: Alfred Knopf, 1998), p. 77. Used with permission.

chronic activation of stressful thoughts can harm the body, wearing down its immune system, elevating blood pressure, and impairing memory.[2] Ways to calm the mind, including prayer, have been clinically demonstrated to improve health.[3]

And *vice versa*—body may affect mind. Right now, try taking a deep breath and slowly exhaling. You feel relaxed, don't you? Your body has relaxed your mind.

Some seekers of holistic wellness are agnostic, convinced that mind and body are ultimate dimensions of human nature, and that there is nothing spiritual beyond them. Others are theists, intuiting a third principle of human nature—"spirit" or "soul." They believe in spiritual holism and endeavor to bring body, mind, and spirit into vital rapport with a further, overarching reality: God.

Many who are drawn to spiritual holism have found Eastern philosophies particularly congenial to their outlook. A look at the eight-part system of Raja Yoga, a spiritual discipline of Hinduism, suggests why this is so. As you look at a listing of its eight parts below, notice how Raja Yoga tries to integrate the moral sense, the body, the intelligence, and subtle spiritual capacities, for a unified ascent to the condition of enlightenment:

ethical don'ts—*yama*
ethical do's—*niyama*
body postures—*hatha*
breathing exercises—*pranayama*
withdrawing the senses—*pratyahara*
mental concentration practices—*dharana*
meditation—*dhyana*
spiritual unity with God—*samadhi*[4]

---

[2] Herbert Benson, M.D., Jule Corliss and Geoffrey Cowley, "Brain Check," *Newsweek,* September 27, 2004, p. 46.

[3] *Ibid.,* p. 47.

[4] Robert S. Ellwood and Barbara A. McGraw, *Many Peoples, Many Faiths: Women and Men in the World Religions,* seventh edition, (Upper Saddleriver, NJ: Prentice Hall, 2002), p. 74.

Because contemporary teachers of Hinduism and Buddhism often accent integral spirituality, many people conclude that the spiritual homeground of holism must be Hinduism or Buddhism, or some other far Eastern religion or philosophy.

An Intuition of Wholeness

Clearly, for some people, holism's appeal rides far beyond its health benefits, but resonates more deeply, even to the soul. Depth psychology suggests as much. Carl Jung suggested that the essential human drive is not the quest for power (Alfred Adler), or the sex drive and the death instinct (Sigmund Freud), but the quest for wholeness, for self-unity. Perhaps the enchantment of holistic healing therapies springs from this universal inner drive.

But another level of inspiration may be posited. Beyond psychological explanations of holism's attractiveness, our passion for interconnections may ultimately arise from our immeasurable metaphysical roots—our roots in Spirit, which inspire in us a divine nostalgia for the oneness of God, the ultimate Whole. Made in the "image of God," the exemplar of all unity, we innately yearn for wholeness and integrity.[5]

A venerable maxim of Christian philosophy speaks to this: the cause is seen in the effect. There are traces, vestiges, imprints, of causes in all effects. Touch a flame to the tip of an incense stick and the cause (heat of the flame) now appears in one of its effects—the radiant red-orange glow of the stick. So it is that the unity of God, the First Cause of all, appears as microcosmic effects in the human person—including in our profound aptitude for wholeness.

But the maxim itself suggests that the mind-body holism does not go far enough. For if God is ultimate Wholeness and the cause of all things seen and unseen, then the unitary effect of this supreme Cause must ramify throughout all creation. In other words, great unities must exist far beyond the mind-body partnership.

[5] Genesis 1:27.

A Surprisingly Holistic Christianity

Christianity agrees with holism that the mind and body are powerfully interactive. We are not angels, insisted St. Thomas Aquinas, a giant of medieval Catholicism, we are not partless, non-material beings, but a unity of matter and mind, humming with vital parts. Moreover, Christianity agrees with spiritual holism that the soul and God are intrinsic to life as a whole. A vision of life that would leave them out no more resembles the fullness of life than a bucket of yellow paint resembles sunshine.

Many versions of spiritual holism are presented today in books and workshops, each affiliated with a particular religious or philosophical outlook. Each distinctly describes the dynamics of the mind-body-spirit partnership, and some offer visions of unities beyond this partnership, including supernatural and cosmic unities. But my purpose in this book will not be to describe this multitude of views.

Rather, I will be suggesting that the mind-body-spirit partnership, and the remarkable and vast unities that exist beyond it, may be richly elaborated in the framework of Christianity. This conclusion will surprise many, as popular opinion seems to look everywhere but Christianity to locate a spiritual context for holism, especially in far Eastern religions and philosophies, as noted.

Surely, sublime holistic intuitions exist in non-Christian religions and philosophies. But my thesis is that Christianity, particularly Catholic Christianity, is uniquely equipped to carry the holistic intuition to its full fruition. I will try to show how Catholicism discloses most truly an intricate profusion of unities which harmoniously criss-cross seen and unseen worlds, like many-colored ribbons in a spring breeze.

"The whole of Christianity," wrote Emile Mersch, S.J., "is unity."[6] To borrow an exquisite phrase from C.S. Lewis, Christianity reveals the "Great Dance" of God's interacting with creation, a grand procession

---

[6] Emile Mersch, S.J., *The Theology of the Mystical Body,* trans. Cyril Vollert, S.J., (St. Louis, MO: B. Herder Book Co., 1952), p. 37.

of personal meaning and divine providence, an interlacing that Lewis called "enamored and inter-inanimated circlings."[7]

We might say that the mind-body-spirit partnership is one such circling—with Spirit as its graced center. But many other circlings exist (termed in this book *holisms,* in the plural). They exist because God, the ultimate Unity, creates unities as a rose exhales perfume. As revealed by Christ, God is a Trinity, a sacred mystery of Three-in-One. "Since He is a communion of Persons within a unity of a single life, His work will be one of community and unity"[8] (Roger Hasseveldt, S.J.). In sum, God's work is intrinsically holistic.

An Interlacing Brightness

"God," said St. Bonaventure, "is a sphere whose center is everywhere and whose circumference is nowhere." God is equally present at every point in creation, making every point equally a divine Center. Look around you now. At every point in your immediate environment, God is equally, centrally present! And this divine Everywhere is knocking on our hearts even now in myriad ways. To meditate on holisms is to ponder many ways that God is interacting with us through divine spheres of influence.

We will be meditating on fifteen holisms of the Christian revelation, each flowering from a distinct dimension of the divine and enlivening a specific kind of wholeness:

- Holism of the Mind-Body
- Holism of the Absolute
- Holism of the Sacraments
- Holism of Christ's Mysteries
- Holism of Existence
- Holism of the World's Religions
- Holism of Prayer and Patience
- Holism of the Beatific Vision
- Holism of the Christ-Logos
- Holism of Unitive State
- Holism of Knowledge
- Holism of the Face of Love
- Holism of Woman and Man
- Holism of the Mystical Body
- Holism of the Incarnation

---

[7] C.S. Lewis, *Perelandra,* (New, York, NY: Scribner, 1996), p. 219.

[8] Roger Hasseveldt, *The Church: A Divine Mystery,* trans. William Storey, (Notre Dame, IN: Fides Publishers, 1964), p. 21.

As you encounter these holisms in upcoming chapters, please notice two points in their presentation. First, they are illustrated as flowers to evoke their organic interlacing to the whole of life, and to the divine Life of the whole: "I am the vine, you are the branches" (John 15:5). For example, below is the flower that will represent the *Holism of the Unitive State.*

Water Lilies

Why choose the water-lily to represent union with God? A traditional symbol of spiritual understanding, the lily floats very brightly on the surface of a pond, with its blossom open to the sky and its roots in the rich silt below. Likewise, the soul in union with God is involved in the wide experience of life while open, surrendered, receptive to the Spirit.

That was why I chose the water-lily. I chose the other flowers in the same way, for their symbolic and aesthetic impressions. I do not elaborate these associations in the text but leave connections between each flower and the holism it designates to your imagination.

Also, notice that these fifteen holisms are not strangers to one another, but pour over their riches unto a shared, spreading treasure. As each holism has immediate links or affinities to others, in our text you will find a second flower representing a related holism next to the first. And underneath both you will find the word *Affinity* and an explanation of how each of these two holisms resonates with the other and, so finally, with them all.

Think of a garden. When two types of flowers grow side by side (for example, roses and jasmine) the proximity of their perfumes, colors, and shapes produces an integral impression different from that produced by their separate impressions. So it is with the holisms of Christianity. To view holisms side by side is to find how one integrates with the other, synergistically.

A Holistic Vision Discloses Hidden Unities

My aim in applying *holisms* and *holistic* to Christianity is modest. I am not elaborating a new Christian theology, but simply employing the holistic principle to highlight the unitary character of traditional Catholic teaching, especially its mystical theology. In so doing, I am trying to correct an unfortunate tendency to consider in isolation from each another the integral truths which Christ revealed. Such an unwarranted fragmentation sadly obscures their unitive radiance.

I will not be using *holism* in a singular sense, but analogically. For example, the dynamics of the *Holism of the Mind-Body Partnership* are utterly different from that of the Trinity, the *Holism of the Absolute,* because the first involves a divine-human interaction and the second describes the perfect harmony of Love in the uncreated Godhead.

I am surely not developing a comprehensive holistic theory in these pages, but simply suggesting through the metaphor of holism something of the unified character of reality as it redounds from the Holy Trinity. In sum, my hope in applying *holism* to Christianity is to illumine from a new angle the meaning of Christ's prayer:

> I pray…
> that all of them may be
> one,
> Father,
> just as you are in me and I am in you.
>
> —*John 17:20-21*

When John Paul the Great traveled to lands distant from Rome, he would immediately kiss the ground of each land on disembarking from his plane. We may find in this lovely gesture an analogy to Christian holism, which honors the divine brightness where it may be found—in many lands, in diverse fields of reality.

The Great Wreath of Being

In many ways, our journey into the holistic character of Christianity will be a meditation on catholicity, truly grasped. Suggestively, *Catholic* and *holistic* share a Greek root, *kath'holou*, which portrays both universality and intrinsic wholeness.[9] The earliest recorded description of the Christian church as *Catholic*, by St. Ignatius of Antioch in the late first century, C.E., envisioned its unity on earth. *Catholic* indicated that the grace of Christ remained one, unified and universal, even as it spread to many lands and diverse peoples. Yet the catholicity of the Church was not only conceived in physical terms but in metaphysical ones, embracing unseen dimensions, including that of the angels and the blessed of heaven. For the Church is "his body, the fullness of him who fills everything in every way" (Ephesians 1:23). The whole Church is both immediate and transcosmic, as it spans earth and heaven. This immensity of light and love is traditionally called the Mystical Body of Christ.

Just as forms of conventional holism envision a creative give-and-take between mind, body and spirit, so an analogous interaction exists in the Mystical Body. The heavenly blessed (fully abiding in Christ) intercede for the wayfarers of earth, even as the prayers of friends and family rise to bless the journey of the departed, in a circulation of grace. We are thus justified to speak of the *Holism of the Mystical Body*— one of fifteen divine-human interactions, or holisms, of the Christian revelation.

In his classic work, *The Great Chain of Being*, Arthur Lovejoy sketched St. Thomas Aquinas' vision of creation as a Chain of Being

---

[9] Avery Dulles, S. J., *The Catholicity of the Church,* (Oxford: Clarendon Press, 1985), p. 8.

mounting from earth to heaven. We might supplement the hierarchical vision of the Chain of Being with a holoarchical one: a Great Wreath of Being, perhaps. As evergreen fronds are twined into a wreath, so fifteen "enamored and inter-animated" holisms twine through reality, originating in the Holy Trinity. (See figure on the following page.)

The Great Wreath of Being represents all that God, the Trinity, has created, seen and unseen, as well as its uncreated divine Source, Christ. According to classic Christian theology, the Father is the transcendent dimension of God, wholly beyond all creation. So in our Wreath of Being you will find the name of the Father placed above it. The Son, the omnipresent Christ, is throughout all creation—and so the name of the Son is found inside the Wreath. And as the Holy Spirit is the transforming power of God within creation, the name of the Spirit may be found at the divine center of the Wreath. This understanding of the Trinity's relation to creation has been the teaching of the undivided Church for two millennia. Olivier Clement writes:

> The Father is the *God beyond all,*
> the origin of all that is.
>
> The incarnate Son is *God with us,*
> and he who becomes incarnate is none other
> than the Logos who gives form to the world
> by his creative words.
>
> The Spirit is *God in us,* the Breath, *the Pneuma,*
> who gives life to all and brings every object
> to its proper perfection.[10]

[10] Olivier Clement, *The Roots of Christian Mysticism,* (New York, NY: New City Press, 1995), p. 63.

The Great Wreath of Being

The Father-above all

Holism of the Beatific Vision

Have I always appreciated the unitive character of the Christian revelation? Certainly not! For many years I was convinced that Christianity (in its orthodox expressions) was merely a washed-out Churchianity: a superficial, ritualized, external faith that spoke neither to the most poignant yearnings of the heart nor to the most sublime inquiries of the mind, and even less so to the dynamic vitalities of the body.

The possibility of a rapprochement between Christianity and holistic spirituality was to me quite inconceivable. To me, Christianity was unmystical, unphilosophical, unholistic.

In sharp contrast, I viewed certain non-Christian schools of wisdom, especially Hindu yoga, Buddhism, and Taoism, as particularly mystical, philosophical, and thoroughly coherent with holistic principles. I was eventually astonished to discover the holistic character of Christianity. I describe my path to this insight in the first chapter of this book.

I have come to see that love and sacred beauty are the first steps in holistic Christianity and its last steps.

I found that to be true to the Light that holistic Christianity reveals is to discover maturing in us a contemplative, intuitive sensitivity to the knock of truth. We begin to marvel at bright glimpses of the real world. "There is only one real world and that is the world Jesus reveals to us, a world of utter love and security which he has made our own"[11] (Sr. Ruth Burrows).

We discover within our souls a mysterious, shattering, upsurging love for God. We are visited by touches of understanding beyond ordinary knowledge. We see blossoming in our being a strangely crisp awareness of the natural world. And we marvel at a strange sensation rippling through us at odd moments in daily life: an overwhelming gratitude.

Life thanking Life.

[11] Ruth Burrows, *Fire Upon the Earth,* (Denville, NJ: Dimension Books, 1981), p. 63.

CHAPTER 1

Discovering Christianity's Mystic Heart

"Ah, Catholic Church, how utterly I share with you in my own way your passion for the universe!"[1]
—*Paul Claudel*

Imagine a man uncovering a certain rock while clearing some land. A grey, green-tinged rock, quite unremarkable. But then he strikes it with a pick, and it cracks open like a big egg! When he peers into its curious interior, he sees jagged translucent crystal, regal purple. Unexpectedly, he has discovered a huge amethyst egg or "geode," valued for its ethereal inner beauty.

The discovery of this amethyst geode resembles in some ways my discovery of a holistic Christianity. In my superficial understanding of it, Christianity appeared plain-crusted—until I discovered its inner secret.

As noted, for many years I was convinced that Christianity was merely a banal Churchianity, curiously unmystical, unphilosophical, and unholistic, especially given the obvious depth and dynamism of its founder.

That is why I left the Catholic Church when I was sixteen for far Eastern spirituality, which I saw as essentially contemplative, philosophical, and holistic—integrative of body, mind, and spirit.

---

[1] Paul Claudel, *I Believe in God,* Agnes du Sarment, ed., trans. Helen Weaver, (USA: Holt, Rinehart and Winston, 1963), p. 187.

But fifteen years ago I returned to the Church. Why? Think of an architect who has been asked by a king to design a colossal castle. The architect summons a young assistant, new to his duties, to get some parchment so that the architect can sketch his ideas for the expansive castle. But the inexperienced boy returns with just a small bit of parchment. The architect laughs, knowing that his design for the grand castle will not fit on the small page.

I found myself in the position of that assistant when I took a second look at Christianity. I discovered that my idea of Christianity had been absurdly smaller than its stunning realities. I found that the little bit of parchment I had reserved for it could not contain the illimitable Christian mysteries. The mystical, philosophical, and holistic resources I had been seeking elsewhere all of my life were in the Church all along—*par excellence.*

My spiritual journey, like your own, has been filled with curious twists and turns. When I was six years old my father suddenly passed away of a heart attack. I witnessed great pain in my family. In fact, much of my childhood was spent watching my family and friends go through their lives wearing brave masks of good cheer, when I knew that behind those coverings stood fortresses of pain, confusion, and despair. Despite the boisterous Italian temperament of my family, their deepest feelings and yearnings were unspoken. In a deep, intuitive way I resolved, as I moved out of my teenage years and into young adulthood, to find healing wisdom that would mend the divide between the inner and the outer, the personal and the social. That is why the following anecdote, which I came across many years ago, has continued to exercise powerful meaning for me.

One evening in 1808, a gaunt man entered the offices of Dr. James Hamilton in Manchester, England. The doctor, struck by the melancholy appearance of this unexpected visitor, asked: "Are you sick?"

"Yes, doctor. I feel sick unto death!"

The doctor leaned forward on his desk, and carefully studied the man's drawn face. "What are your symptoms, sir?"

Sighing pitifully, the man began: "Doctor, I'm frightened of the world around me. I'm depressed by life. I'm terribly unhappy, nothing amuses me, and I have nothing to live for. If you can't help me, I swear I'll kill myself!"

The doctor regarded the man with sincere compassion. "Good sir, listen to me. Your case is hardly hopeless. You only need to laugh! You need to get some pleasure from life!"

The man looked down and flatly said, "What do you mean?"

"Sir, look at me," said the doctor, in a gentle tone. The man slowly raised his eyes. "The answer to your problems is simple. I advise you to go to the circus tonight to see Grimaldi, the clown. I tell you, he's the funniest man alive! The laughter he will bring you will be your salvation!"

"Doctor," said the man with infinite weariness, "I am Grimaldi."

I learned early the truth of the Grimaldi Syndrome: that secret pain is widespread, poignantly hiding behind fixed social smiles. I remember hoping as a child that this was not the way it had to be. Looking back, I see that I had sensed that religion must play a key role in our deliverance from mere social expressions of happiness and success, though it had not been clear how it would do so.

Fortuitously, these yearnings arose in me in 1968 when I was twelve and the larger culture also seemed to be searching. Conflict over the Vietnam War, Woodstock, the Beatles, the Generation Gap, the assassination of John F. Kennedy, Martin Luther King, Jr., and Robert Kennedy was forcing people to ask the basic questions: Who am I? What is the purpose of my life and my community? Politics was in the air in 1968, both on the international front—the Vietnam War—and the domestic, in the civil rights movement. The philosophy of Martin Luther King, Jr., in particular, held a profound attraction for me. I was drawn to his incisive articulation of an ethic of love, peace, and justice—inspired, he affirmed, by the vitality of Christ's Sermon on the Mount.

As a high school freshman, I devoured King's books (more meditative studies than political tracts), which promised a mending of social division. I also memorized much of the Sermon on the Mount which, through the courageous social witness of King, had sprung to life for me. Though a cradle Catholic, I had never studied the Sermon in close detail, and its discovery was exhilarating. This was a breakthrough for me, this disclosure of the interior dimension of religion: "Blessed are the pure of heart, for they shall see God," (Matthew 5:8); "Be perfect, therefore, as your heavenly Father is perfect" (Matthew 5:48). I was thrilled to see in Christ's words a Way of interior transformation that pointed to a life beyond the Grimaldi Syndrome!

Not only was King's work my introduction to the Sermon, it also introduced me to a noble spirituality of another sort, one that changed my life with equal force. One of King's chief influences was the Hindu sage and activist, Mahatma Gandhi. King saw Gandhi's philosophy of *satyagraha*—truth-power—as a way to apply Christ's Sermon on the Mount in daily affairs and political struggles. My study of Gandhi's life led me, in turn, to study one of his formative influences: the Hindu mystical classic, the *Bhagavad-Gita,* the "Song of God."

The *Gita* is one of India's most beloved texts, as it renewed and expanded the wisdom of Hinduism's most ancient text, the Vedas. The *Gita* teaches a series of spiritual disciplines termed *yoga* (from the Sanskrit root, *yuj* to join or yoke) that invite both self-unity—a unity of body, mind, and soul—and unity with God. God is conceived in the *Gita* as the inmost Reality of human beings, the peaceful Center of the soul beyond the nervous "false self" of cramped egotism. This seemed to me—to continue a motif—an esoteric yet practical way of mending the Grimaldi Syndrome.

Moreover, though my knowledge of Catholic tradition was superficial, I had always been fascinated by the saints' mystical experiences of the divine. (A mystical experience is a vivid contact with God, and a Christian mystic is someone who has often experienced such soul-transforming contact).[2] How remarkable, I thought, that a ray of heaven had broken upon their souls while on earth! I was intrigued by the *Gita's* promise that ecstatic soul-experiences could be systematically cultivated: "When, through the practice of yoga, the mind ceases its restless movements, and becomes still, he [the yogi] realizes the

[2] This preliminary definition will be more precisely elaborated in Chapter 6.

Atman"—the *Atman*, the true Self which the yogi takes to be divine.[3] I was particularly moved by the *Gita's* accent on the indwelling presence of Spirit, the immanence of God, for it spoke to me of God's radical nearness to each of us.

Yes, of course, I thought it highly ironic that the divine realities described by Christ could be most effectively realized through Eastern disciplines *outside* the fold of Christianity. But knowing little of true Catholic tradition, I simply accepted a rather naive explanation of this: that (a) Christ's teaching had been hijacked by the Church and eviscerated of mysticism, and (b) that yoga drove intrinsically and systematically to spiritual transformation, while Christianity fostered such transformation only accidentally.

For about two decades, I was an ardent yoga student, studying with a number of gurus, and with one guru, a swami (a Hindu monk) for eight years. Mark Twain quipped, "I never let my schooling interfere with my education," and his wise comment was not lost on me; I sometimes played hooky from my high school classes in New Jersey, taking buses into Manhattan to study with renowned gurus visiting from India. In addition to enjoying the mystical element of their teaching, I relished its holistic character, including instruction in yogic body postures and rhythmic breathing techniques, meant to artfully center the whole person in Spirit.

I also appreciated yoga's definition of God as supernatural Bliss; indeed, a famous and remarkably beautiful Sanskrit name for God is *Sat-Chit-Ananda,* or "Existence-Knowledge-Bliss." The gurus taught a smooth, relatively unbumpy path of meditation to realization of this Bliss. No wonder I was puzzled and disconcerted when, still in my teens, I came across St. John of the Cross' phrase the "dark night of the soul," which had been briefly footnoted in a yoga book I had been studying. (Tellingly, the author cited St. John as a mystic whose exalted experiences of God proved that he must have transcended Christianity!) As a teen yogi on the fast track to enlightenment, I found St. John's "dark night of the soul" thoroughly unappealing, as it was quite at odds

---

[3] Swami Prabhavananda and Christopher Isherwood, trans., *The Bhagavad-Gita,* (New York, NY: Penguin Books, 1972), p. 66.

with the gurus' sweetness-and-light outline of the spiritual path. I felt sorry that John did not have the benefit of a guru to tell him that God is Bliss, and that he should abandon his morbid nickname, for the inner path to Bliss is, well, blissful (in the insuperable logic of a sixteen-year-old).

Yet, truth be told, all was not sweetness and light in yoga circles. Charlatanism was rife in California ashrams in the 1970s, with self-ordained gurus inventing outlandish neo-yogas to appease egotism rather than to challenge it, as the ancient yoga tradition had. Only years after my apprenticeship in yoga did I realize the extent of the shenanigans. Here and there I came to learn of the fall of many well-known yoga teachers of the 1970s and 1980s in hair-raising scandals that typically didn't make the mainstream press: well-substantiated charges of egomaniacal authoritarianism, sexual abuse, and bilking disciples out of life savings. Fortunately for me, I managed to avoid these gaudy side-shows and study with a number of decent, even sagacious, gurus.

Today I can say that my appreciation endures for what is true, noble, and sublime in yoga and other ancient wisdoms. I know that many true spiritual intuitions came to me through yoga, including the significance of interior quiet, the exposure of the ego's shallow games as key to spiritual reception, and the perception of our cosmos as a temple of God. As I see it, these insights—bright swatches of truth—finally pointed me to what C.S. Lewis referred to in one of his allegories as "the deeper magic still"—the trackless mystery of Christ and His Church, and the Wreath of Being braided by the Trinity.[4]

My re-evaluation of Catholicism came about shortly before my doctoral studies in comparative religion at the University of Southern California. My research into mysticism had led me to a number of extraordinary books authored by Catholic contemplatives, contemporary and ancient. I found in the work of the nineteenth-century Carmelite, Blessed Elizabeth of the Trinity, the doctrine of the indwelling Trinity in the soul, which opened my eyes to the personal interiority of God elaborated in Christianity.

---

[4] C.S. Lewis, *The Lion, the Witch and the Wardrobe,* (New York, NY: HarperCollins, 1978), p. 163.

I found in the masterwork of the twentieth-century Catholic philosopher Jacques Maritain, *The Degrees of Knowledge,* a grand synthesis of the ways of insight, from the simplest sensory perception of a blade of grass to the soul's eternal vision of God, termed by Catholics the *beatific vision.* I was stunned by the contemplative and metaphysical depths of these works. I started to attend noon Mass at the Catholic Church across the street from the USC, and was amazed by the mystical character of the Mass. I began to see that Catholicism was not accidentally, but essentially, mystical. I saw that a view of the Church that left out its mystical foundation would be as incomplete as a version of *Gray's Anatomy* that left out all charts on the circulatory system.

> Purify yourself and you will see heaven in yourself. In yourself you will see angels and their brightness, and you will see their Master with them and in them. The spiritual homeland of the person whose soul has been purified is within. The sun that shines there is the light of the Trinity. The air breathed by the entering thoughts is the Holy Spirit the Comforter. With the person dwell the angels....Such a person rejoices every hour in the contemplation of his soul, and marvels at the beauty that appears, a hundred times brighter than the brightness of the sun....That is the kingdom of God hidden within us, according to the words of the Lord.[5]
>
> —*Isaac of Nineveh*

Here was a God of joy and a way of transformation that was a far, far cry from the superficial "organized religion" I had regularly excoriated in my yoga years. To return to an earlier analogy, the small bit of parchment I had reserved for Christianity vanished, and I began to see that the far-flung cosmos was itself a bit of parchment on which Christ the "Word," the creative *Logos,* had deigned to write a poem of Life.

The gurus of my youth and beyond had typically dismissed Christianity—especially Catholicism—as a watered-down "organized religion," contrary to the personal and committed spirituality of yoga.

[5] Olivier Clement, *The Roots of Christian Mysticism,* (New York, NY: New City Press, 1995), p. 253.

Jesus Christ, they regularly taught, was a Self-realized yogi and not the founder of the religion bearing his name. "Organized" Christianity was the invention of priestcraft and political contrivance.

In a wider context, the gurus' dismissal of organized religion is routinely reinforced by contemporary media, which regularly expresses animus against mainstream Christianity.[6] In this vein I remember, during my yoga days, seeing on television Franco Zeffirelli's cinematic masterpiece, *Jesus of Nazareth,* and nodding in approval at a scene which seemed to support my yogic distaste for organized religion.

Zeffirelli set the scene at night, with Jesus and his twelve apostles talking around a high, sputtering fire. The cinematographer somehow captured the figures in hues reminiscent of rich Michaelangelo-like oils. Evocative, magical, persuasive—it is one of the movie's most haunting scenes. A close-up frames Jesus speaking heartfully to Simon: "And so now I will call you Peter, the rock. And upon this rock I will build *what I must call* my church—the gates of hell will not prevail against it." Years later, when I read the scripture passage which inspired this scene, I realized that the scriptwriter had put words in Jesus' mouth. Jesus never said that He would build "*what I must call* my church" but simply, "I will build my church" (Matthew 16:18). To put a fine point on this, we might contrast a husband's introducing his wife with the words, "I'd like you to meet someone whom I must call my wife," to "I'd like to introduce my wife." The movie scene is a small but suggestive clue to the routinized prejudice against Christianity and organized religion.

The tendency of certain teachers of Eastern mysticism to alienate Christ from the Church is of a piece with their treatment of the Christian mystics. Recall that a mystic is one who has direct, vivid, and transforming experiences of God. The so-called Christian mystics, the yogis assert, are only nominally Christian, not really Christian, because all mysticism is beyond religion. Yoga teachers are not alone in this view. In diverse spirituality circles today the consensus is that all mysticism is the same, and all mystics have come upon the same

---

[6] Bernard Goldberg, *Bias: A CBS Insider Exposes How the Media Distort the News,* (Washington, DC: Regnery Publishing, 2002), pp. 126-130.

high realities of the Spirit. The so-called "Christian" mystics simply use a Christian vocabulary to describe transcendent realities common to Hinduism and Buddhism. The mystics of every religion have come to identical, interchangeable revelations.

Hence the tendency, in these circles, to segregate the Christian mystics from the Church to see them as spiritually belonging to a kind of separate esoteric league of their own, existing above the "unenlightened" teachings of organized Christianity. The mystics are the major leaguers; Christianity is the little league. The mystics have the truth fresh off the fruity bough of transcendental experience; the Church has only stale-crust dogma.

Well-meaning phrases such as "All religions are one" and "All mysticism is one" are repeated so often that the sheer momentum of their repetition appears to substantiate them. I believed these mottos, too, for twenty years, but eventually my studies in comparative religion led me to question these assertions.

My coming to understand the distinctiveness of Christian mysticism was pivotal to my re-awakening to Catholicism. I came to see that Christian mystics such as St. John of the Cross and St. Teresa of Avila were not "Christian" by accidents of historical conditioning, nor merely by their employing "Christian" vocabulary. They were Christian mystics because God disclosed to their hearts certain superlative realities of Christ and of the mystery of the Holy Trinity.

This last point is important because it implies the integral, or holistic, relationship between the Church and her mystics. I came to realize that Church dogma is hardly opposed to authentic mysticism, as many spirituality teachers insist. Rather, dogmas are the fruit of mystical insight; contemplatively pondered, dogmas are mysteries that catalyze the soul's quest for intuitive understanding. These dogmas have been living realities to the Church's mystics—not "stale crust."

This suggests a second point. I saw that Christian mystics were able to give their sublime gifts to the Church only after the Church, the Mystical Body of Christ, first gave to them. The wisdom of the Christian mystics flowered under the regime of the Church's sacraments and were nurtured by the living dogma that fed their meditations. Teresa of Avila succinctly put the true relationship of the mystic to the Church: "I am a daughter of the Church."

Two final points on a pejorative characterization of Catholicism as "organized religion." First, implicit in this critique is the premise that the mystery and beauty of absolute Truth surpasses organization, a premise crystallized in these words: "The mystery is larger than the visible structure and organization of the Church."[7]

That statement sounds like something I might have heard during my yoga years. What would Christian theologians think of it? What would they say about the idea that divine mystery "is larger than the visible structure and organization of the Church"?

Pope John Paul II liked it. I am sure he did because I found those words in a book he authored, *Crossing the Threshold of Hope* (the quote is from the Second Vatican Council). The pope knew well that the divine mystery exceeds the visible structure of the Church.[8] Yet he also knew that Christ has called the Church to transmit His life through the sacraments to each generation and bear witness to His truth.

Let us also remember there is nothing wrong with organization *per se*. You do not need a theologian or philosopher to prove it. Just ask any botanist if she has ever come across an unorganized rose. Indeed, "organization" and "organic" are root-linked words. The Church has an intrinsic organic unity because she has a unifying Soul: the Holy Spirit. The unity of Catholic doctrine, spirituality, mysticism, sacraments, and liturgy is not surprising, given the underlying unicity of her Spirit.

My aim is to make clear in these pages that the mind-body-spirit partnership is a good start at an organic, holistic vision of life, but it is only a hint at the expansive unities to which God is inviting us, "to bring all things in heaven and on earth together" (Ephesians 1:10).

---

[7] John Paul II, *Crossing the Threshold of Hope,* Vittorio Messori, ed., (New York, NY: Alfred A. Knopf, 1994), p. 142.

[8] See especially the Vatican II documents *Gaudiam et spes: Pastoral Constitution on the Church in the Modern World* and *Nostra aetate: Declaration on the Relationship of the Church to Non-Christian Religions.*

Holism limited to the mind-body-spirit partnership bears an unlikeness to holistic Christianity as a nightlight does to the Aurora Borealis.

I recall a letter written by the philosopher Maritain in the mid-1960s to a teenager who had written to him, describing herself "in quest of Beauty." The teenager felt alienated from Christianity, and wondered if Maritain might help her. When I first read Maritain's reply to her I was in my thirties but it resonated with the boy I had been who had taken buses to Manhattan to meditate on God with the gurus, a boy who had dismissed a Christianity he did not really know, only to later discover its secret. Wrote Maritain:

> Yes, you are "in quest of Beauty, of the absolute, of a God who is not one of hate." And how right you are! Your revolt is healthy, because it is a revolt against a God who is not a true God.
>
> The Christianity you were taught as a child is a child's religion. At seventeen your eyes have begun to open on the world as it really is. You are asked to realize that Christianity is a terrible mystery of love, and that the Cross is not a pleasant and comfortable figure of speech protecting those joys over which popular preachers wax so eloquent, but actually a gallows of horror on which God was hanged for love of us.... And God restores all things—invisibly by His love, and the love of his saints who lay down their lives for their friends. Perhaps what I am writing to you here seems to make no sense, but I am writing it all the same because it is the truth, and someday you will see that it is.[9]

---

[9] Bernard E. Doering, *Jacques Maritain and the French Catholic Intellectuals,* (Notre Dame, IN: University of Notre Dame, 1983), p. 239.

CHAPTER 2

How to Experience God's Presence Vividly

"The Catholic is at home in the whole universe...."[1]
—Paul Claudel

Relax your spirit now. Let it settle into a place of unknown energy, purity, wellness. Go ahead, try. Take your time. Become quietly attentive to your breathing for a time. Follow your breath, in and out. Relax.

There—you've done it.

Now from this poised point of departure, set your spirit free, let it travel as it lists. It is moving now, journeying, following an intuition. It moves effortlessly through these pages and back through time, in an easeful piercing of the density of two thousand years to a plain room, a room filled with the scent of roasted lamb, freshly baked bread and bitter herbs.

An upper room of a Jerusalem inn. But what was to be a festive evening has turned to dark confusion. Jesus is speaking of his impending arrest and death. This is the end. The end of days walking together on hilly paths and resting in fragrant groves—days laughing on windswept boats, days amid humble, plaintive crowds and among shoving, raucous enemies. Of lamp-lit intimate evenings together, just fifteen friends or so, with good food and drink—conversation heartily pointing to a new dawn.

---

[1] Paul Claudel, *I Believe in God,* Agnes du Sarment, ed., trans. Helen Weaver, (USA: Holt, Rinehart and Winston, 1963), p. 187.

And it is the end of spare days and solitary desert retreats, when the clothing on one's back was greater than a king's palace, and the constellations were gems enough. Somehow, all of this is ending tonight—racing toward an incredibly tragic end. But Jesus' words and gaze belie this. As usual, he is stealing life from death, and conjuring honey from barren rock. No, this is not the end, somehow. You listen in awe and wonder, as Jesus speaks to the Father:

> All I have is yours, and all you have is mine.
>
> —*John 17:10*

With these words hanging in the air, your spirit is mysteriously drawn elsewhere. It moves through a moonlit night, above the French countryside of the sixteenth-century. Here is the sparsely furnished room of Sister Marie—later to be known as "Blessed Marie of the Incarnation" and recognized as a Christian mystic of profound insight.

She is reflecting on the seventeenth chapter of St. John's Gospel—on the same words you heard uttered a moment ago in the upper room. By the candlelight that flickers on the page before her, her lips suddenly lift in a smile; the Spirit has overshadowed her understanding with new light. Effortlessly reading her thoughts now, you too are caught up in the ecstatic vision of truth she has been given: Marie no longer finds herself a spectator to Jesus' affirmation of unity with the Father, but knows that she too has been qualified by lavish grace to personally affirm

> All I have is yours, and all you have is mine.

She opens a daybook and her quill is swift on the page:

> Glorify yourself in me and triumph over her who belongs to You because my glory consists in belonging to you and you to me. Everything you have is mine.[2]

[2] Ronda De Sola Chervin, *Prayers of the Women Mystics,* (Ann Arbor, MI: Servant Publications, 1992), p. 147.

May I suggest that the journey we have just taken from Jerusalem to rural France has revealed a wondrous Gospel truth for us: that Christ's affirmation, "Father, everything of yours is mine" can be *our* grateful words to the Spirit.

We can begin by noting that the spiritual truth, "Father, everything of yours is mine," means that right now, in this present moment, the Spirit is inviting us to an expansive way of being. It is welcoming us to the spiritual vitalities of peace, love, depth, beauty, truth, naturalness, tenderness, and freedom right now.

For these are qualities that inhere in the very nature of the Spirit who created us and who is now, even in this split-second, lovingly sustaining our being in existence: the same Spirit who is "closer than your very breath," as St. Augustine said. Since the very nature of Spirit includes peace, love, freedom, and truth, then right now these spiritual vitalities must be knocking at the door of our hearts! The Christian mystics have testified that these vitalities of being are meant for us now!

> True though it is
> that these are things
> which the Lord gives to whom He wills,
> He would give them to us all
> if we loved Him as He loves us.
> For He desires nothing else
> but to have those to
> whom He may give them.[3]
>
> —*Teresa of Avila*

Yet how many of us fall into the horrible self-hoax of projecting some ideal future moment, some rainbow-tinted "someday," when circumstances will be just right to experience qualities such as peace, soul-depth, freedom, and spiritual rest? The German mystic Meister Eckhart knew better: "Time is what keeps the Light from reaching us. There is no greater obstacle to God than time."

---

[3] Teresa of Avila, *The Interior Castle,* trans. Kieran Kavanaugh, O.C.D., and Otilio Rodriguez, O.C.D., (New York, NY: Paulist Press, 1979).

Yes, Jesus invites us NOW, within the rich and varied texture of daily living, to the vitalities of Spirit:

> I have told you these things,
> so that in me you may have peace.
> In this world you will have trouble.
> But take heart! I have overcome the world.
>
> —*John 16:33*

The purpose of this chapter is to convey the accessibility of the Light, and to offer two keys to experiencing holistic Christianity in daily life. We will start with an revealing exercise. Below you will find a partial list of vitalities which inhere in the Spirit—and therefore are accessible to your spirit NOW. I invite you to take each quality in turn as a soul-focus: a magic window into spiritual possibilities NOW.

As you proceed with the exercise, let each spiritual quality call to your depths. Let it evoke images and feelings from your "spiritual unconscious,"[4] as Jacques Maritain put it—your center in God, which knows the influx of spiritual intuitions. Let each quality tap sublime images and feelings, as in a kind of soulful "Rorschach" test.

To do this, mentally place one idea at a time (peace, love, freedom) in the first blank of the special sentence below, then invite your spiritual unconscious to fill in the second blank. (Re-read the sentence a number of times with the same idea in the first blank, to evoke a rich personal response.) Take your time.

"The flowering of ______ in my life now would mean that____."

- peace
- meditativeness
- wholeness
- naturalness
- self-command
- rest
- awareness
- love
- honesty
- uniqueness
- wisdom
- healing
- listening
- freedom
- depth
- creativity
- adventure
- empathy
- growth
- kindness
- enchantment

[4] Jacques Maritain, *Creative Intuition in Art and Poetry,* (New York, NY: Pantheon Books, 1953), pp. 242-243.

I hope the exercise prompted you to new ways of understanding. Notice this superlative fact: we can invite as much of each of these vitalities as we want. Nothing stops our openness to these vitalities—except our own refusal of them. Look again at the list and notice how each one relates to the others; their interrelationship and symphonic reinforcement constitute the *Holism of Existence.*

The *Holism of Existence* finds all human endeavor that seeks to please God enchanted with spiritual significance.

Holism of Existence

Holism of Woman and Man

Affinity: The *Holism of Woman and Man* (Chapter 15)

Whatever thoughtfulness, generosity, and delight we experience in marriage and family that draw us into the divine milieu—these are very bright participations in the Spirit.

Union With God

Imagine yourself a visitor to a tropical land, spending some time on a tour. The guide directs your attention to some flowers in the distance, a low-growing palm she identifies as the "Bird of Paradise." As you walk toward it, she points out that from this distance, orange-winged birds appear to cluster around its long green stalks. But as you reach them, you see how the mild optical illusion works. The "birds" are really winglike orange and blue flowers that blossom from the long stalks.

A much more subtle illusion confuses us in daily life: the false and disastrous belief that happiness and meaning can be found separate from God. Because meaning and vitality are indivisible from God, Christianity orients us to union with God in daily life, and anticipates not only our coming to a permanent union with God in this lifetime, but finally to the tranquil light and love of the Trinity.

It is commonly thought that only Eastern religions and philosophies posit a radical change in being in this life—a transformation traditionally termed enlightenment. Not so. Christianity too posits a radical change, a permanent transformation beyond the ego in this life—enlightenment in Christ, if you will. The Christian mystics have called this transformation variously the unitive state, transforming union, and the unitive way.[5] The experiments in truth you will be invited to in this chapter will be initiations into two great means to union with Christ.

Experiments in Truth

A friend once said to me that his Buddhist approach to truth, unlike that of Christianity, can be verified by practice. Christians, he said, walk by faith (which to him meant a memorized belief system), while the truths of the Buddhist path are experimentally verifiable.

My friend's critique speaks to the grand human yearning to directly experience the ultimate reality—a most noble yearning, and one for which Christians ought to be grateful to Buddhists for sounding down through the ages. And yet his critique misunderstands Christianity on two points.

First, it misconceives the Christian understanding of faith, as it confuses faith with mere memorized belief, which faith is not. Faith, most deeply fathomed, is thoroughly mystical. As the mystic St. John

---

[5] *The Collected Works of St. John of the Cross,* trans. Kieran Kavanaugh, O.C.D., and Otilio Rodriguez, O.C.D., (Washington, DC: ICS Publications, 1991), p. 477.

of the Cross said, faith is "divine light exceeding all understanding."[6] Yes, Christians do walk by faith—but that faith is far more than memorized belief, as we shall see.

Second, the critique incorrectly imagines that the truth of Christ is not verifiable through practice. It is verifiable at its deepest core. Nor did Christ discourage this experiment, but explicitly invites us to it:

> If anyone chooses to do God's will
> he will find out whether my teaching
> comes from God or whether I speak
> on my own.
>
> —*John 7:17*

The balance of this chapter invites you to undertake two specific experiments in truth. Practiced earnestly and consistently, these experiments will reveal to your heart the mystic character of Christianity—reveal it like the sounding of a bell reveals its hidden musical lustre. The first experiment is in prayer, a practice we will call the *Self-Release Prayer.* The second experiment involves the principle, *Resent Not Evil.* At the end of the chapter, we will integrate these practices to unveil their holistic unity.

The Self-Release Prayer

Christ said: "Love the Lord your God with all your heart and with all your soul and with all your mind" (Matthew 22:37). The meaning of the commandment "Love God" is manifold—infinite, really, for God's very nature is Love. But one particular meaning has our attention now, a meaning prominent in the works of the Christian mystics. They taught a specific disposition of prayer that expresses love and invites transforming grace: the *Self-Release Prayer.*

Though the phrase *Self-Release Prayer* is not found verbatim in the literature of Christian mysticism, this approach to communion with God has been taught for millennia under many other names. The

[6] *Ibid.,* p. 177.

description of the Prayer and its fruits remains from century to century essentially the same.

To understand this Prayer, we start with the commonsense premise that to love someone is to desire the beloved's presence. So when Christ says, "Love God," He would have us cleave to God's Being here and now. This adhering to God in a simple movement of love is the Self-Release Prayer.

What does this prayer ask for? Only the blessing of God's presence.

How is it prayed? By turning away from self (which means letting go of self-absorbed thinking, if even for a moment) in loving openness to God's immediate presence. Try this now. Let yourself go silent within, and in that state of simple being become aware of God's silent presence to you.

Silence is your openness to God who is beyond thought. And God answers your loving receptivity with a benediction of divine healing silence.

This is the great secret of the mystics' sayings—

> "If thou goest out of self, God without doubt goeth in" (Blessed Johannes Tauler).
>
> "Empty yourself for the love of God" (Teresa of Avila).
>
> "Go out of what is your own" (Meister Eckhart).

Try the Self-Release Prayer again, this time a little differently. Open up your senses. Look around you, but without self-reference—simply look. Now let the space of silence that this quiet looking has opened in you become an openness to God's immediate presence. Let your silence invite God's silent presence to you. If a bird is chirping outside (as one is as I write this), simply listen to its song in the context of God's silent presence. Listen without ego-focused thought for a moment, in loving receptivity to the divine. Delight in the mystic stillness that visits your heart, bespeaking a contact beyond words with your Creator.

Perhaps you have never prayed in this way. There are many authentic forms of prayer, each a distinct way of openness to God. The Self-

Release Prayer is one. It is a true and transforming communion with the Supreme.

A Practical Expression of Contemplative Prayer

A matchless description of the Self-Release Prayer comes from the Carmelite contemplative, Blessed Elizabeth of the Trinity (1880-1906); its purport is:

> Go out of yourself
> in order to adhere to God
> by a very simple, wholly loving movement
> which allows God to imprint Himself on you and
> *to transform the soul into Himself.*[7]

Certainly it is not wrong to ask God to help us in prayer, even in our smallest concerns. But that is not the purpose of this Prayer. Let us take each part of Elizabeth's instructions in turn, as they are an eminently practical expression of the contemplative dimension of Christianity.

"Go out of yourself." It is important to emphasize that Elizabeth's meaning here is quite specific, lest we conceive her instruction as abstract. We go out of self by dropping unnecessary thoughts, and not filling the interior space that ensues, but wordlessly welcoming transforming stillness—an expression of God's immediate presence.

As for unnecessary thoughts—we have plenty of them every day. Many more than we now think we have, as the Prayer will show us in time. They include negative mental reactions, endless trivia, replayed arguments with absent antagonists, repetitive thoughts, sad daydreams, self-justifications, rationalizations, contradictions, mechanical prejudices, self-deceptions, and useless worries. As Montaigne

---

[7] M.M. Philipon, O.P., ed., *Sister Elizabeth of the Trinity: Spiritual Writings, Letters, Retreats, and Unpublished Notes,* (New York, NY: P.J. Kenedy & Sons, 1962), p. 122. Elizabeth's exact words are: "It seems to me that in heaven my mission will be to attract souls by helping them go out of themselves, in order to cling to God with a very simple and loving movement, and to keep them in the great interior silence which allows God to imprint Himself on them, to transform them into Himself."

said, "My life has been filled with terrible misfortunes, most of which have never occurred."

Certainly we can do without some of these thoughts. Doing without more would even be better, for such negative thoughts are subreality. St. Augustine observed truly that evil has less metaphysical substance or being than good: that good is rich in being, but evil is a hole in existence, a dire absence in being.

So to let go of such thoughts is really a momentary liberation from subreality and a welcoming of being—indeed, Supreme Being. To let go of subreality honors God, for it is an embrace of Being. It is answered by a benediction of transforming Stillness. This silence is a nameless fragrance that carries to the finest dimensions of inner space to incense the meeting court of God and the soul.

> Be still, and know that I am God.
>
> —*Psalms 46:10*

This exchange is a secret between ourselves and God—this cleft we make for Him, this inner valley which knows the misty billows of divine Being.

How to Practice the Self-Release Prayer

This is the Self-Release Prayer:

1. Become aware of a thought or daydream that you can let go.
2. Let it go to make a space for God in interior silence.
3. Tend to the flash of Silence that replaces the thought, for it is an intuitive communion with God. "Grace fills empty spaces but it can only enter where there is a void to receive it, and it is grace itself which makes this void"[8] (Simone Weil).

As you see, to enact the Self-Release Prayer takes but a moment, yet its inner Stillness savors of an expansive aesthetic, a beginningless

[8] Simone Weil, *Gravity and Grace,* trans. Emma Craufurd, (London: Routledge and Kegan Paul, 1963), p. 10.

innocence, a hidden eternity. Think of an explorer planting a flag on a new land, claiming it for his king and queen. The Self-Release Prayer is like that. The moment we let go of subreality to love Being by a quiet receptivity, the flag of our Sovereign is planted here and now—planted in the empty space susceptible to God. It is our delight to see His banner.

The Self-Release Prayer is holistic, involving many dimensions of being. It involves our will, as it is a will-to-God. It involves awareness, as our consciousness of petty thoughts allows us to drop them. It often involves the senses, for a gaze at nature facilitates self-release. It is mystical, as it is a reception of transforming grace. It is humanistic, as it invites well-being.[9]

Mystic Stillness Intuits God

To deepen our practice of the Self-Release Prayer, we need to consider what the Christian mystics mean when they ask us to "adhere to God"—"Go out of yourself in order to adhere to God," in Elizabeth of the Trinity's words.

Since God's nature transcends any image and concept the mind can confect, we may adhere to God by letting the mind go silent before God's presence, an acknowledgement of the transconceptual majesty of God.

As even thought's highest activity cannot comprehend divinity, we let thought go into non-action to adhere to God. When we do this, God sees that we understand His Being transcends our mental capacity to grasp Him and blesses our humble seeing of this by visiting us, in a timeless moment, as the Stillness which existed before all things existed.

Though our minds can hardly fathom *what* God is, we know *that* God is, and THAT is enough. The thirteenth-century anonymous classic, *The Book of Privy Counsel,* instructs us:

---

[9] Herbert Benson, M.D., Jule Corliss and Geoffrey Cowley, "Brain Check," *Newsweek,* September 27, 2004, p. 46.

[Do not let your mind be] clothed
in any special thought of God's nature
or any of His works,
but only that He is.
Let Him be like this I beg you,
and do not form Him in any other manner.

Seek no further for Him
by the ingenuity of your mind...

"What I am Lord, I offer to you,
without any regard for any attribute of Your being,
but only that You are
as you are,
and nothing else."[10]

John of the Cross asks us to do the very same thing: "Preserve a loving attentiveness to God with no desire to feel or understand any particular thing about Him."[11] Why? Because, says John, "the language [God] best hears is silent love."[12]

This Prayer Cooperates With Christ's Mysteries In Us

Elizabeth of the Trinity concludes her instruction by speaking of its mystical effects: this Prayer "allows God to imprint Himself on you and *to transform the soul into Himself.*" We alluded to a holy process earlier, to a sacred path that leads to union with Christ in this life, and beyond death to the light and love of the Trinity. This is what Elizabeth is speaking of: Christ's recapitulating His Mysteries in us.

In our early days of practicing the Self-Release Prayer, the flash of silence that answers our going out of self to God may seem more like

---

[10] *The Cloud of Unknowing and The Letter of Private Direction,* Anonymous, Robert Way, ed., (Trabuco Canyon, CA: Source Books, 1986), pp. 113-114.

[11] Kavanaugh and Rodriguez, *op cit.*, p. 92.

[12] *Ibid.*, p. 95.

a curious blankness than God's presence. Either way, it is still soul-transforming because God answers every desire for His presence with transforming grace, whether we feel it or not. God's healing response to Self-Release is instant and never-failing.

I am reminded of this when I see the traditional representation of the "Descending Dove," symbolizing the Holy Spirit, the Spirit that God sends to the soul to transform it in Christ's likeness.

The Descending Dove

Consider the angle of the Dove's descent. It is not leisurely gliding to its mark. It is not taking its sweet time to fulfill its mission. It is nose-diving! By representing the Spirit in this way, the artist has given us a superb symbol of the instantaneous character of God's grace. The Dove's cast-all-caution-to-the-wind mad impatience to make us whole is poignant—and even sweetly comic.

The point is: the instant our heart is open to God's holy Presence, as in the Self-Release Prayer, grace is there—whether palpable or not. Grace has descended—with the mad, headlong haste of healing Love. As we invite God through this Prayer many times a day, we will soon find that God turns the tables on us—as the Holy Spirit solicits us often to this life-giving Prayer.

As we continue to grow with the Self-Release Prayer, the holy Stillness it acquaints us with takes on a new significance, as the deeper dimensions of our being come to recognize its replenishing reality:

> Everything happens as though,
> by a miraculous favor,
> our very senses themselves had been made
> aware that silence is not the absence of sounds,
> but something infinitely more real than sounds,
> and the center of a perfect harmony

more perfect than anything
which a combination of sounds can produce.
There is a silence in the beauty of the universe
which is like a noise
when compared with the silence of God.[13]

—*Simone Weil*

From Self-Release to Soul-Seeing

You will find, too, that your practice of the Self-Release Prayer soon turns into what we may call *Soul-Seeing.* Unlike the Self-Release Prayer described above, which takes but a moment to enact, Soul-Seeing is an ongoing state of interior silence. It may last for half a minute or five minutes or more, if you are inclined to invite it. It is a way to use some of our leisure time to commune with God in the natural world.

You are taking an early evening walk. You have used your mind on many practical matters today. The sky is greying darkly in the east, but is still a grey-blue in the west, where there is one little cloud, with an astonishing gold underbelly. This gentle twilight is drawing you out of yourself, luring you out of self-concern, evoking the interior quiet of the Self-Release Prayer. Just as the single peal of a bell may fill a town, so this interval of inner silence spreads upon all things. "We see the same colors; we hear the same sounds, but in not the same way"[14] (Simone Weil).

But now instead of going back to thinking as you usually do following the "simple movement" of Self-Release, you gently continue in receptive silence. In this way, the Self-Release Prayer turns into Soul-Seeing. "Let us be silent, that we might hear the whispers of the gods"[15] (Ralph Waldo Emerson).

---

[13] Simone Weil, *Waiting for God,* trans. Emma Craufurd, (New York, NY: Harper & Row Publishers, 1973), p. 213.

[14] *Ibid.,* p. 159.

[15] David Simon, *The Wisdom of Healing: A Natural Mind Body Program for Optimal Wellness,* (New York, NY: Random House, 1997), p. 83.

In the cool of the evening, as you walk down the street just observing, without self-reference, all the elements of nature throng together in a nameless poignancy. The evening is exquisitely dappled with meaning; not a meaning expressible in words, but a wordless significance, one of inexplicable, delicious value.

The first star appears shyly over the tree tops. The moon is ivory and blue. You walk on, susceptible to these innocent glories, and to the One who is the evening's spreading grace. You let go of thoughts as they arise, as no single thought can distill the depth of this scene. The earth tonight is so lovely, and it is only our self-contracted hearts that resist its renewing spell.

Above, the stars glimmer in their well-charted courses. But the voyage of a quiet spirit with the enchantment of starlight upon it is uncharted.

The Principle, *Resent Not Evil*

We will now study another principle that, like the *Self-Release Prayer,* is pure spiritual magic. That principle, *Resent not evil,* draws us into communion with our Creator right in the middle in daily life.

A science exhibit was once set up to show how energy is transferred. A lab floor was covered with hundreds of mousetraps, grouped tightly together and set to snap. A single ping-pong ball was tossed into the room. The ball hit one mousetrap which snapped at it—and both trap and ball flew into the air. They fell onto two other traps, setting them flying. More traps snapped, then others. In a matter of seconds, all the traps had been sprung with a clatter—a practical illustration of the transference of energy.

Just as the flying ping-pong ball and mousetraps passed on the energy that had been passed onto them, so emotional states are passed on all day long, from person to person—at work, on the road, on the telephone, in stores, at home. These include negative emotional states—which pass through us so routinely that we have ceased to be horrified by their impudent usurpation. But rather than mechanically reacting (as when someone speaks to us rudely, and we immediately internalize it or speak rudely back), we can put into action Jesus' exalted words (in the King James Bible), "Resist not evil" (Matthew 5:39)—or in a clarifying paraphrase, *Resent not evil.*

The Bewitching Baton

Think of a relay race. A baton is handed off from runner to runner and travels far. In much the same way, resentment snakes its way in daily life from person to person as a bewitching baton, causing hurt, confusion, anxiety, bitterness, and emptiness—as one person passes it on to the next, hardly aware of what its passing is costing him, or costing the one who receives this hideous baton.

To the extent that we are apart from the Spirit of Life, there accrues in us a certain life-frustration level, a kind of vague, inarticulate resentment against life itself. Though generalized life-frustration is most clearly seen in expressly bitter people who evince resentment in nearly every human transaction, it is just as often hidden behind Grimaldi-like smiles that quickly turn to scowls when frustrated, even in little matters.

When we are in situations that frustrate us, even minor ones, we tend to mechanically manifest our general life-frustration level, either inwardly, in unspoken irritation, or outwardly in rebuke. Often the rebuke is out of proportion to the offense; that is because our vehement reaction is more a function of our general frustration level than a response to the specific event.

When you are on the receiving end of this, you see it clearly. You see that you were not the real target of that person's frustration, but that you were simply a convenient symbol for his or her overall life-frustration—a symbolic victim of it. You were handed the bewitching baton. He was trying to pass the pain inside him to you. You typically accepted the baton, in one form or another, either by mechanically answering rudeness with more rudeness, or silently internalizing your resentment.

But Christ has given us three words to reverse all this, words of pure spiritual magic: *Resent not evil.* As we practice this principle, the Holy Spirit within teaches us something truly astonishing: that we are never under any compulsion either to receive the bewitching baton or to pass it back. Never. Let that sink in. It means that starting right now and even unto eternity, you need never have a single internalized enemy. This insight frees us from subrealities such as resentment, calcified grudges, and negative preoccupations.

> Reality is the life, the world, of the risen Jesus, where there is utter security and joy, where all is well and will be well. This is where we must live, not in our miserable subjective states…measuring life as it seems to us, as we feel it to be instead of as it is.[16]
>
> —*Ruth Burrows*

Outwardly, of course, certain people will continue to oppose us, seek to frustrate us, and wish us ill. And we must deal practically with all that, but we need not internalize any of it.

The World Is Too Burdened With Pain

The following insights can help us truly live the principle of *Resent not evil* with clarity and without spurious dodges.

Let us agree that the world is too burdened with pain. You and I must resolve not to further add to the pain of the world. A saying traditionally attributed to Plato capsulizes this wisdom: "Be kind, for everyone is fighting a great battle."

Think of a person who has recently tried to pass on to you the bewitching baton—and know that secretly he or she is fighting a great inner battle against exterior or interior forces that you and I know nothing about. We must try to see things from the other's position, aware of his or her difficulties. He passed on the bewitching baton because he did not know better; now that we are beginning to know better, we must neither internalize it nor pass it back, but dissolve it through the magic of *Resent not evil.*

"Be kind, for everyone is fighting a great battle."

---

[16] Ruth Burrows, *Guidelines for Mystical Prayer,* (Denville, NJ: Dimension Books, 1981), p. 63.

Instant Spiritual Justice

Perhaps we are concerned that if we do not answer rudeness with a sharp comment, we fail the principle of justice. But on a spiritual level perfect justice always prevails. Instant spiritual justice is this: everyone must live with his own nature, the quality of his inner being, twenty-four hours a day. The person who passes on the baton is instantly punished by the self-contracted state of mind which causes him or her to pass it. Self-contracted emotions and thoughts are closed from the Light, an alienation which is intrinsically punishing. "To cut oneself off from God for a single moment is strictly speaking to die"[17] (Jacques Maritain). To die within, but to keep on walking around. So spiritual justice is instant and inexorable. That is why Christ asks us to pray for enemies and not tempt them further away from the Light by resentful reactions.

Responsibility for the Light

"Let your light shine before men, that they may see your good deeds and praise your Father in heaven" (Matthew 5:16). Connect this with *Resent not evil.* When you and I do not mechanically pass back the bewitching baton, the bit of Light that emerges in our patient non-reaction may change hearts: it certainly will change our own. God wills that this Light shine before others, to attract them to the one Healer, as He "wants all men to be saved and to come to a knowledge of the truth" (1 Timothy 2:4).

But if I refuse my brother the opportunity to see the Light of patience, I block God's invitation to him. May I claim to really love God if I hide His Light from my neighbor? "Those who do not love their neighbor abhor God"[18] (John of the Cross). Further, if we are be transformed into union with God—a "union of likeness," according to the mystics—we must will what the Spirit wills, and that is Light.

---

[17] Jacques Maritain, *Notebooks,* trans. Joseph W. Evans, (Albany, NY: Magi Books, 1984), pp. 121-122.

[18] Kavanaugh and Rodriguez, *op cit.,* p. 97.

Love your enemies...
that you may be sons
of your Father in heaven.

Be perfect, therefore,
as your heavenly Father is perfect.

—*Matthew 5:44-45, 48*

Beyond the Mediocrity of Mechanical Reactions

Here are three especially insidious ways we justify resentment and impatience:

- "I'm not angry for my sake, of course—I'm angry because of the principle of the thing!" When we find ourselves loudly and rigidly insisting on the "principle of the thing" in petty matters, we are probably rationalizing: using the situation to vent some personal frustration quite unconnected to simply getting the business at hand right.
- "The customer is always right!" we declare, and think this allows us to speak rudely as consumers. But we are not Christians in one moment and consumers the next. As a friend of mine memorably said, we cannot leave our Christianity behind when we go shopping as we might leave a pet in the car. The slogan, "The customer is always right," does not trump the principle of patience.

To be patient is not to be impractical; if, say, we are unsatisfied with a product we have purchased, we should be plainspoken about it. We stay in communion with our Creator as we speak by remembering that the other person is a beloved creation of God for whom God wills all good. "Speaking the truth in love," as St. Paul says, we can take care not to make others into symbolic victims of some ulterior frustration.[19] "[T]here is nothing that

---

[19] Ephesians 4:15.

can be done with anger that cannot be done better without it"[20] (Dallas Willard).

- "This isn't ordinary anger! I'm righteously angry, like Christ Himself was when He cleansed the money-changers from the Temple!" This is a dangerous misuse of scripture, readily abused to justify all sorts of ego-driven rages.
- "He had no right to say that to me!" He probably did not. Nevertheless, was what he said true? Am I especially upset because it is true, and part of me knows it and resents his seeing a truth I don't want to face? We are often most touchy, most defensive, on hearing self-exposing truth.

So instead of automatically resenting criticism and dismissing it, we might stand back and objectively ask ourselves if the criticism is true, even if it has been rudely expressed. John of the Cross advises, "Do not excuse yourself or refuse to be corrected by all; listen to every reproof with a serene countenance...."[21] John even asks us to be grateful to those who try our patience. Without knowing it, they have given us opportunities to show our love for God, to put Him before our touchy egos. "Virtue and strength of soul grow and are confirmed," says John, "in the trials of patience."[22]

Do note the holistic character of *Resent not evil.* It integrates many dimensions of life and being. It involves our emotions, for it invites empathy for others and acknowledges their pain that would pass itself on in the bewitching baton. It entails psychology, as it glimpses unconscious forces at work below surface-motivations, and deals honestly with them. It includes self-knowledge, for it recognizes the desperation of our own pain, which looks for symbolic targets. It exercises our will, for it endeavors to will what God wills—goodwill toward all. It is mys-

---

[20] Dallas Willard, *The Divine Conspiracy, Rediscovering Our Hidden Life in God,* (New York, NY: HarperSanFrancisco, 1998), p. 151.

[21] Kavanaugh and Rodriguez, *op cit.,* p. 96.

[22] *Ibid.,* p. 86.

tical, as it flies to God and asks for Love's help to love. It is ethical as it seeks conciliation. It is health-related, as freedom from stress caused by ongoing, caustic resentment invites physiological rejuvenation.[23]

The Transforming Power of *Resent Not Evil*

Now to gather some of these insights together in a practical scenario: In daily life, a situation irritates us. We are about to overreact to it because the irritation symbolizes for us, unconsciously, other life-frustrations unconnected to this moment.

We are about to pass on the bewitching baton. Here is a symbolic victim on whom we can vent some of our general resentment toward life as a whole. But then by some grace, we intuit the Master's voice, *Resent not evil,* illumining our understanding like the sudden flaring of a campfire that clarifies a dim map.

By this light we see the ongoing pain of the world in the anguished look or the hard look of the other, and the possibility of Light. And a miracle happens. We chose patience, not mechanical resentment—and the Light is there, for the other and for us.

The other person senses, if unconsciously, that something different is happening. What is different is that the hideous baton has just been dissolved by the spiritual magic of *Resent not evil.* It has neither been internalized in us nor passed back to him as it routinely has been. In the recesses of his being, a new hope has been awakened by this manifestation of the Light—a budding realization that a Life exists that is not merely defensive and reactive, but a source of quiet goodwill.

That is the first part of a two-part miracle. The second is this: The moment we enact *Resent not evil,* the Light also shines within us, irradiating with healing our own life-frustration level. The work of this Light is to turn our heart of stone into a heart of flesh. Indeed, when the Light has completed its work in us, our heart will participate in Christ's own Sacred Heart: for he is transforming our humanity into his.

This requires discipline. As philosophy professor Dallas Willard reminds us, *discipline* is cognate with the word *disciple.* As disciples of

---

[23] Jordana Lewis and Jerry Adler, "Forgive and Let Live," *Newsweek,* September 27, 2004, p. 52.

Christ, whose Holy Spirit is Love, we are responsible for love on earth, especially as it pertains to our immediate situation. John of the Cross puts the significance of all this as plainly as it can be put: "Anyone who complains or grumbles is not perfect, nor even a good Christian."[24]

A sacrifice is involved in our not answering rudeness with rudeness. But what we sacrifice, strangely, is only subreality: the immature part of ourselves that thrives on negative excitement and judging, which uses judgment to feel itself to be a little false god. "So, when you feel like being impatient, or inclined to say something uncharitable, turn towards Him, and in order to please Him, allow the natural movement to pass. How many acts of self-denial, known to Him alone, we can offer Him"[25] (Elizabeth of the Trinity).

Yes, suffering is involved: but we are suffering only our raging ego that is not getting its way. It is screaming within us: 'You have the right to be angry! Go on!' We suffer this by not mechanically giving into the ego's demands. "What does anyone know who does not know how to suffer for Christ?"[26] (John of the Cross). As said, it is a strange sacrifice, because all we are really sacrificing in this moment is a cloying nothingness, a subreality, an absurdity. Yet God loves this little sacrifice of trivia and rewards it, incredibly, by giving Himself to the soul.

The Feverish Feeling of Life

To conclude our reflections on *Resent not evil,* we will consider one more facet of the complex lure of resentment: the *Feverish Feeling of Life.* You have experienced this. You are driving the speed limit on the freeway—then discover you are being dangerously tailgated by another driver. Two lanes to the left of the tailgater are wide open, but instead of taking either and driving at any speed he chooses, he stubbornly insists on driving recklessly close behind you.

---

[24] Kavanaugh and Rodriguez, *op cit.,* p. 97.

[25] Philipon, *op cit.,* p. 56.

[26] Kavanaugh and Rodriguez, *op cit.,* p. 97.

Why? What is his motivation? Tailgating gives him or her a *Feverish Feeling of Life*—a feeling of mad ego-triumph. The *Feverish Feeling of Life* is an exhilarating but false sense of power through outbursts of resentment.

> But man, proud man,
> dressed in little brief authority,
> most ignorant of what he is most assured
> —his glassy essence—
> like an angry ape
> plays such fantastic tricks
> before the high heavens
> as make the angels weep.
>
> —*Shakespeare, Measure for Measure (Act 2, sc. ii)*

Excitement in itself is innocent, a natural part of life. But the feverish feelings of anger, bitterness, one-upmanship, revenge, sniping, and power plays—these further degrade our life-frustration level and add to the already deep pain of the world.

Twenty-five percent of drivers surveyed in a university study said that on their daily commute they unleash frustrations about their jobs and home life on other drivers. (Though the study surveyed women only, we may assume the percentages are at least comparable for men.) The adrenaline-rush of cutting off other drivers electrifies us with a *Feverish Feeling of Life.* Our momentary road-dominance makes us feel, unconsciously, in control of our lives as an artificial compensation for the lack of control we feel.

> All our mental and emotional resources are marshaled to nurture and tend...anger, and our body throbs with it. Energy is dedicated to keeping the anger alive: we constantly remind ourselves of how wrongly we have been treated.[27]
>
> —*Dallas Willard*

But in the memorable terms of Jesus, to call upon resentment to save us from life-frustration is to mistake darkness for light.

---

[27] Willard, *op cit.*, p. 150.

> If then the light within you
> is darkness,
> how great is that darkness!
>
> —*Matthew 6:23*

The tailgater takes as his false light the shallow thrill of intimidating another, the thrilling throb of resentment, the hypnotic thrill of egoistic power. In that moment, these seem to be rewarding. Speaking of such confused rewards, Jesus said:

> I tell you the truth,
> they have received their reward in full.
>
> —*Matthew 6:16*

Perhaps Jesus' larger point is that you and I must choose between fictitious rewards and real ones, for they are mutually exclusive. I cannot have them both. I can have the fiery thrill of resentment—or the peaceable Spirit. I can have the thrill of passing on the bewitching baton or the healing inner silence when I let it pass. I can have the momentary relief of attacking a symbolic victim or the real relief of contact with the everlasting Light. I can have the phony rewards of frantically keeping up with the Joneses or a natural pace of life.

Resentment is merely one element of the light/darkness mix-up in daily living. We may take a morose self-pity for the light—or passive aggression, addictions, or cynicism.

The Meeting of Self-Release and *Resent Not Evil*

As we practice the Self-Release Prayer and *Resent not evil* we begin to see how at points they interpenetrate, like the conjunction of two stars that cast a great light.

The bewitching baton has just been thrust toward you. You are on the receiving end of some impatience. But instead of inwardly accepting it (going into a state of resentment) and then mechanically passing it back, you become objective to the situation. You approach it from a standpoint higher than egoism. You sense that other's anger toward you is more toward a symbolic victim (to vent life-frustration) than toward you personally.

You remember that God wills a healing Light for all, ever-more so for the troubled. "Be kind—for everyone is fighting a great battle." This understanding prompts you to let go of resentment you feel, to disidentify with the inner yell of pride, *He can't say that to me!* You let go of unhelpful self-focused thought:

> Go out of yourself
> in order to adhere to God
> by a very simple, wholly loving movement
> which allows God to imprint Himself on you and
> to transform the soul into Himself.

This is the conjunction of *Resent not evil* and the Self-Release Prayer. At that instant, there is an exquisite burst of healing Silence at the center of consciousness, a Stillness that is unwithering, aesthetic, renewing. It radiates from the deepest point of your being.

You overlook the bewitching baton—it vanishes in a flash. You respond to the other person from a perspective higher than the uproar of egoism. Oh, this is true magic! It all takes place in a blessed split second. But it is pause enough to permit a breeze of eternity to enter time here and now. By your *no* to the Feverish Feeling of Life, and your *yes* to God in this situation, a bright confluence of *Resent not evil* and the Self-Release Prayer thrives in your soul and gently commands the scene.

The Self-Release Prayer and *Resent not evil* are both movements beyond egoism. In prayer, the soul goes out of itself, Godward, in a consecrated silence. Likewise, patience is a God-united act of the will. Patience lets go of resentment to invite Light.

As one lets go of resentment, a flash of tranquil silence visits the heart—a blessed conjunction of prayer and patience. This is the *Holism of Prayer and Patience.*

Dahlia

Holism of Prayer and Patience

Apple blossoms

Holism of the Mind-Body Partnership

Affinity: The *Holism of the Mind-Body Partnership* (Chapter 8)

Resentment is not a disembodied reaction, but has biochemical components that can overwhelm the wisdom of patience.

An artful knowledge of how this works—how the Mind-Body Partnership operates—supports the Holism of Prayer and Patience. The old wisdom of taking a deep breath in a moment of frustration, for example, has been scientifically demonstrated to interrupt the body's spiral toward anger by eliciting the "Relaxation Response."

You put the book down, as you have an appointment to keep. As you walk out to your car, a phrase from Ruth Burrows comes to mind: "The real world of Truth and Love." It held a strange attraction for you on first reading, and so it does now. You feel refreshed by it. You open the door of your car, but pause before getting into it, as your attention is drawn to the graceful lines of a maple tree nearby. *How odd,* you think, shaking your head a bit. *This is the first time I've really looked at that lovely tree in months.*

You feel the pretty naturalness of the sunlight on the leaves gently twining with Burrow's saying, "the real world of Truth and Love." Your body, strangely charmed, sighs on its own. The phrase *Self-Release* comes unbidden to you. A wholesome, healing quiet spreads through your spirit. "Is this some part," you wonder, "of what the mystics mean?" Another dimension, of sorts, has stolen into the scene, and you notice it with a start—an innocent Presence, gladdening the sun and the leaves.

What did the nineteenth-century essayist James Russell Lowell say? "One day, with life and heart, is more than time enough to find a world."

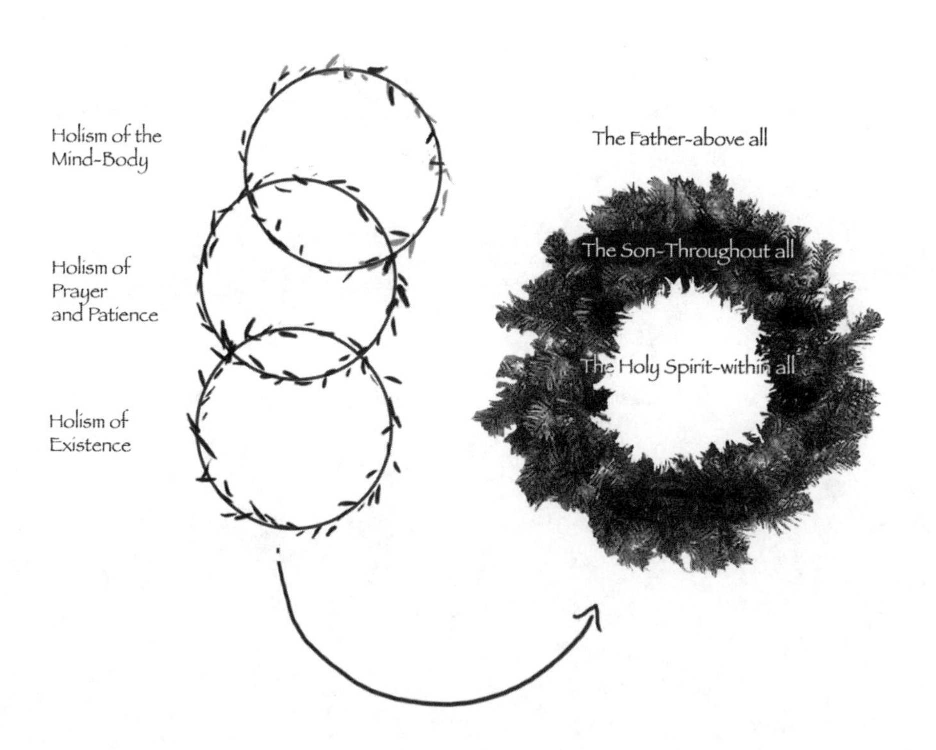

CHAPTER 3

The Thrice-Loved God: The Holism of the Absolute

"The knowledge of the Trinity in unity is the fruit and end of all our life."[1]
—St. Thomas Aquinas

"Thus to be a Christian is to be born into the life of the Trinity, which is the incorruptible life of God, possessed by the Three Persons and conveyed by Them in the pattern of incomprehensible love."[2]
—Jean Danielou, S.J.

The story is told of two great composers—let us just call them Brahms and Liszt—standing on a bridge, pondering the future of music. Brahms stares bleakly at the rushing waters, shakes his head and says darkly: "All the great music has been written! There is just a finite number of notes to work with, Liszt. And a limited configuration of patterns. Soon it will be impossible to write an original melody!"

Liszt listens in silence for a time. Then a wry smile appears, and a shout: "Look, Brahms! Look there!" He points agitatedly to the water

[1] Jacques Maritain, *The Degrees of Knowledge,* trans. Bernard Wall, (New York, NY: Charles Scribner's Sons, 1938), p. 465.

[2] Jean Danielou, *God and the Ways of Knowing,* trans. Walter Roberts, (New York, NY: Meridian Books, 1957), p. 149.

just disappearing beneath the bridge. "Oh no! There it goes—the very last ripple!"

Listz is wryly suggesting that just as the river will not stop raising ripples, music is infinite and will never lack soaring complexities. To put this metaphysically, there is a basic generosity in creation. The good of each created thing is expressive, outpouring, fertile. The rose breathes its perfume, the dawn uncurls the little leaf, a mother's smile awakens her baby's first smile, star-sparkle travels a trillion miles to give itself to our gaze, the robin presses her warmth to her eggs.

The generosity of the universe glints with God. Each created thing is made in the image of God, and so reflects the outpouring nature of its Creator, who is Love itself (1 John 4:16).

Christ revealed God as a Blessed Trinity, a thrice-holy generosity. The Trinity is the fountainhead of all holisms in heaven and on earth. All of holistic Christianity mystically cascades from the viewless height of the Trinity. Like cherry blossoms lilting from a measureless branch, the brightest wonders of Christian wisdom extend from the Tri-Personal God.

What Christ Revealed About God

Reflecting on the nature of God that Christ revealed, let us first note that God is infinitely different from the white bearded old man in the sky that Christianity's detractors insist Christians believe in. Christianity has never affirmed this absurdity; it only exists in cartoon caricatures of the faith. Rather:

> God is
> the Infinite, the Absolute.
> He possesses being, intelligence, love, beauty
> to an infinite degree.
> We should not say he *has*
> being, intelligence, love;
> rather,
> that he *is* Being itself,
> Intelligence itself, Love and Beauty themselves.

> He dwells within himself;
> he is lacking in absolutely nothing.[3]
>
> —*Cardinal Charles Journet*

Two thousand years ago God came to earth in the person of Jesus Christ to reveal the intimate Life of God. He revealed the innermost secret of the divine nature: that the one God has a Tri-Personal Existence. So important was this revelation that God did not inspire a prophet to reveal it, but rather came Himself to lift the veil.

Many have objected to the idea of a Triune God, chiding Christians for gratuitously introducing an esoteric puzzle into religion. But we must understand that the Trinity was not the pipe dream of early Christians who had nothing better to do than complexify monotheism. Nor was the Trinity a tendentious abstraction produced later by Christian philosophers. Rather, Jesus Christ thrust the truth of the Trinity onto the stage of history, like a conductor thrusting a baton that solicits a startling peal of music. Because Christ taught by signs and words the Tri-Personal unity of God, his followers had no choice but to accept this new understanding of divinity and pray for grace to receive the wonders this new vision implied.

At the earliest point of the Christ's Incarnation, the Annunciation, the Trinitarian mystery began to be disclosed. The angel announces to Mary that she is to conceive the Son of God:

> The HOLY SPIRIT will come upon you,
> and the power of the Most High [the FATHER]
> will overshadow you.
> So the holy one to be born will be called
> the SON OF GOD.
>
> —*Luke 1: 35*

There it is, the Trinity: Father, Son, and Holy Spirit. Thus a young virgin of Israel was the first person on earth to hear of the innermost nature of God, as it had never been revealed before in any land, in any religion (as we shall presently see).

---

[3] Charles Journet, *The Meaning of Grace,* trans. A.V. Littledale, (New York, NY: P. J. Kenedy & Sons, 1960), p. 3.

Many years later, at the baptism of Jesus, the Trinity was again disclosed:

> As soon as Jesus
> was baptized,
> he went up out of the water.
> At that moment heaven was opened, and he saw
> the SPIRIT of God
> descending like a dove
> and lighting on him.
> And a voice [the FATHER]
> from heaven said,
> "This is my SON, whom I love;
> with him I am well-pleased."
>
> —*Matthew 3:16-17*

Then the final hour of Jesus Christ's historical incarnation, Christ says:

> Therefore go and make disciples of all nations,
> baptizing them in the name of
> the FATHER, and of the SON, and of the HOLY SPIRIT,
> and teaching them to obey
> everything I have commanded you.
>
> —*Matthew 28:19*

In the face of this irresistible testimony, what was the earliest Church to do, but recognize the Three-in-One and worship in awe?[4] Writes Alan Schreck of Franciscan University: "The central belief of the Catholic Church is that God is one in three persons—Father, Son, and Holy Spirit. These three persons are distinct, but equal in power, majesty, and divinity. The 'Trinity' is the name that the early Christians gave to the one God comprised of three equal and distinct divine persons."[5]

---

[4] Bertrand de Margerie, S.J. *The Christian Trinity in History,* trans. by Edmund J. Foreman, S.J., (Still River, MA: St. Bede's Publications, 1982), pp. 3-72.

[5] Alan Schreck, *Catholic and Christian: An Explanation of Commonly Misunderstood Catholic Beliefs,* (Ann Arbor, MI: Servant Books, 1984), p. 14.

Because of the paradoxical nature of the Trinity—the Three in One—some despair of getting any deep understanding of it, and regard meditation on it as futile, or at least impractical. "It's a mystery of faith," they say, and would leave it at that. They are certainly right that it is a mystery. It is the farthest shore of the Christian mysteries.

But that is the last reason to not meditate on the Trinity. To do otherwise is like saying that since gold is the heaviest metal, it is too burdensome to carry. The very metaphysical opulence of the Trinity is cause for our meditation. Perhaps those who dismiss pondering the Trinity as futile misunderstand the theological meaning of "mystery." A "mystery" in Christian terms is not a frustrating, even incoherent, puzzle. A mystery is not a truth we cannot know anything about, but a truth that we cannot know *everything* about, as theologian Frank Sheed suggested. It is a divine truth, utterly trustworthy, for it has been revealed to us by God (as in Christ's sayings)—a truth that cannot be completely contained by human concepts, yet one that still yields true and profound meaning for human understanding. That is why we can reflect on the mystery of the Trinity here.

Has God Always Existed as a Trinity?

Before this genesis of time and space, before the big bang posited by astrophysics, before a single particle of matter quivered in surprise at its own existence—God IS! But has God always been a Trinity? The question arises because the Son of the Trinity—Christ—was born on earth only two thousand years ago. The universe had existed for 14 billion years before the Son was born, and God existed before the universe began. So the question is again: has God always been a Trinity, or did the fullness of the Trinity only come into existence with the birth of the Son two thousand years ago? What does Christianity teach about this?

When I have put this question to university students (many of them Christians), I invariably get many puzzled looks—and more than a few sheepish expressions which seem to say, "Hey, I should know this!"

Did the Son of God exist before Bethlehem? *Yes* has been the great consensus of the historic Church. Catholic, Orthodox, and Protestant Christian believers all hold that God has ever been a Trinity, even before the Incarnation, and even before a single wave-particle sparkled into being. In other words, the Son existed in the Trinity pre-cosmically (before the universe) and pre-Incarnationally (before Jesus was conceived by Mary).

But if the Son has always existed (with the Father and the Spirit), in what manner did the Son exist before the universe and the Incarnation? Certainly we must not imagine that Christ existed in hyperspace with a beard, garment, and sandals before the universe existed, as earthly elements did not yet even exist to comprise these.

What was the nature of the Son's existence? The Son existed even before the universe as an absolute, ultimate dimension of the Trinity. Although the exact character of the Son's existence is wholly unimaginable to consciousness, we can say that the Son is the Eternal Manifest of God, God's creative potency. The Son is perfect divine Knowing, "the Father's Mind"[6] (St. Athanasius). The Father creates the universe through His divine Potency, the Son. The Son is the creative Word (Greek, *Logos*) of the Father. The apostle John described the Son in this way:

> In the beginning was the Word [Son],
> and the Word was with God [Father],
> and the Word was God....
> Through him all things were made....
>
> —*John 1:1, 3*

Picture the earth in space. It was created through the Son ("through him all things were made") and even at this instant is being creatively continued in existence by the Son, Christ! We can see that our typical vision of the Son has been too limited. Too often we have only thought of the Son as Jesus of Nazareth, the Incarnation of God. But we lose

---

[6] St. Athanasius, *On the Incarnation,* trans. and ed. by Sister Penelope Lawson, C.S.M.V., (New York, NY: Macmillan Publishing, 1981), p. 13.

much by limiting our vision of the Son to the incarnate Christ, for the Son is also the eternal *Logos*, the divine Knowing of God, who is even in this instant upholding in being all space and time.

Take a breath, become aware of your physical body, and note that the divine mystery undergirding your form and the form of all that exists is the Christ-Logos. "For those who can see, Christ shines in a diaphany, through the cosmos and in matter"[7] (Francis Klauder).

Just as the Son is the divine Knowing of the Trinity, the Father is the Trinity's utterly transcendent dimension. The Father is the Unmanifest of God beyond all creation. The Father is the shoreless glory of the Son, the bliss of heaven in which the Son everlastingly abides.

The Holy Spirit is the Manifesting dimension of God—the Eternal Movement of the divine, the everlasting circulation of love between the Father and the Son. The creativity of the Son is manifested by the Spirit who implements the designs of the Son—creates what the Son wills.

Father and Son also send the Spirit into us to transform us by degrees into the divine likeness. First into the likeness of Christ's humanity—what we have been calling the unitive way or transforming union. And beyond the grave, the Spirit transforms the soul into the very Son of the Trinity, for only the one Son wholly knows the Father.

Even as a towering sequoia might give its own sap to a parched blade of grass, so the Spirit imbues us with its sap, raising us to the Son. "Christ is the way, Christ in us"[8] (Emile Mersch).

A Trinitarian Thought Experiment

The following thought-experiment will aid our meditation on the Trinity. Begin by thinking of yourself when you were five years old. Now picture yourself as a teenager—your physical appearance, attitudes,

---

[7] Francis Klauder, *Aspects of the Thought of Teilhard de Chardin,* (North Quincy, MA: Christopher Publishing House, 1971), p. 74.

[8] Emile Mersch, S.J., *The Theology of the Mystical Body,* trans. Cyril Vollert, S.J., (St. Louis, MO: B. Herder Book Co., 1952), p. 89.

thoughts, projects, feelings. Now at your high school graduation. Now your college years. Now as you are today. Finally, try to picture yourself as you might be in five years.

Would it be possible, now, to bring all these images together into one master image of yourself? Quite impossible, as you have just discovered. For one, such as master image can not be conceived because of the dynamic character of the self—we change from year to year in countless ways, and these "selves" are incommensurable. Also, our knowledge of even our present self is partially obscure, incomplete, and endangered by rationalization and self-deception. Finally, what we shall become tomorrow is unknown. As such, the very character of the human self excludes complete self-knowledge.

Now juxtapose our limited self-knowledge to God's knowledge of God. God knows God with complete, timelessly true understanding. And this is where our understanding of the Son of God must begin. Because the pre-cosmic, pre-incarnational Son (having no human form and no body of earthly elements) existed in supersubstantial Form as God's perfect divine Knowing.

This venerable doctrine of the Son is analogically capsulated by Sheed:

> Whatever is in the Father
> must be in his idea of himself,
> and must be exactly the same
> as it is in himself.
>
> Otherwise God would have an
> inadequate idea of himself,
> which would be nonsense.
> Thus, because God is infinite, eternal, all-powerful,
> his idea of himself is infinite, eternal, all-powerful.
>
> Because God is God,
> his idea is God.[9]

---

[9] F. J. Sheed, *Theology for Beginners*, (Ann Arbor, MI: Servant Books, 1981), p. 34.

Hence, God's perfect Understanding, or Intelligence, is the Eternal Son. And just as you are not two beings—you and your understanding—so God is not two, but one. Notice how this view preserves the absolute unity of God, the core of monotheism, yet reveals two distinct Dimensions of God: Father and Son. (Still, we must be careful not to imagine that God literally has an "idea" of Himself, as you and I do of ourselves. The Son is not an idea of the Father as in a human idea; the Son is all that is Manifest of the Unmanifest Father.)

What of the Third Person of the Trinity, the Holy Spirit? To approach this mystery, think of a beloved friend. Isn't the love you share a palpable presence between you two? So it is with God's love for God, but infinitely so—the Father's love for the Son, and the Son's love for the Father. Their Loving relation is so real that it is the Third Person of the Godhead, the Holy Spirit. It pours forth continually within the divine abyss as their Love, their infinite bond. Sheed writes: "The uttered love of Father and Son is infinite, lacks no perfection that they have, is God, a person, someone."[10] Thus the Holy Spirit is the very personification of Love within the Godhead.

W. Norris Clarke, S.J., a Christian philosopher, summarizes the supreme wonder of the Trinity:

> ...the very inner nature of the Supreme Being itself—even before its overflow into creation—is an ecstatic process (beyond time and change) of self-communicating love: the Father, the originating possessor of infinite fullness of the divine nature, communicates ecstatically his entire divine nature to the Second Person, the Son or the Word, in an act of loving self-knowledge...
>
> Then both together, in a single act of mutual love, pour forth the same divine essence again in all its fullness to their love image, the Holy Spirit, the third Person. Thus the very inner life of God himself...is by its very nature self-communicative Love,

---

[10] *Ibid.,* p. 36.

> which then flows over freely in a finite communication that is creation.[11]

In this way, the Tri-Personal God is at once distinctly dimensional, yet indivisibly One. The ultimate whole, the *Holism of the Absolute.*

At this point, with even a few rays of the Trinitarian mystery upon our understanding, we begin to see the overarching significance of the Trinity in Christianity. The Trinity *is* Christianity.

> The first word a child hears the Church speak over him is,
> "I baptize you
> in the Name of the Father,
> and of the Son, and the Holy Ghost."
>
> He is thrown as a creature of flesh and blood,
> into the abyss of the Trinitarian life,
> to which all life and all eternity
> *will have no other object than to accustom him.*[12]
>
> —*Jean Danielou.*

The Distinctiveness of the Christian Trinitarian Doctrine

Before Christ revealed the Trinity, the Triune character of God remained obscure even to the loftiest ancient religious and philosophical wisdoms. Hebrew prophets sang majestically of the divine Oneness of God; the great prayer of the Jews, the *shema,* poignantly proclaims, "Hear, O Israel: The Lord our God, the Lord is one" (Deuteronomy 6:4). But when Jesus unfurled to Israel the further truth of this Oneness, the truth of God's Tri-Personal unity, the chief priests of the Temple and many scribes and pharisees rejected it as incompatible with the monotheism of the Abraham, Moses, and the prophets.

From the minarets of Islam the Oneness of God is sung daily: "There is no God but God." The Koran was written nearly six centuries

[11] W. Norris Clarke, *Person and Being,* (Milwaukee, WI: Marquette University Press, 1998), pp. 11-12.

[12] Danielou, *op cit.,* p. 140.

after the Christian gospels, and explicitly rejects the Trinity. The Trinity was not a teaching of Christ, says the Koran, but an invention of later Christians; the Trinity is a distortion of the "prophet" Jesus' original teaching of the oneness of Allah. The Koran (4:40) states: "Believe therefore in God and his apostles, and say not, 'Three:' (there is a Trinity)...God is only one God!"[13]

To conceive of God as multiple, which Islam accuses Christianity of doing, is the worst possible sin: *shirk,* which means associating anyone with God. Therefore, Islam rejects as *shirk* the Trinity and as *shirk* the idea that Jesus Christ was God on earth.

Buddhism does not speak of a God at all, and so the matter of a Trinity is moot; the Buddha's reference to an "unborn one" (the closest he came to speaking of an original divine Reality) is to an unconditioned reality—not a Trinity.[14]

Hinduism does not recognize a Trinity. Devout Hindus reverence a *trimurthi* of three chief gods—Brahma, Vishnu, and Shiva—but also billions of other gods. Philosophical Hinduism takes a different tack, but also one that does not recognize the Triune unity of God. The chief philosophy of Hinduism, *advaita vedanta,* posits a God that is so radically One that from its standpoint the universe itself is an illusion (*maya*). Brahman is an undifferentiated One in *advaita* philosophy: there is no creation, and no divine Tri-Personality.

The Trinity Is the Basis of "God Is Love"

We have found that Christ alone revealed a Triune Godhead. He also revealed that God is personal. This prompts another question. Is God "personal" even apart from being a personal God to us? That is: Is God intrinsically personal, personal in Himself?

---

[13] *The Koran,* trans. J. M. Rodwell, (North Clarendon, VT: Tuttle Publishing, 1994), p. 66.

[14] For a compelling study of Buddhism and the question of God, see Paul Williams, *The Unexpected Way: On Converting from Buddhism to Catholicism,* T & T Clark, Edinburgh & New York, 2002.

A parallel question relates to the phrase, "God is love" (1 John 4:16). Is God Love only in relation to us, or is God innately Love, Love itself, even apart from God's loving His creation? Would God be Love without a universe to love?

As it turns out, the answers to these questions are surprisingly interconnected. As we shall see, these are not abstract matters, but go to the heart of the Christian faith.

Let us start by reviewing our comparative study of religions. On the one hand, we found that many faiths affirm with Christianity that God is One. On the other, we discovered that non-Christian religions deny the Trinity. Turning to another point, let us find out what the world's religions have to say of the relation of God and love. Christianity does not only say God is loving, but says, "God is love," affirming their identity (1 John 4:16).

Mainstream Islam describes Allah as just, benevolent—a providential Sovereign who rewards and punishes His believers equitably. God is merciful, kind, compassionate—but not "Love" *per se.* Nor is God's relation to humanity the relation of a Father to His children, as Judaism and Christianity say. Such an idea is another form of *shirk,* says Islam. We are not children of God, for a child is like his parents and nothing is like God.

Judaism does speak of God as a loving Father to humanity. Yet Judaism—which shares Islam's non-Trinitarian understanding of God—does not make an identity between Love and God. God is good, just, eternal, creative, unfathomable, providential, but the phrase "God is Love" does not occur in the Hebrew scriptures.

Hinduism's *advaita vedanta* describes God as bliss, as consciousness, and existence—but not as Love. As a radically monistic philosophy, *advaita* says finally that there is no *other* one to love or to be a lover, as there is just the undifferentiated One.

That none of these religions affirms "God is Love" hardly means that these faiths lack profound principles that conduce to charity and goodness. Surely all of these religions have raised up women and men of exemplary kindness and goodness—and love.

Yet we are led to a remarkable conclusion: the Triune Personality of God, found only in Christianity, is the very basis of the principle,

"God is Love." Put another way, as Christianity alone affirms the Trinity, it alone affirms that God is Love. Because God is Triune and not an undifferentiated Monad, God is an Intra-personal circulation of love, even apart from God's true love for creation. "If God were not threefold...God wouldn't be love in himself—or in order to love he would need creation, and then he wouldn't be God anymore"[15] (Hans Urs von Balthasar).

So now we have answers to the two questions we raised about God's personality and love, and we see they are related. Christianity affirms that God is personal even apart from creation, because God is intrinsically Tri-Personal. Correlatively, God is intrinsically Love even apart from His love for the universe because the Triune God is a communicative circle of Love itself.

The Holism of the Trinity Is the Master-Clue to God's Plan

God as Three-in-One is perfect wholeness, the *Holism of the Absolute.* A whole is a harmony of elements. We encounter many instances of wholeness in the created universe, to a greater or lesser degree. But the wholeness of the Holy Trinity is a matchless harmony of light and love. The three divine Persons are insuperably distinct, yet impartibly one. The perfect Holism of the Trinity is synonymous with the perfect Love which is the Trinity. And we will see now that Love, the unity of the Trinity, is the master-clue to God's plan for creation. "The circle of love, by the Incarnation of the eternal Son, was extended to include men in this life of knowledge and love"[16] (Roger Hasseveldt).

In a free act of generosity, God creates the universe through the eternal Son, who becomes the continuous *Logos* foundation of all matter and energy: a mysterious Whole in which the whole of creation inheres. As Love, God wants to share divine Life with all He has created, so the *Logos* incarnates as Jesus Christ to impart His own Holy

---

[15] Hans Urs von Balthasar, *Who Is A Christian?,* trans. by John Cumming, (New York, NY: Newman Press, 1968), p. 95.

[16] Roger Hasseveldt, *The Church: A Divine Mystery,* trans William Storey, (Notre Dame, IN: Fides Publishers, 1964), p. 54.

Spirit to women and men. The Spirit "pours Himself into creatures and lives in them"[17] (Matthias Joseph Scheeben). In this way they are joined to the Trinity by no less bond than the Spirit that has from eternity united the Father to the Son.

Then the indwelling Spirit recapitulates Christ's Mysteries in us (His life, death, resurrection and ascension), raising us to union with Christ's humanity in this life, and ultimately to participation in His divinity. As Jesus Christ changes bread and wine into his Being, so the Spirit ultimately elevates all creation in Christ to the bliss of the Trinity, the heavenly circle of love. "If God is gift within himself, he is also Gift for the Others, the Creator. He can communicate his Joy and his Life"[18] (Jules Monchanin, S.J.).

The Trinitarian God of the Christian Mystic

The Trinity reveals itself to the intuition of Christians through transforming graces. The more the soul matures, the more sublime its intuitive knowledge of the Trinity becomes.

An old philosophical motto goes to this principle: knowledge is a function of being. To elevate the being of the knower is to create a corresponding expansion in the kind and amount of knowing. To learn about something in our basic orbit of experience does not take much of a change in our being, just a slight adjustment. But to come to know something so unlike us as the infinite Trinity takes a radical elevation in our being. Thus the Holy Spirit, God-in-us, unfolds the Mystery of the Trinity by unfolding us: by elevating our being, expanding our ability to know and love, transforming us to the core. The Door to the Trinity opens us.

The writings of the Christian mystics, our elder brothers and sisters in the Spirit, are full of Trinitarian illuminations. As these men and

---

[17] Matthias Joseph Scheeben, *Mysteries of Christianity*, trans by Cyril Vollert, S. J., (St. Louis, MO: B. Herder Book Co., 1964), p. 411.

[18] J. G. Weber, ed. and trans, *In Quest of the Absolute: The Life and Work of Jules Monchanin,* (Kalamazoo, MI: Cistercian Publications, 1977), p. 122.

women were transformed ever more deeply into Christ, their understanding of the Trinity achieved lambent clarity.

Authentic mystics of every religion have experienced God. What is distinctive about Christian mysticism is its foundation in the Trinity. If you can imagine a book that discusses the collected works of Mark Twain but does not mention the Mississippi River, then you can imagine a book by a Christian mystic that leaves out the Trinity. Teresa of Avila said on entering the "seventh mansion" of prayer:

> It sees these three Persons,
> individually, and yet,
> by a wonderful kind of knowledge which is given to it,
> the soul realizes that
> most certainly and truly
> all these
> three Persons are one Substance...[19]

The English mystic, Blessed Julian of Norwich wrote:

> The Trinity is our maker.
> The Trinity is our keeper.
> The Trinity is our everlasting lover.
> The Trinity is our endless joy.

Blessed Elizabeth of the Trinity aspired ever to be

> retired, as it were, into the depth of my soul, so as to lose myself, to be transmerged into the Blessed Trinity Who dwells there.[20]

The Self-Release Prayer is Trinitarian

But you and I do not only want to read about the Trinity—we want direct intimacy with our Creator too. A vital means to that, as we have

[19] Thomas Dubay, S.M., *Fire Within: St. Teresa of Avila, St. John of the Cross, and the Gospel—on Prayer,* (San Francisco, CA: Ignatius Press, 1989), p. 104.

[20] M.M. Philipon, O.P., ed, *Sister Elizabeth of the Trinity: Spiritual Writings, Letters, Retreats, and Unpublished Notes,* (New York, NY: P. J. Kenedy & Sons, 1962), p. 114.

seen, is the Self-Release Prayer. To practice it is to receive piquant Trinitarian intuitions. That is because to go out of self to God is to participate in Christ's own Trinitarian prayer in us, a prayer that is always going out from the Son in the Spirit to the Father.

To review the Self-Release Prayer:

1. Become aware of a thought or daydream that you can let go.
2. Let it go to make a space for God in interior silence.
3. Tend to the flash of Silence that replaces the thought, for it is an intuitive communion with God. To enact the Self-Release Prayer may last only a few seconds—yet its Stillness robes the soul in eternity.

All Christian prayer is Trinitarian, a participation in the circulation of love in the Trinity. As a lake reflects the sun and the strolling cloud, so the soul in prayer reflects the eternal Love-movement of the Trinity. The eternal movement of the Spirit is the Son's love for the Father and the Father's Love for the Son. When we sit in prayer, we do not create this movement, but may raise sails into it and be borne afar in it.

> It is our conviction
> that the central message of the New Testament
> is that there is really only one prayer,
> and that this prayer
> is the prayer of Christ.
> It is a prayer that continues in our hearts
> day and night.
>
> I can describe it only
> as the stream of love that flows constantly
> between Jesus and the Father.
> The stream of love is the Holy Spirit.[21]
>
> —*Fr. John Main*

Strictly speaking, it is not we who love God, but the mystery of Christ-in-us who loves the Father in prayer. Think of a breeze blowing through a fragrant orchard, carrying the breath of its fruits and flowers. Christ-in-us is the fragrant orchard; His Spirit is the breeze; and we are the blessed field through which it lists to the Father.

---

[21] John Main, *Moment of Christ,* (New York, NY: Crossroad, 1985), p. x.

An Enchanted Convivium of Being

To reflect on the Trinity as we have is also to enrich our contact with God's vivacity in nature. The next time you are outdoors, notice the outflowing and community of the natural world. The sun giving itself to the earth, the dew rising to the sky to form clouds, the birds calling to one other, the garden exhaling hues and perfumes—a festal sharing and intermingling of life and energy in the Wreath of Being.

And as you drink in this diversity in unity, remember that it is ultimately sourced NOW in the Holy Trinity, the serene society of light and love with each divine Person wholly giving its Life to the others, yet All remaining impartibly one.

Look anew at nature. Really see in every convivium and generosity of the natural world a vital reflection of the Trinity's circle of Love as it is happening now! "God has sown the world with His likeness"[22] (Paul Claudel).

God is communicative Love, with the unmanifest Father timelessly begetting the Son, His eternal Manifest, and both lovingly spirating the everlasting movement of the Holy Spirit. This Three-in-One is the *Holism of the Absolute—the foundation of all natural and supernatural holisms.*

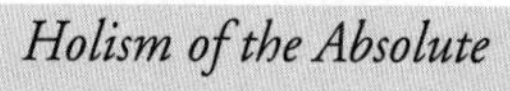

Holism of the Absolute

Holism of Existence

Affinity: The *Holism of Existence* (Chapter Two)

[22] Paul Claudel, *I Believe in God,* Agnes du Sarment, ed., trans. Helen Weaver, (USA: Holt, Rinehart and Winston, 1963), p. 35.

All the inter-relationships we see in the natural world—as among the earth, the sky, the trees, and the human body—all of them reflect the Intra-Communion of God, the Trinity. Is it not obvious that the Trinity is the taproot of all holisms, the vital joint of all things? "To be a person is to *be with*..., to be a sharer, a receiver, a lover. Ultimately the reason why all this is so is that this is the nature of the Supreme Being..."[23] (W. Norris Clarke, S.J.).

[23] Clarke, *op cit.*, p. 112.

CHAPTER 4

The Universe Is the Kaleidoscopic Shadow of Christ

"All created beings exist through Christ and are sustained in their being by Christ's activity. He is the Logos, the image according to which not only man but all creation was fashioned."[1]

—*George Maloney, S.J.*

Imagine Sandro Botticelli applying a final stroke of greenish-blue to *Birth of Venus.* As he lifts his brush off the canvas it disappears. Or think of the master at the end of his life. As he passes out of this world, all his works—all his sculptures, oils, sketches—all instantly dissolve into nothingness.

While there is an intimate connection between the artist and his work, it is not so intimate that minus his attention or presence it evaporates.

But God is so intimately joined to what He creates, that its very being indicates that God is there. There is simply no existence possible apart from God's sustaining Presence. So look around you now, right now, and marvel—whatever you see, it exists because God is behind it here and now, substantiating its existence. What more breathtaking thought may one have?

[1] George A. Maloney, *The Cosmic Christ; from Paul to Teilhard,* (New York, NY: Sheed and Ward, 1968), p. 7.

Though cosmic creation initially occurred billions of years ago, God has not for a second taken His hands off his work, but has continued to conserve its existence, lest it lapse into nothing. "My Father is at work until now, so I am at work" (John 5:17).

All the structures of matter—from grass to grasshoppers to galaxies—radically borrow their created being from the ONE self-existent Being, God. How is this so? Frank Sheed explains:

> God can confer existence upon all other beings,
> precisely because he has it in his own right.
> It is his nature to exist.
> God does not have to receive existence,
> *because he is existence.*[2]

God is the ever-blossom, rising from God the ever-earth, into God the ever-sky.

In this chapter we will study how God's creative and conserving activity connects specifically to the Son of God. We will reflect on the *Holism of the Christ-Logos* and the rootedness of the whole created universe in an uncreated, mysterious Whole: Christ.

The Creed Distills the Mysteries

The mystery of the Son and the other Mysteries of the faith are harmonized in the Church's statement of faith—the Nicene Creed. This masterpiece of mystagogy was written by the bishops at the Council of Nicea in the fourth century. Though its authors were astute in theology and philosophy, the wisdom of the Creed was not principally a product of academic study; it was a fruit of the mystical theology of the Church Fathers, the early teachers of Christianity after the Apostles.[3] Only several hundred words long, the Creed would fill a single sheet of parchment. Small and exquisite, it is an ivory cameo upon the neck of the Bride of Christ, the Church.

---

[2] F. J. Sheed, *Theology for Beginners*, (Ann Arbor, MI: Servant Books, 1981), p. 18.

[3] Mystical theology is intuitive understanding of the Christian mysteries by illuminating and transforming grace.

This life-giving Credo
which we repeat faithfully every day,
what is it but a distillation of mysteries?

Each of its successive articles is
the revelation of a fact
which our intelligence is incapable of controlling,
and which we have no choice but
to accept and absorb—
to our delight.

For each of these drops,
these distilled nights, is quickened and impregnated with light,
love, power, and joy.[4]

—*Paul Claudel*

The Creed begins

We believe in one God, the Father, the Almighty,
maker of heaven and earth,
of all that is seen and unseen.

We believe in one Lord, Jesus Christ,
the only Son of God,
eternally begotten of the Father,
God from God,
Light from Light,
True God from True God,
begotten not made,
one in Being with the Father,
through Him all things were made.[5]

---

[4] Paul Claudel, *I Believe in God,* Agnes du Sarment, ed., trans. Helen Weaver, (USA: Holt, Rinehart and Winston, 1963), pp. 9-10.

[5] Alfred McBride, O. Praem., *Celebrating the Mass, A Guide for Understanding and Loving the Mass More Deeply,* (Huntington, IN: Our Sunday Visitor Publishing Division, 1999), p. 30.

Ah, there it is—in that last line. Notice that "all things were made" through the Son, the Father's creative Potency.

When Catholics recite the Nicene Creed each week at Sunday Mass, perhaps we hurry too quickly over this six-word phrase about the Son. Our attention is drawn to the drama which follows it:

> For us men and our salvation,
> he came down from heaven:
> by the power of the Holy Spirit
> he was born of the Virgin Mary,
> and became man.
> For our sake, he was also crucified
> under Pontius Pilate,
> suffered, died and was buried...[6]

But we are missing much by our relative neglect of the six words that precede it—"through Him all things were made." For in glossing over them, we miss a most mystical dimension of the Son: the Son as the Cosmic Christ, the uncaused *Alpha* of the universe, the bright Axis of all the unfathomably complex operations of space and time. The natural world is the color-swathed empire of the Son. Its banners are the waving trees, its anthem is composed on the fly each morning by little birds of the dawn.

The *Logos* in the Bible

The key to the sacred Mystery of the Cosmic Christ is a single word in scripture mentioned in the last chapter: the *Logos.* In English translations of the New Testament the Greek word *Logos* is rendered "Word." Here again are the opening chords of John's Gospel:

> In the beginning was the **Word,**
> and the **Word** was with God, and the **Word** was God...
> Through him all things were made;
> without him nothing was made that has been made.
>
> —*John 1:1, 3*

---

[6] *Ibid.*

Unfortunately, the English word *Word* quite misses the richness of the original Greek, *Logos*. To uncover the extraordinary depth of John's designation of Christ as *Logos*, let us explore its Greek context.

Imagine yourself in Greece at a time several hundred years before St. John's writing, near a site called the "Painted *Stoa*" (*stoa* is Greek for "porch"). Close by, a Stoic philosopher is in a discussion with students. Not much time passes before we hear the word *Logos* spoken. This is not surprising because for the Stoics, the *Logos* is the Axis of all reality. The *Logos* is God.

Hundreds of years before Christ's coming, these philosophers were awed by the colossal architecture of the universe and posited at the burning summit of being a *Logos*: the Mystery of matter supporting all the universe. For them, the *Logos* was:

- the divine principle that suffuses and directs the cosmos
- the Source of cosmic complexity,
  as well as the orchestrator of its unity
- the Creative Mind behind all pacific beauty

Because of Hellenic influences on Jewish culture, the Stoic principle of the *Logos* was familiar to the Jews.

St. John called Jesus Christ the *Logos* because he knew Him as the Incarnation of the eternal Son who existed before the universe came to be. John was enlightened to understand Christ as the divine Knowing "though whom all things are made." Tellingly, it is John's gospel that records Jesus' saying to Pharisees, "I tell you the truth, before Abraham was born, I am!" (John 8:58). By His use of the distinctive Hebrew phrase, "I am," Christ suggests that His divine nature is eternal, because "I AM" ("Yahweh" in Hebrew) is the Name by which God designated Himself to Moses (Exodus 3:14).

As we see, the English translation of John's word *Logos* as "Word" is severely limited. Writes Jaroslav Pelikan, a distinguished Christian scholar:

> But the "Logos of God," when applied to Jesus Christ meant far more than "Word of God," more even than divine revelation;

> there were many other Greek vocables that would have sufficed to express that much and no more, and several of them were being used in the New Testament and in other early Christian literature. Employing the specific name Logos implied in addition to this that what had come in Jesus Christ was also the Reason and Mind of the cosmos.[7]

Back to the Stoics' conception of the *Logos.* It was indeed remarkable, prophetic. And yet their intuitions of the *Logos* were still fragmentary, limited, and even at points misleading. But this is hardly surprising, as centuries would pass before the *Logos* would take flesh and be born to the world as Jesus Christ.

Ironically, the Stoics themselves would not believe that the *Logos* could be born as a God-man. The *Logos* in the flesh? This was an absurdity to the Stoic mentality, scandalous gibberish. What on earth would the Super-Intelligence of the universe be doing on earth—even dying on a wretched cross! Hence St. Paul was moved to write that the Cross was "foolishness to the Greeks"[8] (1 Corinthians 1:23).

The Stoics conceived the *Logos* as a passively benign divinity, as pleasant but as impersonal as sunshine. In contrast, Christians believed the *Logos,* incarnate in Jesus, was actively merciful, not beneath dying on a Cross to disclose God's love and reveal the Mysteries of the Way back to God.

As revealed in Christ, the *Logos* is not an immobile, stony gate of the divine, through which only the high wisdom of sages passes. It is a God of compassion who would run out through the gate to meet His lost sons, his prodigals—calling back over his shoulder to his servants, *Ready the feast!* "In the first place it should be known, that if anyone is seeking God, the Beloved is seeking that person much more"[9] (John of the Cross). This is the true *Logos.*

---

[7] Jaroslav Pelikan, *Jesus Through the Centuries: His Place in the History of Culture,* (New Haven, CT: Yale University Press, 1985), pp. 62-63.

[8] This translation is from the King James Bible.

[9] *The Collected Works of St. John of the Cross,* trans. Kieran Kavanaugh O.C.D., and Otilio Rodriguez, O.C.D., (Washington, DC: ICS Publications, 1991), p. 684.

The Rhapsody of Christ

We see that the Apostle John's application of the *Logos* to Christ was revolutionary. For John the *Logos* was not a concept in the whistling lecture of a philosopher; it was Life itself. With this background in mind, let us look again at the Prologue, with the original Greek inserted and now clarified:

> In the beginning was the **Logos,**
> and the **Logos** was with God, and the **Logos** was God.
> Through him all things were made;
> without him nothing was made that has been made.
>
> —*John 1:1, 3*

To describe God throughout creation was the chief passion of French priest and paleontologist, Teilhard de Chardin, S.J. (1881-1955). This apostle of the *Logos* dimension of God wrote:

> The prodigious expanses of time
> which preceded the first Christmas
> were not empty
> of Christ:
> they were imbued
> with the influx of his power...
>
> When Christ first appeared before men
> in the arms of Mary
> he had already
> stirred up the world.[10]

The Christ-Logos, then, is the holy Pith of all things:

> That Light whose Smile kindles the universe,
> That Beauty in which all things work and move....
>
> —*Percey Bysshe Shelley, Adonais, LIV*

[10] Teilhard de Chardin, *Hymn of the Universe,* trans. Simon Bartholomew, (New York, NY: Harper & Row, 1965), p. 77.

Even as you read these words, you are being fountained into being by the Christ-Logos. Become aware of your next heartbeat: it is the rhythm and meter of the poet Christ—His rhapsody in your being.

> For in him we live and move and have our being.
>
> —*Acts 17:28*

The *Logos* is "smiling in flowers, then rising and waving His hands in the trees"[11] (Kahlil Gibran).

Please personalize this. Think of one of your favorite natural scenes. Get it clearly in mind. What is it? The ocean? A mountain? A forest? The desert at sunrise? Please realize this: the Christ-Logos, the Son, is the animating Beauty of that natural wonder. The color, the fragrance, the shapes, the myriad pulses of life of that particular place—all rise from the Son. Teilhard de Chardin was given to see by mystical graces Christ as the unifying uncreated Element of nature:

> Like those translucent materials
> which can be wholly illumined
> by a light enclosed within them,
> the world manifests to the christian mystic
> as bathed in an inward light
> which brings out its structure,
> its relief, and its depths…
> a tranquil, mighty radiance…[12]

The castle of the whole cosmos is moored in the Cosmic Christ, the living Rock. Even as Jesus' human body cast a shadow at noon on the grasses of Judea, so too his vaster Body, which existed before time, also casts a shadow—our universe. And the colorful shadow of his vaster Body is all that is.

---

[11] Kahlil Gibran, *The Prophet,* (New York, NY: Alfred Knopf, 1998), p. 79.

[12] Teilhard de Chardin, *op cit.,* pp. 88-89.

The Christ-Logos is the uncreated, infinite One, everywhere the same, behind the diverse, finite forms of creation in the Great Wreath of Being.

Glorious Lord Christ...
you who gather into your exuberant unity
every beauty, every affinity, every energy,
every mode of existence;
it is you to whom my being cried out
with a desire as vast as the universe,
In truth you are my Lord and my God.[13]

—*Teilhard de Chardin*

The myriad infinitesimals of existent matter and energy are like magic seeds ever-cast from the Sower's hand. To the fourteenth century mystic, Blessed Julian of Norwich, Christ vividly revealed Himself as the *Logos* who renews universal creation each moment. In one "showing," as she called them, Christ said to her:

See! I am in everything!
See! I never lift my hands off my works,
nor will I ever.
See! I lead everything toward the purpose
for which I ordained it, without beginning,
by the same Power, Wisdom, and Love by
which I created it.

"I have often said God is creating this entire world full and entire in this present now"[14] (Meister Eckhart). In other words, the whole created universe is arising right now from an unseen Whole, the Son. We might say that Eckhart is describing the *Holism of the Christ-Logos.*

---

[13] Chardin, *op cit.,* p. 34.

[14] Matthew Fox, *Breakthrough: Meister Eckhart's Creation Spirituality in New Translation,* (New York, NY: Doubleday Books, 1980), p. 65.

All of creation, seen and unseen, is rooted in the Christ-Logos—the Mystery of matter. All that is good, true, and beautiful in creation arises from the *Holism of the Christ-Logos.*

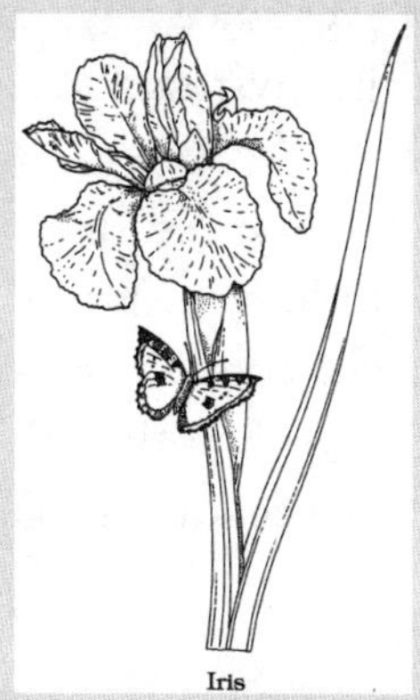

Holism of the Christ-Logos

Holism of the Unitive State

Affinity: The *Holism of the Unitive State* (Chapter Nine).

To come to the unitive state—union with God—is to be graced with heightened awareness of the *Logos* shining through creation.

The Son Is the Innermost Secret of Matter

Verses from the prologue of St. John's gospel are only several of the very many New Testament verses which reveal Christ as the divine Secret of matter. Time and again in scripture and in diverse ways, the Son (rather than the Father or the Spirit) is directly linked to matter. Let us gather together some of these references, to see clearly how often the Son in particular is associated with material creation.

With the Apostle John, St. Paul mystically perceived that the Logos-Son holds all material worlds together:

> For by him all things were created:
> things in heaven and on earth, visible and invisible…
> He is before all things,
> and in him all things hold together.
>
> —*Colossians 1:16, 17*

Eventually the Son incarnates as Jesus Christ, assuming a material body. Then on the eve of His Passion, the Son takes two material elements, bread and wine, and says, "This is my Body. This is my Blood. Do this in remembrance of Me." And ever since then, at every Mass, the Son becomes materially present in the mystical Eucharist, and will do so until the end of time.

After his passion and crucifixion, the Son resurrects His glorified material body and later ascends bodily to heaven. You see the pattern: the Son's manifesting again and again His connection to matter. The conclusion we must draw is compelling: the Son-dimension of God is the Mystery of matter. Not matter as science knows matter—but the Unknown of matter, its *Logos* source.

The Numinous Spell of Beauty

"How sense-luscious the world is," begins Diane Ackerman in her lyrical *A Natural History of the Senses.* "In the summer, we can be decoyed out of bed by the sweet smell of the air soughing through our bedroom window."[15]

Not only can nature's beauty lure us out of bed and into the day, but can even bespell our spirits into the "divine milieu"—enchant us to God's threshold, for the *Logos* undergirds the beauty of Nature.[16] Fair nature magnetizes us to Beauty itself; and the Christ-Logos is the honey within the branches of beauty. "God is called 'super-beautiful,' namely, because He possesses in Himself eminently, and prior to all other beings, the source of all beauty"[17] (James Anderson).

---

[15] Diane Ackerman, *A Natural History of the Senses,* (New York, NY: Random House, 1990), p. xv.

[16] Though Christianity reveals the *Logos* omnipresent in creation, its doctrine is not pantheistic. The created universe is distinct from the uncreated Whole, the *Logos,* which gives it being.

[17] James F. Anderson, *Introduction to the Metaphysics of St. Thomas Aquinas,* (Chicago, IL: Henry Regnery Company, 1953), pp. 91-92.

The mystics know the Christic character of creation, and how God touches the heart in pure nature. At Monte Calvario, John of the Cross would lead his friars to a rocky lookout or cool stream, and after speaking to them of God's splendor, ask one monk to sit over here on the mountain, another over there, to commune in solitude with God. "Beauty is to things what sanctity is to the soul" (Simone Weil).

Teilhard de Chardin ecstatically slaked his soul-thirst on the beauty of Christ omnipresent:

> Lord,
> it is you who,
> through the imperceptible goadings
> of sense-beauty,
> penetrated my heart in order to
> make its life flow out into yourself.
>
> You came down into me
> by means of a tiny scrap of created reality;
> and then, suddenly, you unfurled your immensity
> before my eyes and displayed yourself to me
> as Universal Being.[18]

Out of the blue, the Christ-Logos may at any time cast a spell of numinous beauty on a heart, to turn it Godward. Consider this conversion experience of an officer who served in the First World War:

> I walked eastward for about two miles along the towpath and turned. The nearer I drew to the village, the more alive my surroundings seemed to become. It was as if something which had been dormant when I was in the wood were coming to life. I must have drifted into an exalted state. The moon, when I looked up at it, seemed to have become personalized and observant, as if it were aware of my presence on the tow-path. A sweet scent pervaded the air. Early shoots were breaking from the sticky buds of the balsam poplars which bordered the canal;

[18] Teilhard de Chardin, *op. cit.*, p. 91.

> their pleasant resinous odour conveyed good-will....A feeling that I was being absorbed into the living surroundings gained in intensity and was working up to a climax. Something was about to happen. Then it happened. The experience lasted, I should say, about thirty seconds and seemed to come out of the sky in which were resounding harmonies. The thought: "That is the music of the spheres" was immediately followed by a glimpse of luminous bodies—meteors or stars—circulating in predestined courses emitting both light and music. I stood still on the tow-path and wondered if I was to fall down. I dropped to one knee and thought: "How wonderful to die at this moment!"[19]

"Here I am! I stand at the door and knock," said Christ in a mystic vision given to St. John (Revelation 3:20). The Lord of Beauty knocked on the door of this soldier's heart through a preternatural intensification of nature's loveliness.

The *Logos* as Goodness, Truth, Beauty

In addition to Beauty, all the great "transcendentals" (as metaphysics calls them) are holistically rooted in the omnipresent Christ-Logos: the transcendentals of oneness, truth, and goodness. Therefore, all healing and enlivening contacts we have in daily life with unity, beauty, truth, goodness, and love are contacts with Christ, though we may never have so named them.

This idea inspires a maxim of holistic Christianity: *Wherever there is the reality of healing, there is Healing Reality*—God. When anyone experiences a truly healing insight, it is ultimately sourced in the Christ-Logos—the living Truth, Healing Reality. Writes Charles Malik in *The Wonder of Being:*

> Indeed, whatever excellence and glory
> exist in earth and in heaven—

[19] Sir Alister Hardy, *The Spiritual Nature of Man: A Study of Contemporary Religious Experience,* (Oxford: Clarendon Press, 1979), p. 41.

> the order and lawfulness of nature,
> great music, science, philosophy,
> knowledge, reason, poetry and literature,
> company and friendship,
> the joy and zest of living,
> truthfulness, contentment, peace, strength, love—
> do not come from earth and heaven
> but from outside earth and heaven altogether—
> from the Lord God.[20]

Any truth or experience we have that is genuinely healing, must be from the Christ-Logos, even if we do not explicitly grasp His presence in it, because "apart from me you can do nothing" (John 15:5). Of course, there is not an iota of egotism in Christ's saying; he is speaking of his hidden *Logos* nature. So whenever we are healed or transformed by contact with any goodness, truth, and beauty, we are healed and transformed by Christ.

You see a beautiful orange-petalled rose. You lean toward it, and draw in its exquisite scent. Trivial self-preoccupation vanishes. In this relaxed moment you feel the reality of healing. The eternal Son of God, the Christ-Logos, is here.

The devout Hindu woman tenderly nursing her baby is, in the tenderness of her love, worshipping Christ, even if she does not think the word "Christ"—for "apart from me you can do nothing." Her love for her baby is a participation in goodness, and so she is connected to Christ. *Wherever there is the reality of healing, there is Healing Reality.*

This hour a scientist discovered a medicine that will bring wholeness to shattered bodies. In her discovery is a spark of the Cosmic Christ, for "apart from me you can do nothing." Perhaps the scientist is an atheist, and she does not acknowledge the Christic character of the good she has come upon. But God will bless her if she has compassionately worked to heal bodies, regardless of her disbelief in Him. Christ tells a story of a king who says on judgment day:

> "For I was hungry and you gave me something to eat...I was sick and you looked after me...."

---

[20] Charles N. Malik, *The Wonder of Being,* (Waco, TX: Word Books, 1974), p. 68.

> Then the righteous will answer him, "Lord, when did we see you hungry and feed you...?"
>
> The king will reply, "I tell you the truth, whatever you did for one of the least of these brothers of mine, you did for me."
>
> —*Matthew 25:35, 37, 39-40*

Wherever there is the reality of healing, there is Healing Reality.

Several times in these pages we have quoted the poet Paul Claudel, who converted to Christianity as a young artist in Paris. By his art he consciously glorified Christ. But now think of a poet who has not known Christ, yet his work is alive with the truth of life. Wherever there is healing truth, there is Christ. Jacques Maritain had many such artist-friends; he writes of them:

> In the last analysis all genuine poetry
> is religious.
>
> Even if the poet
> has no conceptual knowledge of God,
> even if he is or believes he is an atheist,
> it is toward the primary source of Beauty
> that in actual fact his spiritual effort is oriented.
>
> And thus, if not intellectual or moral hindrance
> thwarts this spiritual dynamism,
> he will naturally be led by poetry
> to some conscious notion and awareness
> of the existence of that God
> at Whom he is unconsciously looking,
> in and through
> his art and his work.[21]

As the *Logos* is the substratum of all reality, the truths of science and math resonate in holistic harmony with the divine Whole; wrote the twentieth-century Christian philosopher Simone Weil:

---

[21] Jacques Maritain, *Man's Approach to God,* (Latrobe, PA: The Archabbey Press, 1960), pp. 18-19.

The solution of a geometry problem
does not in itself constitute a precious gift,
but the same law applies to it
because it is an image of something precious.

Being a little fragment of a particular truth,
it is a pure image of the unique, eternal, and living Truth,
the very Truth that once in a human voice declared,
"I am the Truth."[22]

In this way, the Christ-Logos is the ultimate ground of the arts and science, aesthetics and ethics, religion and philosophy. This confluence is the *Holism of the Christ-Logos* with the *Holism of Knowledge,* to be further discussed in Chapter Six.

The Self-Release Prayer Invites Contact with the Christ-Logos

Think of yourself on a late September day in New England, a hundred fifty years ago. You are walking leisurely through a woods with your good companion, Ralph Waldo Emerson. You say little to one another, a remark here and there, for mostly you and he are simply taking in the leafy autumn sights, textures, and scents. Emerson would later write:

> In the woods, too, a man casts off his years, as a snake his slough, and at what period soever of his life is always a child. In the woods is perpetual youth.....Standing on the bare ground,—my head bathed by the blithe air and uplifted into infinite space,—all mean egotism vanishes. I become a transparent eyeball; I am nothing; I see all; the currents of the Universal Being circulate through me....[23]

Is not it obvious by his description that Emerson knew the ways of the Self-Release Prayer? Note how the sights and sounds of nature solicited him to this prayer of quiet, which intimated to him "Universal Being."

---

[22] Simone Weil, *Waiting for God,* trans. Emma Craufurd, (New York, NY: Harper & Row Publishers, 1973), p. 112.

[23] http://www.emersoncentral.com/nature1.htm

We see now how the Self-Release Prayer may invite contact with the omnipresent Christ-Logos. The sunlight on the bark of a tree, a crowd of orange and yellow flowers in the window box of a local shop, a protective rebuke from a mother jay guarding her nest—the Christ-Logos is the invisible Wonder in which all this is nested. By the Self-Release Prayer, we may be graced with glimpses of the One behind the many.

To pray this Prayer in the context of nature:

1. Glimpse natural beauty.
2. Let go of self-preoccupations.
3. Intuit a flash of silence, the door that opens upon the Christ-Logos in nature.
4. Commune for a wordless, timeless moment with the omnipresent Son in the natural world.

It is Saturday morning and you open the door to get the newspaper. You are met unexpectedly by a gentle spring breeze, ecstatic with jasmine. You had not realized spring was imminent, and now it is pleasantly upon you. You remember, in that instant, the Self-Release Prayer. Experiencing the breeze, you let go of any self-preoccupation. When you opened the door to get the paper, you had been daydreaming about a mishap at work. Now you become aware that a flash of gentle silence has replaced the worried daydream. You notice that the silence mingles magically with the beauty of the jasmine breeze, revealing a new, striking depth to the moment. The flash of silence becomes an open mystic window that allows you to savor the warm fragrant breeze and to intuitively commune with the source of its beauty—the Christ-Logos.

Having meditated for a time on the *Logos*, perhaps the next time we hear someone casually say, maybe even as a mechanical cliché, "The beauty of the world speaks of God," we will be drawn beyond the cliché to the metaphysical profundity to which it points: the Son-Dimension of the Trinity, the *Logos* that unifies the natural worlds.

CHAPTER 5

Lightning Made Eternal: The Incarnation of God

"There is much to fathom in Christ, for he is like an abundant mine with many recesses of treasures, so that however deep individuals may go they never reach the end or the bottom...."[1]

—John of the Cross

He entered the world as a tumult of lightning, as a May breeze coming silently across a field, as a healing dream that unlines a restless sleeper's brow.

Sky-Heart, Knight of our fairer dream,
You do still tread the day,
Nor bows nor spears shall stay your steps.
You walk through all our arrows.
You smile down upon us,
And though you are the youngest of us all
You father us all.[2]

—Kahlil Gibran

---

[1] *The Collected Works of St. John of the Cross,* trans. Kieran Kavanaugh O.C.D., and Otilio Rodriguez, O.C.D., (Washington, DC: ICS Publications, 1991), from *The Spiritual Canticle,* p. 616.

[2] Kahlil Gibran, *Jesus the Son of Man,* (New York, NY: Alfred A. Knopf, 1995), p. 256. Used with permission.

In his Divinity, he is the *Logos,* the eternal Son of the eternal Father—the omnipresent, generative Christ before Bethlehem. And then, two thousand years ago, in a second dawn after the world's first dawn—

> The Word [Logos] became flesh
> and made his dwelling among us.
>
> —*John 1:14*

In an elementary school art class this morning, children are drawing pictures of whatever they want. A visiting educator, walking around the classroom, spies a drawing of one little girl—a truly remarkable drawing.

"My, what an interesting picture," she says, bending toward the illustration. "What exactly are you drawing?"

The little girl looks up and, frowning at the lady, says, "God"—and goes back to her drawing.

The visitor chuckles softly to herself. "My dear, you know that no one knows what God looks like!"

The girl just continues drawing. "They will when I'm finished."

The child spoke better than she knew. God has indeed desired to reveal His countenance to us in a way we could understand.

> He made himself like me so that I might be clothed in him
> I had no fear when I saw him,
> for he is mercy to me.
> He took my nature so that I might understand him,
> my face so that I should not turn away from him.[3]
>
> —*Odes of Solomon 7*

[3] Olivier Clement, *The Roots of Christian Mysticism,* (New York, NY: New City Press, 1995), p. 37.

Christianity's Innovation

Truth be told, philosophy and religion have not always understood even the idea that God is seeking to communicate with human beings. This idea would be considered absurd, even scandalous, in the thought of ancient Greek philosophy. This is made clear in a summary of the matter by Jacques Maritain, in his commentary on a colossus of early philosophy, Aristotle:

> As far as Aristotle is concerned, "it would be ridiculous," he says, "to reproach God because the love we receive from him in return is not equal to the love we give him, just as it would be ridiculous for the subject to make a similar reproach to a prince."[4]

But Christianity offered a revolutionary vision:

> For Christianity, in any case, grace, by raising the human person to the supernatural order, makes him partake in the very life and goods of God... *God is no longer enclosed in his transcendence but communicates it. Between God and man, as between friends, there can be love from person to person, with all its extravagances...*[5]

Hence, Jesus' striking statement at the last supper:

> I no longer call you servants....
> Instead I have called you friends.
>
> —*John 15:15*

There is a hidden profundity in Jesus' saying that exceeds even its obvious magnanimity. The key to unlocking this profundity is the dictum of John of the Cross: *Love demands equality.* John writes in *The Spiritual Canticle:*

---

[4] Jacques Maritain, *Moral Philosophy: An Historical and Critical Survey of the Great Systems,* (New York, NY: Charles Scribner's Sons, 1964), p. 82.

[5] *Ibid.*

> The soul's aim is a love equal to God's. She always desired this equality, naturally and supernaturally, for lovers cannot be satisfied without feeling they love as much as they are loved.[6]

John is saying that when we understand the true bounty of another's love for us, we thirst to rise to the sublimity of that love, to love the beloved as we are loved. This is what we should keep in mind in reflecting on Jesus' words, "I have called you friends." Befriending us, Christ is implicitly promising to help us attain the divine amplitude of love, to love Him with the same illimitable love He bears for us—for love demands equality. Pause for moment to ponder how amazing this is. Since Christ's love for us is infinite, He is promising us an infinite growth in our capacity to love!

Not Idly Called Christians

But how can we love infinitely? For that would mean to love exactly as God loves. What kind of promise is God making? How can God fulfill it—to infinitely stretch our capacity to love so that it spans God's love in every dimension?

To understand this, we need to draw on our discussion of the Trinity. Recall that the Third Person of the Trinity, Holy Spirit, is Love absolute: the infinite Love shared by the Father and the Son. Also recall that Christ promised that he would send this Spirit into anyone who would welcome it, to join him or her perfectly to the Trinity, as He and the Father are united. It is a gift of His very divinity; He wills that the Spirit "take from what is mine and make it known to you" (John 16:15).

Imagine that the sun has promised to light a little wax candle—and then itself perches upon its wick and humbly remains there to be its flame! An immensity has come to indwell us, and we do not know it.

But we shall. The Spirit of Love is silently, inexorably transforming our soul into itself. And that is how we will fulfill the truth, *Love demands equality*. Our soul will be transfigured in eternity into the

---

[6] Kavanaugh and Rodriguez, *op cit.*, p. 618.

one perfect Lover of God, the Son, and so will come to wholly love God as God loves God. "We are not idly called Christians"[7] (Martin Darcy, S.J.).

Eternity and Eviternity

God incarnate, Jesus Christ, was both God and man. Christ's human nature was like our own in all ways, according to sacred tradition. Yet there are important differences between us and Christ, the unique God-man—differences we will now reflect on.

You may be wondering what place differences have in a study of holism. Isn't holism about unity? Yes. But unity can include difference, as in complementarity, which is not identity. Spouses may become one in their love, but they are not identical. Their oneness is of complementarity, not of identity. Similarly, Christian holism envisions the oneness between self and God as complementary. We are one with God not because we *are* God (identity), but because God completes our being (complementarity). Christian holism also knows oneness through transformation. We are one with God now, but God is transforming us into ever deeper oneness with Himself. Finally, beyond death, God will complete our transformation in Him, transfiguring our souls into Christ, for only the divine Son fully knows the Father in the Spirit. That is why our study of differences, as well as likenesses, is in keeping with the holistic intuition of unity. In the phrase of Jacques Maritain, we must distinguish to unite.[8]

We begin by noting that human beings are truly called children of God, as God loves us with the solicitude of a mother and father. "For you created my innermost being, you knit me together in my mother's womb…." (Psalms 139:13). We are all sons and daughters of God in this sense, as God is our Creator and loving provider.

---

[7] Martin C. Darcy, S.J., *Of God and Man: Thoughts on Faith and Morals,* (Notre Dame, IN: University of Notre Dame Press, 1964), p. 173.

[8] Jacques Maritain, *The Degrees of Knowledge,* trans. Bernard Wall, (New York, NY: Charles Scribner's Sons, 1938), p. ix.

But there is only one Son who existed before creation: the *Logos* who is eternally begotten of the Father, even before the worlds were created. Only this *Logos,* this Son, existed before he was biologically conceived in the womb of Mary. You and I did not exist before our biological conception. Think of the day of your birth. Now count back nine months from that, to the moment you were conceived. Before that, you did not biologically exist (or spiritually exist, as the soul does not pre-exist embodiment.) In contrast, the Son has always existed as the eternal *Logos,* the verdant Spring of innumerable galaxies—Christ has ever existed timelessly before His conception in Mary's womb. "The one who comes down from above is above all. . . ." (John 3:31).

So only one Son is eternal, timelessly existent. In contrast, you and I are *eviternal:* that is to say, we had a beginning in time, but are now on a journey to God's eternity.

Christ's Egoless Beginnings

Consider another difference: The Son, sacred tradition tells us, was born without sin. This is tantamount to saying that the Son was born without an ego. For it is only the ego that can choose away from God, which is sin, and it is unthinkable that the Son—being God—could choose contrary to His own will. This does not mean that Christ was born without a self. Christ was born with a self, but one innately and unwaveringly centered in God.

What is the difference between ego and self? Self is synonymous with consciousness, which is the specific mode of human knowing. (Animals are aware, but their mode of knowing is sensory awareness unmediated by self, whereas our knowing is self-reflexive: consciousness.) Consciousness includes the whole of self-reflexivity, including emotions, the unconscious, thoughts, body-awareness, and ego.

So consciousness is not synonymous with ego. The ego is the original, deepest point of self or consciousness, but it is not the whole of consciousness. Ego is will-for-self: that central point in us that seeks our own good (however truly or foolishly we conceive that good). When truly oriented, the ego seeks God as its highest good, realizing that only God can fully satisfy its quest for meaning. When badly oriented, the ego restlessly seeks identity in the hypnotic dazzle of prestige, power, and ostentatious possessions.

God wants to transform us beyond the fickleness of the ego, to a condition in which we consistently will what is truly good for us—which is simply God and God's will, as God is our highest good. God transforms us to that condition (the unitive state) by ending the ego in a stroke of grace at the right season of our spiritual journey, and becoming Himself our new inner reference point in daily life.

Back to our discussion of Christ. He did not come to the egoless unitive state through a spiritual quest, but was uniquely born into it. From birth, Christ's humanity was united to the Father. If our spiritual journey should take us to the unitive state, we thereby catch up with Christ's humanity by grace. We then become truly his brothers and sisters, as He was born only to be "the firstborn of many brethren" (Romans 8:29). In coming to union with him, we fulfill our humanity, for he is "the image of humanity as it had originally been intended to be..."[9] (Jaroslav Pelikan).

The Unsung Passion of Christ

That the Son of God existed before his Incarnation as the *Logos* (whereas we began to exist only nine months before our birth) has surprising implications. Christ knew the transcendental bliss of heaven (in his words, the "glory" of the Father) before Incarnating, but we did not. How could we, for we did not exist before our biological conception. We were not plucked from expansive heavenly bliss and plunged into a few cells of flesh, as was Christ. Our biological beginnings were natural, unconscious, perhaps even euphorically "oceanic," as Freud speculated.

But Christ's biological conception was a precipitous stepping down—from the inconceivable bliss of the Absolute, the Trinity, to the manifold limitations of human consciousness.

---

[9] Jaroslav Pelikan, *Jesus Through the Centuries: His Place in the History of Culture,* (New Haven, CT: Yale University Press, 1985), p. 74.

In an infinitely sublime act of love, Christ

> being in the very nature God,
> did not consider equality with God
> something to be grasped,
> but made himself nothing,
> taking the very nature of a servant,
> being made in human likeness.
>
> —*Philippians 2:6*

When we think of the suffering of Christ we typically put it at the end of His life, in His passion in the Garden of Gethsemane and in the agony his cross, with its physical and metaphysical horrors. But there is an unsung passion of Christ—the first moments of His Incarnation. These entailed immeasurably greater suffering than even the most oppressive agonies of his last moments on the cross. His Incarnation was a transcendentally awful suffering.

We conventionally remember Christ's beginnings in this world as placid and mild. Swathed in the lilting tenderness of Mary and girded by the calloused hands of good Joseph, the infant God sleeps in heavenly peace. His dolorous days, his passion and crucifixion, are far off from these tranquil, dulcet beginnings. But this view does not do justice to the unspeakably dreadful price that the Son paid just to cross the infinite abyss between the Uncreated Trinity and the created world, to undergo the process of Incarnating as Jesus Christ. It was the kind of suffering that only God could endure, and only the noblest God would endure for our spinning atom.

The process of Incarnating entailed the Son's uniting his divine Person to human consciousness. Though we experience consciousness as expansive intelligence and freedom, the Absolute is so transcendent to consciousness that the Son's assumption of it was a like a torturous imprisonment. It was a voluntary reduction of shoreless Eternity to grains of time, a "cramped condition that God, the Perfect, the ineffable Being, chose to take upon Himself with all humility and meekness"[10] (Paul Claudel). The Trinitarian Son voluntarily accepted this crude

---

[10] Paul Claudel, *I Believe in God,* Agnes du Sarment, ed., trans. Helen Weaver, (USA: Holt, Rinehart and Winston, 1963), p. 51.

imprisonment for our sake, sacrificing His experience of the Father's glory to come in perfect solidarity with our humanity and make the passage through consciousness and beyond back to the heaven of the Father. "How could we be partakers of adoption as God's sons without receiving from Him, through the Son, the gift of communion with Him?...This is why He passed through all ages of human life, restoring to all men communion with God"[11] (St. Irenaeus).

The Superlative Holistic Icon

> When the original chaos rose up, all the elements
> that in the fullness of time
> would go to form the body of the Savior were there,
> scattered throughout the universal mass.
> God was even then fashioning a body for Himself.[12]
>
> —*Emile Mersch*

At the first moment of Creation, in the first gold-red instant of time, the elements that would eventually form the body of the Incarnate God, Jesus Christ, were present in the cosmic plasma, which diffuse Presence, even then, was a benediction and a call—"when I am lifted up from the earth, I will draw all men to myself" (John 12:32).

As we try to better understand the God-man, we may unexpectedly be aided by a picture commonly reproduced in psychology books. You may have seen it. At first glance, you see a white goblet. A moment later, the dark background appears as two other images—two figures facing each other. Then as your perception subtlety shifts again, you see the goblet once more.

Something analogous to this occurs when one gazes on a crucifix. Imagine yourself in Catholic Church, pondering the crucifix near the

---

[11] Irenaeus, *The Scandal of the Incarnation: Irenaeus Against the Heresies,* ed. Hans Urs von Balthasar, trans. John Saward, (San Francisco, CA: Ignatius Press, 1990), p. 59.

[12] Emile Mersch, S.J., *The Theology of the Mystical Body,* trans. Cyril Vollert, S.J., (St. Louis, MO: B. Herder Book Co., 1952), p. 135.

altar. As you first gaze on it, you see the figure of a man who has bled his life out for God. A man wholly given to doing God's will. In short, you see True Man, Man-for-God. (Christ's Godward will is here designated by an ascending arrow.)

Scala/Art Resource, NY

But as you continue to gaze, the form before you changes. You no longer find the figure of a Man aspiring upward toward God, but now see an incarnate God descending from above: the descent of God to man, God coming to be with wounded and aspiring humanity. You see a God who has abandoned the experience of heavenly glory to be nailed between criminals. A thorn-crowned God voluntarily anointed with a darkling distillation of human pain—the pain of the despised, the forgotten, the misjudged. (A descent designated as follows by a descending arrow.)

Scala/Art Resource, NY

This is God wholly in solidarity with the prisoner at Dauchau, the starving villager oppressed by a dictator, the abused child, the bereaved, the forgotten elderly in the nursing home. He is "God with us"—*Emmanuel,* in the Hebrew (Matthew 1:23). The images shift back and forth. Now you see Man-for-God. Now God-for-Man.

In this icon, we find the perfect Holism: the unity of God and humanity, perfect God and perfect Man, wholly one in Jesus Christ. Man-for-God, God-for-Man.

> Thus are supernaturally realized in this sublime mystery God's desire to give Himself as much as possible to man, and man's yearning to be united as much as possible to God.[13]
>
> —*Reginald Garrigou-Lagrange*

[13] Reginald Garrigou-Lagrange, *Our Savior and His Love for Us,* trans. A. Bouchard, (Rockford, IL: Tan Books and Publishers, Inc., 1998), p. 90.

> The mystery of Jesus Christ consists in this *really standing on both sides* of the line that divides God from his creatures in the purely natural order of creation.[14]
>
> —*Karl Rahner, S.J.*

As we will see in upcoming chapters, the meaning of Christ's death includes but far exceeds those just explored. In studying the final Mysteries of Christ in Chapter Eleven, we will discover that by his death Christ demonstrated a particular mystic transition that is *sine qua non* to his and our truly knowing the Father.

God unites His uncreated *Logos* nature to the created nature of humanity in Jesus Christ in the *Holism of the Incarnation.* By his Incarnation, Christ has united himself with the humanity of all; tellingly, the Nicene Creed does not say that eternal Son become *a* man but became MAN. "Jesus Christ is, so to speak, the concrete universal"[15] (Karl Rahner). Christ forms a holistic union with our humanity.

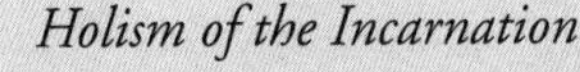

Holism of the Incarnation — *Holism of Existence*

Affinity: The *Holism of Existence* (Chapter Two)

---

[14] Karl Rahner, *Mary, Mother of the Lord: Theological Meditations,* (New York, NY: Herder and Herder, 1963), p. 12.

[15] Avery Dulles, *The Catholicity of the Church,* (New York, NY: Oxford University Press, 1985), p. 9.

That God would become man—assume humanity—is a poignant affirmation of the human condition, our nature and daily existence. God's affirmation of the dignity of the human person is amplified even more in His living for thirty years incognito in Nazareth—whose people knew Him simply as Jesus, the Carpenter. Thus does the *Holism of the Incarnation* support the *Holism of Existence.*

Christ, the Unprecedented

"The more profound a work is," observed Henri De Lubac, "the less its antecedents explain it. We must, in order to understand it, evaluate what will come of it or—if it is still too early—guess at it."[16]

Too often historians, sociologists, and psychologists reductively approach Christ's life according to typological antecedents, slotting him into the standard categories of their disciplines. For example, a political scientist may insist that Christ is best understood as a social revolutionary. More esoteric theorists tend to do the same, presenting Christ as a yogi, or a bodhisattva, or a philosopher, or a gnostic enlightener. But none of these attempts is satisfactory. Jesus Christ, God incarnate, is metaphysically without precedent: a divine-human Whole that had never been before, the man-God. Let us consider two popular but reductive categorizations of Christ: Christ as philosopher, in the manner of Socrates, and Christ as gnostic redeemer.

Socrates and Christ

Though separated by four centuries, Christ and Socrates were wandering teachers. Both consecrated their lives to the truth, both were guileless, and both were put to death rather than renounce truth. But these likenesses are limited, and casually pressed to wrong conclusions, said G.K. Chesterton in *Everlasting Man,* his study of world religions. Chesterton certainly does not begrudge the greatness of Socrates; but he maintains that the commonalities between Socrates and Christ are

---

[16] Henri de Lubac, *The Church: Paradox and Mystery,* (Staten Island, NY: Alba House, 1969), p. 33.

wildly overdrawn. Chesterton points out that Socrates and certain other "great philosophers give us a vague impression of having little to do except to walk and talk."[17]

Socrates and his students would be at home in your local cafe—this lovable curmudgeon inquiring endlessly and brilliantly of the virtues, while his young entourage choke back guffaws as they watch him innocently deflate the pretensions of those reputed to be wise.

But Jesus' life, says Chesterton, gives an altogether different impression:

> Now, compared to these wanderers the life of Jesus went as swift and straight as a thunderbolt. It was above all things dramatic; it did above all things consist in doing something that had to be done. It emphatically would not have been done if Jesus had walked around the world for ever doing nothing except tell the truth.[18]

His teaching mission has the vividness of lightning—of "lightning made eternal as the light,"[19] says Chesterton.

Christ is on the move; he has something specific to do. "Didn't you know I had to be in my Father's house [teaching]?" says the twelve-year-old Jesus to Mary and Joseph.[20] From beginning to end, the story of Christ "is the story of a journey, almost in the manner of a military march...."[21] To study Christ's public life in the gospels is to see cyclonic energy combined with placid poise. It is to hear a reposeful fugue—march, a Way, a passage through human consciousness by God. The major episodes of this passage are traditionally called Christ's "Mysteries."

---

[17] G.K. Chesterton, *The Everlasting Man,* (London: Hodder and Stoughton, 1925), p. 235.

[18] *Ibid.,* pp. 236-237.

[19] *Ibid.,* p. 312.

[20] Luke 2:49.

[21] Chesterton, *op cit.,* p. 237.

Christ is not a man making his way through life, as the good Socrates was, but the Way making its Life known to man. Christ is not simply one self among many, but the other Self of all who have ever lived or will be. He is not a blade of grass among other blades, but the green strength of the whole field. Socrates was a great man; Christ was the greatness of man. For Christ was Man-for-God, Man Essential—the heart of the jewel of which Socrates and we are many facets.

The Gnostic Misconception of Christ

Christ is also misconceived as a gnostic redeemer, a view of him popularized in the novel, *The Da Vinci Code*.[22] A major theme of the novel is that Christ's true significance and message are best revealed in ancient gnostic writings such as the *Gospel of Mary*, rather than in those of the New Testament. That is because, the novel tells us, the New Testament was shaped under irresistible political pressure from Emperor Constantine, who forced the Church to exclude the real story of Christ from its official testament: that Christ was a gnostic redeemer. Christ's divinity was fabricated by the Church in the fourth century to consolidate Constantine's power: "Jesus was viewed by His followers as a mortal prophet…a great and powerful man, but a man nonetheless. A mortal." So says one of the novel's main characters, Sir Leigh Teabing.[23] The Church sealed its hoax by adopting Matthew, Mark, Luke, and John as official gospels, as these were more congenial to Constantine's imperial aspirations than were the gnostic gospels.

But the *Code's* portrait of Christ is absurd. To say, as Teabing does, that Christians did not consider Christ divine until the fourth century is patently inaccurate. New Testament scholar J.N.D. Kelly rightly insists that "the all-but-universal Christian conviction in the [centuries

---

[22] Gnosticism is an umbrella term for a variety of teachings, some of which presumed to represent Christ's teaching. They presented a false gospel quite different from that of the Apostles and the early Church, and a mysticism inconsistent with Trinitarian Christianity.

[23] Dan Brown, *The Da Vinci Code,* (New York, NY: Doubleday, 2003), p. 233.

before Nicea] had been that Jesus Christ was divine as well as human. The most primitive confession had been "Jesus is Lord" [Romans 10:9; Philippians 2:11], and its import had been elaborated and deepened in the apostolic age."[24]

More, *The Da Vinci Code*'s explanation of how the canon of Christian scripture came to be is completely untenable. The truth of the matter is found in *The Hidden Gospels: How the Search for Jesus Lost Its Way,* by Philip Jenkins, professor of History and Religious Studies at Pennsylvania State University. (That Jenkins' book was written several years before the *Code's* publication underscores that *The Da Vinci Code* simply rehashed an old canard.) Three points in Jenkins' study are especially important. First, the process of determining the canon of the New Testament was well under way long before Constantine became emperor. A century and a half before Constantine's reign the Church's great teachers such as Justin Martyr were using a four-fold gospel collection, the same as is used today: Matthew, Mark, Luke, and John.[25]

Second, the so-called gnostic gospels were not unjustly excluded from the New Testament canon, as the novel insists. They were never legitimate candidates for inclusion, as they were written a hundred years or more after the gospels of Matthew, Mark, Luke and John:

> This doesn't mean apocryphal texts such as the gospels of Mary and Philip have no historical value. A text written in, say, 225, can by priceless for what it tells us about the intellectual, cultural, and social world of the early third century, and particularly for the history of the churches or communities which created that work. But it is as far removed from the world of Jesus as we today are from the time of Thomas Jefferson or Napoleon, and a third-century gospel stems from a cultural and political

---

[24] J.N.D. Kelly, *Early Christian Doctrines,* rev. ed. (San Francisco, CA: Harper & Row, 1978), p. 138. Also see Bertrand de Margerie, S.J., *The Christian Trinity in History.* Trans. by Edmund J. Foreman, S.J., (Still River, MA: St. Bede's Publications, 1982), pp. 101-105.

[25] Philip Jenkins, *Hidden Gospels: How the Search for Jesus Lost Its Way,* (New York, NY: Oxford University Press, 2002), p. 85.

> environment utterly different from Palestine in 30. It can tell us nothing whatsoever of the life or sayings of Jesus, or the environment of his earliest followers....[26]

Third, gnostic writings are unreliable accounts of Christ's life and teaching, produced by schools of thought decidedly alien to his original teaching: "What became the orthodox view has very clear roots in the first century," writes Jenkins, "and indeed in the earliest discernible strands of the Jesus movement; in contrast, all the available sources for the Gnostic view are much later, and that movement emerges as a deliberate reaction to orthodoxy."[27] *The Da Vinci Code,* then, tells us as little about early Christian history as *The Wizard of Oz* tells us about farm life in the Midwest.

No doubt many have picked up *The Da Vinci Code* hoping to find a mystic element of Christianity which has eluded them. They are disserved by work which erroneously suggests that Christian mysticism lies outside the revelation and sacramental life of historic Christianity, and distorts the nature and mission of the God-Man.

The Meaning of "I Am the Way"

Christ said, "I am the way, the truth, and the life. No one comes to the Father but through me" (John 14:6). Some Christian churches find proof in this that non-Christians will not be saved—that Hindus, Buddhists, and other non-Christians are doomed to eternal apartness from God if they die without confessing Christ as Savior with their lips and believing it in their hearts.

This is not the teaching of the Catholic Church. Though the Church teaches that salvation is only through Christ, it also teaches that non-Christians who truly love God are saved. To believe that *Christ is the Way* is not to cast a supernatural vote for Christ as Savior—instead of a vote, say, for the Buddha, or Krishna, or Confucius. Rather, it is to affirm that the passage made by Jesus Christ through the human

---

[26] *Ibid.*, p. 93.

[27] *Ibid.*, p. 116.

experience and beyond to the heaven of the Father is the Way it will go for all of us, in Christ.

This passage is the Way of Christ's Mysteries, in the phrase of the undivided Church. The Mysteries are the episodic milestones of Christ's life, as follows:

- Hidden Years in Nazareth
- Public Ministry
- Eucharist
- Death
- Resurrection
- Ascension

This understanding of the Way of Christ illumines the true meaning of His saying, "Follow me!" (John 21:19). Those words were not spoken solely as an ethical injunction as in, "Live as I have lived—follow me," but as statement of the transformations which constitute our journey of grace in Him, a journey that recapitulates his own Mysteries: "Follow Me in My Mysteries to the Father."

Christ's Mysteries propel us forward like implacable billows in sails, to our soul's unity with His humanity in this life, and after death, the transformation of our soul into His divinity, for Christ alone knows the glory of Father which is heaven. This is the *Holism of Christ's Mysteries.*

Holism of Christ's Mysteries

Holism of the Beatific Vision

Affinity: The *Holism of the Beatific Vision* (Chapter Seventeen)

The Beatific Vision is heaven, which is to know God as God knows God. But since only divine Knowing knows God, we must be transformed into Christ, who is that divine Knowing that alone knows the Father.

Christ's "Hidden Years"

God Almighty lived on earth in human form for thirty-three years—but thirty of those years were spent in spiritual anonymity! Consider a spatial metaphor for this. Think of a 12 inch ruler as the whole span of Christ's earthly life. In these terms, Christ's dramatic public ministry amounts to just over an inch! When we think of Christ's life, we usually focus on these three years. That they are chronologically disproportionate to his pre-ministry years should give us pause. What is Christ's message for us in his thirty years in Nazareth? What can his spiritual anonymity during those years teach us about our journey to God? Indeed, the Mystery of Jesus' hidden years in Nazareth (as the Church traditionally calls them) has much to teach us.

> Nazareth's children knew and played
> with God as a little boy;
> growing up with him,
> in time they did business with God as a carpenter.
> All those years He lived with them solely as a man,
> with no hint of more,
> the Lord of the universe dwelling incognito
> among His creatures…
>
> He must have loved the people of Nazareth
> in a special way,
> for they had been companions and brothers
> in God's unique *personal* experience as a man,
> unrecognized in His divinity.[28]
>
> —*Warren H. Carroll*

---

[28] Warren H. Carroll, *The Founding of Christendom, A History of Christendom,* vol. 1, (Front Royal, VA: Christendom Publications, 1985), p. 316.

We may assume that Jesus' spiritual genius (let alone his divine Personhood) went unheralded during these Nazareth years by the town's response to Jesus' return after his first tumultuous season of public ministry. They were incredulous. They had known him simply as a carpenter. As he is about to speak in the town's old synagogue, no one recalls his performing miracles among them (the New Testament records none.) No one speaks of his precocious eloquence; if he had spoken profoundly among them, no one had taken note of it. As they make their way to hear Jesus in the synagogue, no one boasts, "Didn't I tell you? Didn't I predict he would flourish as a great rabbi, and a wonder-worker!"

Instead, the New Testament reports that they were amazed on hearing Him speak. They asked each other: "Isn't this the carpenter's son?...Where then did this man get all these things?" (Matthew 13:54-56).

Where did he? Where did he get his wisdom? There is no evidence, as said, that Jesus' wisdom was the outcome of a spiritual quest. In our time, some yogis and Buddhists have conjectured that Christ's "enlightenment" was achieved during a spiritual quest in the Far East, but this view is wholly unconvincing.[29]

Where then? We have the answer already. We found that Jesus was uniquely born in perfect union with the Father. His soul was innately God-oriented. Just as a nutrient-pulp surrounds the germ of a seed in its shell and fosters its growth, so the Father's grace ever surrounded and perfectly penetrated the understanding of the maturing Jesus. These irresistible graces oriented the understanding of Jesus, harmonizing to the Supreme what he was learning through observation, experience, reflection, relationship, study, and prayer. In this way, "Jesus advanced in wisdom and age and favor before God and man" (Luke 2:51).

Christ's Hidden Years Recapitulated In Us

That Jesus's unitive state was "hidden" from the people of Nazareth should not astonish us. We all know people who are in the unitive

[29] See article, "Did Jesus Travel to India?" http://www.karma2grace.org/Articles/Jesustoindia.htm

state. You don't think so? Do you know someone who has loved God deeply and consistently for many years? It is very possible that he or she is in the unitive state. (This point will be clarified in Chapters Nine and Ten.) There are no spectacular external signs of this union: no iridescent halos, no walking on water, not even eloquence on religious topics. None of these is essential to the unitive state. The unitive state is a secret between God and the soul, not obvious to the world. That is why it is perfectly likely that the carpenter Jesus lived in spiritual anonymity for thirty years in Nazareth, his unity with God hidden. Jesus' simplest, workaday actions were imbued with unity with the Father, but as such unity does not call attention to itself, Jesus just blended in.

That is the great lesson of Christ's hidden years. Christ showed us that no extraordinary circumstances are required for living in union with God—that the fruits and gifts of the unitive life are well-exercised in ordinary contexts. Women and men who come to the unitive Way have families, go to work everyday, delight in their children, fulfill community obligations, and take care of their aging parents. Their unity with God is not spectacular but hidden, an intimate covenant between them and God, recapitulating Christ's anonymity in Nazareth.

Public Ministry and Passion

In contrast to the ordinariness of his hidden years, Christ's public ministry was a stunning fugue of beauty and mercy, miracle and truth, gentleness and adamantine. In Jesus' final hours, when Pontius Pilate saw him mockingly clad by soldiers in a purple robe and crowned with thorns, Pilate said: *"Ecce homo"* ("Here is the man!")[30] Pilate spoke better than he knew.

> He is supremely for the Father, from the Father.
> He is *the man*—
> "Behold the man!"—

[30] John 19:5.

> because of his total fidelity to transcendence.
> The whole of his being was thrown behind
> this ecstatic journey to the Father.[31]
>
> —*Ruth Burrows*

In Nazareth few knew that Jesus was completely Man-for-God. But the Godward cast of his nature was unmistakable during his three years of public teaching. The unconventionality of his message relative to normative Judaism shocked the scribes and pharisees, who confronted him and would silence him. He would not back down, for he was about his Father's business. His love for God and man was now continually open to the gaze of all like an enormous tree lit with every flower of the world.

We might be inclined to imagine this outer change in Christ betokened a radical inner change, but it did not. Christ lived in the Godward unitive state during his hidden years as truly as he did during his public years, but it was expressed in each distinctly.

On the burning noon-time hills of Judea, His wisdom came as spangles of snow that surprised the weary upturned faces of the crowds who ringed Him. The air into which He spoke became a harbor as on a festival day, crowded with colorful sails.

When they left Him, His wisdom continued to tap upon their hearts like a summer's rain on a roof. He was a brisk autumn spirit, stripping the grove of every hiding place. And His song passed through heavy walls that had stopped louder songs.

His light was wide like a foil of gold spread upon the moon, and yet intimately candescent, as words spoken to a friend in the fragile circle made by a single lamp-flame. In this way, His understanding was like a breeze that would visit one leaf, yet in its visit all leaves danced.

Christ's Public Years and Us

Does Christ recapitulate the Mystery of his public ministry in those who come to union with God? Rarely. The life of St. Francis of Assisi

---

[31] Ruth Burrows, *Ascent to Love: The Spiritual Teaching of St. John of the Cross,* (London: Darton, Longman, and Todd, 1987), p. 82.

is one outstanding and rare example of this recapitulation.[32] Few are endowed with Jesus' innate personal magnetism, brilliance, wisdom, and fewer still his charisms of prophesy and healing. (Of course, this work is never done by human beings anyway, only by God.) But in at least one respect all men and women in the unitive state will partially recapitulate Christ's public years. Like Him, they will be given strength to live the courage of their convictions, and will risk reputation, position, and possessions to be true to God.

The Mystery of the Eucharist

At his last supper, Christ shows his apostles their spiritual destiny. He pours them wine: "This is my blood." He hands them bread: "This is my body" (Luke 22:19-20). "Eat, drink." As the bread and wine will unite with their bodies, so are they being united to Christ, his God-united humanity becoming theirs.

Christ's words at this table are not symbolic but creative. As the Creative Word of the universe, its *Logos*, He has miraculously turned bread into his Body Vast and wine into His Elixir-Blood. All miraculous transmutations in scripture only faintly foreshadow the miracle enacted at this table.

God turned rock into water for Moses in the desert. Later Christ turned water into wine at a wedding. Now Christ creates a Wine that drinks the drinker, and a Bread that consumes unto Christ those who bring it to their lips. "While we 'eat' the substance of the true Body of Christ under sacramental species, we ourselves are eaten and absorbed by the Mystical Body of Christ"[33] (Thomas Merton).

"The proper effect of the Eucharist is the transformation of man into God" (Thomas Aquinas). The Eucharist is thus not only the central means of Christian transformation, but the whole of Christianity in little.

---

[32] The recapitulation of this Mystery in Francis of Assisi's life is discussed in Chapter Nine.

[33] Thomas Merton, *The Living Bread,* (London: Burns & Oats, 1956).

In Chapter Eleven we will consider the last Mysteries of Christ—His Death, Resurrection, and Ascension—and the meaning of His recapitulation of them in us.

CHAPTER 6

The Gospel According to the Christian Mystics

"An ancient legend has it that when God was creating the world, He was approached by four angels.
The first one asked, 'How are you going to do it?'
The second one asked, 'Why are you going to do it?'
The third one asked, 'Can I be of help?'
The fourth, 'What is it worth?'
The first was a scientist; the second, a philosopher; the third, an altruist; the fourth, a real estate agent.
A fifth angel watched in wonder and applauded in sheer delight.
***This one was the mystic."*[1]**
—Anthony De Mello

There is in the mystic a deep, ultimate humor, a winged humor, the humor of the triumph of God and His unreserved self-bestowal. Whatever may be the last syllables of recorded time—whether a bang, a whimper, or "Hosannah in the highest!"—the divine reply to it will be Laughter, all things will be steeped and healed in miraculous Laughter. The joy of the mystics anticipates this life triumphant.

---

[1] Anthony De Mello, *The Heart of the Enlightened: A Book of Story Meditations,* (New York, NY: Doubleday Books, 1991), p. 47.

Who is the mystic? "The Christian mystic," writes William Johnston, S.J., "is one who lives the Christ-mystery and is transformed by it."[2] This is a definition of rare excellence on two counts. First, it accents transformation in Christ as the hallmark of the Christian mystic. Too many other definitions simply say that the mystic is one who has profoundly experienced God, and leave it at that. The mystic certainly does experience God:

> My mind in the flash
> of a trembling glance
> came to Absolute Being—
> That Which Is.[3]
>
> —*St. Augustine*

But this encounter is effective, it is ontologically transforming, it changes the very character of the mystic's soul, opening it further to the divine influx.

Second, Fr. Johnston's definition specifies the true means of this transformation: the "Christ-mystery" itself. Christ is recapitulating his Mysteries unto the Father in the life of the mystic. "I wish no longer to live my own life but to be transformed into Jesus Christ…and so that the Father, overshadowing me, may recognize His 'beloved Son in whom He is well pleased'"[4] (Elizabeth of the Trinity). The mystic St. Paul uses the phrase "in Christ" around 170 times in his epistles. And the Christian mystic lives the Christ-mystery in another sense: God's revelation to the mystic is integrally Trinitarian.

What else characterizes the Christian mystic? The mystic not only knows the joy of God's presence, but the pain of transformation, for the mystic comes to a knowledge of things divine by a passion, a suffering,

---

[2] William Johnston, *The Mystical Way,* (New York, NY: HarperCollins, 1993), p. 221.

[3] Dom Cuthbert Butler, *Western Mysticism: The Teaching of Augustine, Gregory and Bernard on Contemplation and the Contemplative Life,* third edition; (New York, NY: Barnes & Noble, 1967), p. 4.

[4] M.M. Philipon, O.P., ed, *Sister Elizabeth of the Trinity: Spiritual Writings, Letters, Retreats, and Unpublished Notes,* (New York, NY: P.J. Kenedy & Sons, 1962), p. 144.

of the Light, which brilliant love exceeds natural human limits and so pains the soul that is being conformed to it. There are dark nights to be passed through, as human nature yields to the divine nature, the limited to the Limitless. The Christian mystics do not placate us with comforting pleasantries, but show us the innocent fire of divinity, humanity, life, death, sacrifice, beauty, truth, ecstasy, suffering, love.

And the mystics are pre-eminently lovers of God. A Love has possessed them to dare straits of experience from which others shrink, to know the truth of the Beloved in full measure, at any cost to self.

> Mystic shadow, bending near me, Who art thou?
> Whence come ye?
> And—tell me—is it fair
> Or is the truth bitter as eaten fire?
> Tell me!
> Fear not that I should quaver.
> For I dare—I dare.
> Then, tell me![5]

Mystical Transformation Is the Fruition of Baptism

Though not all Christians are mystics, all faithful Christians are being mystically transformed, by degrees, to perfect rapport with God. This rapport and transformation are not tangential to Christianity, but its oxygen and its lungs.

Unlike gnostic traditions which involve secret initiations and the communication of esoteric knowledge to an elite, the Christian mystical life begins with baptism. I was about to say "begins with *ordinary* baptism," but that would be a contradiction. What could be less ordinary than baptism? In this rite, the Third Person of the Trinity comes to indwell the soul, to unite it to the Godhead with the same eternal bond of Love as between the Father and the Son! (That is why St. Francis of

[5] Stephen Crane, *The Black Riders And Other Lines.* Certainly I am not implying that Stephen Crane himself was a mystic, but only that he expresses in this poem a true intuition of the mystics' bold receptivity to truth.

Assisi desired to kneel in front of a just-baptised infant, believing that Almighty God had just come to occupy the little one's soul, making it a Tabernacle of the Trinity.)

In the course of a lifetime, any growth in our soul toward God is rightly called mystical transformation because it is a work of grace, Christ's life in us. In other words, to be a Christian growing in grace is to be a Christian being mystically transformed. For the Catholic, the whole secret of this transformation in Christ is sacramental grace and love for God. Such growth requires no secret oaths, techniques, or arcane knowledge.

> If anyone loves me he will obey my teaching.
> My Father will love him and we will love him
> and make our home with him.
>
> —*John 14:23*

Growth requires cooperation with grace through love of God. Tons of drums of rocket fuel may sit in a warehouse unreleased, quiescent, static. Unused, this fuel will not lift a tea cup from a saucer. "This purpose of God never wavers, it is concentrated white-hot on each individual. If then, growth does not happen or happens very inadequately we have to look for the cause in us, not in our Father"[6] (Ruth Burrows).

"How to Be a Mystic"?

Is the mystic vocation self-chosen? Can anyone be a mystic? Is it solely a matter of intensity of dedication to God, or does God choose certain women and men to be mystics? A sub-genre of books today, with titles like *How to Be a Mystic,* insist that all persons are potentially mystics—and become mystics if they earnestly participate in a spiritual quest.

But the truth is otherwise. As said, all Christians are summoned to increasingly profound union with God in Christ, and so to deep spirituality—but only some Christians are called to the mystic vocation. It is not a self-selected vocation, but a distinct calling in the Mystical Body:

---

[6] Ruth Burrows, *Guidelines for Mystical Prayer,* (Denville, NJ: Dimension Books, 1981), p. 27.

> There are different kinds of working, but the same God works all of them in all men....All these are the work of one and the same Spirit, and he gives them to each one, just as he determines.
>
> —*1 Corinthians 12:6, 11*

What chiefly distinguishes the mystic from other Christians? Is it her or his degree of sanctity? No. The non-mystic may be just as faithful as the mystic. Here is the essential distinction: the mystic is graced by a special charism to see and describe the ways of God, particularly how God supernaturally acts upon the soul.

Other Christians will undergo the same transforming work of the Spirit, and know the same intimacy with God, but their impression of God's work in the soul is chiefly by the effects of grace, rather than by a direct seeing of God's working in the depths of their being, which is the mystic's distinguishing charism.

Imagine a magic sea current that carries voyagers through hazardous straits to a good land. While some of the crew witness the journey from the deck, others experience it below deck. The mystics have a deck-view of the journey to union with God, in a ship borne afar by the current of God's transforming grace. The mystics see this current clearly, and bring us tidings of the journey's blissful expanses, its oppressive storms, its doldrums, and finally its irenic harbor.

But other Christians who make this journey experience its buffeting and smooth sailing below deck. They can describe the journey from its felt effects; the mystics are given to describe the voyage by their direct seeing of the current's ways. All Christians are called to the new land of union, as transforming union with God is the proper maturing of baptismal grace, yet the mystics have been specially equipped to vividly see and describe the workings of grace. Their revelatory voyage allows them to map the journey to God for the benefit of the whole Church.

Spiritual director Ruth Burrows calls the mystic's vivid seeing of God's workings in the soul "light on," and sees in it the mark of a prophetic calling, for the benefit of the entire Church:

> A "light on" state, as distinct from an occasional reception of "light on" may perhaps occur no more than once or twice in an

> era. It has a prophetic character. The one so endowed understands beyond the ken of humankind and he or she must enlighten others.[7]

The presence of mystics in the Church is part of the *Holism of the Mystical Body* (discussed in Chapter Fourteen). The common good of the Mystical Body is upbuilt by diverse gifts, including the "light on" prayer of the mystics.

The mystic is the wave that brings the depth of the ocean to the shore, with its breath of seashells and the melodies of its unthinkable wells, then slips below the sand to return to his love, the Sea.

Who Is a Contemplative?

In the literature of Christian spirituality, the term "contemplative" occurs perhaps as often as the term "mystic." Each has a distinct meaning. One way of distinguishing them is to characterize the contemplative as one who travels by a way of an ever-deepening silence. By "silence" I am not indicating the curtailment of speech, but the soul's quiet receptivity before God, and God's silent communication to the soul, the character of which changes as the journey proceeds. The contemplative nature of John of the Cross' life with God is evident in his remark: "Look at the infinite knowledge and that hidden secret. What peace, what love, what silence is in that divine bosom!"[8]

Contemplatives may be especially drawn to the Self-Release Prayer, which invites the divine Stillness. Writes Madame Guyon, a seventeenth-century French contemplative: "It is by the silence of the soul that he communicates with God.…[S]ilence becomes a wonderful transmission and receiving of Divine communication."[9]

Not all contemplatives are mystics—that is to say, not all contemplatives are persons of "light on" prayer. Some contemplatives do not vividly see the Spirit's transforming work in their souls, but only know

---

[7] *Ibid.*, p. 46.

[8] Kavanaugh and Rodriguez, *op cit.*, p. 96.

[9] Jeanne Guyon, *Union with God,* (USA: Christian Books, 1981), p. 73.

it "light off," by the effects of grace. These contemplatives, too, relish God in holy silence.

Yet some contemplatives are mystics—John of the Cross, for example. As John journeyed to God-union by a *via negativa,* a path of divine silence, he was given a most vivid "light on" knowledge of the journey. John also clearly describes a further journey to beatific transformation beyond God-union.[10] (In this beatific transformation, a ultimate silence is known, the silencing or ending of all self in Christ, who transubstantiates the soul into Himself, the One who dwells in the Father's glory.)

Whether mystics or contemplatives or neither, all Christians who love God participate in Christian mysticism because they participate in the life of grace, for essentially Christian mysticism is the transforming reception of Christic grace. There is no separate Christian mysticism apart from Christianity, and no Christianity without the clarifying knowledge of Christian mysticism.

A Mystical Church from the Beginning

From the moment of the Annunciation, the Son began a special mystical relationship with humanity, and so begins Christian mysticism. As the full story of Christian mysticism utterly exceeds this study, we must content ourselves with an impressionistic consideration of a few moments in it.

The Virgin Mary was the first Christian mystic, as she knew Christ within her own depths. She is the first to whom Paul's phrase, "Do you not know that your body is a temple of the Holy Spirit?" (1 Corinthians 6:19) would have applied, and in what a way! As we relish the paradoxes of Jesus' Being, so we do the Blessed Virgin's. A litany of them was sung by an early Christian bard, James Sarug:

> Blessed is she: she within the bounds of her body was contained the Boundless One who fills the heavens, which cannot contain him.

---

[10] Kavanaugh and Rodriguez, *op cit.,* p. 627.

Blessed is she: she gave her womb to him
who lets loose the waves of the sea.

Blessed is she: she has born the mighty giant
who sustains the world,
she has embraced him and
covered him with kisses.

Blessed is she: her lips have touched him whose
blazing made angels of fire recoil.

Blessed is she: she has fed with her milk him
who gives life to the whole world.[11]

Aptly, she is called the Mystical Rose. The Lord of the universe was within her womb, like fragrance in a rose. What the angel Gabriel promised Mary will eventually be enacted spiritually in all the faithful:

The Holy Spirit will come upon you,
and the power of the Most High
will overshadow you.
So the holy one to be born
will be called the Son of God.

—Luke 1:35

The mystic Eckhart found Mary's conception of Christ analogous to our coming to union with God, the unitive state:

As long as we are not like God
and are still undergoing the birth
by which Christ is formed in us
…we are restless and troubled about many things.

[11] Olivier Clement, *The Roots of Christian Mysticism,* (New York, NY: New City Press, 1995), p. 42.

> But when Christ, God's Son, has been formed in us
> so that "we are his true Son" (1 John 5:20)...
> At that time we shall have full and perfect delight....[12]

Because our Lady gave birth to the physical body of Our Lord, she is the Mother of his Mystical Body, the Church. "No one has knowledge of the Mystical Body as she has. With each of us...she experiences a spiritual motherhood" (Jules Monchanin).

Jesus Christ, Mystic

Jesus Christ was the perfect mystic—though not only a mystic. The Incarnation is the zenith of mysticism: "I and the Father are one" (John 10:30). Think of a violin-crafter of the caliber of a Stradivarius. He has made many remarkable instruments for others. Their sound is true, and they have found their way to many lands. But there is one violin he has crafted especially for his own playing. Its timbre is truest, its sound is sweetest, for he has crafted it only to express his own art.

Christ is that violin—his Father, the violin-crafter. All other God-united people are His instruments too, but because Christ's humanity is hypostatically united with His own Divinity, Christ is uniquely both the violin and violin-maker, and the song thereof. We walk the mystic way; He is the mystic Way.

He turns bread and wine into His divine Body and Blood for our strength; and He sends His breath into ours lungs so we might breathe a higher summit. How could we ascend to the unitive state, and higher reaches yet, without Christ's strength and breath? What is the whole cosmos except the Son's outgoing breath? What is all mysticism except the Son's ingoing breath?

The Mystical Genius of St. Paul

At Pentecost, Christ sends very own Light, His Holy Spirit, into the faithful, inviting them to interior communion with the One who had previously been shuttered behind a Temple veil. Paul describes an

---

[12] Richard Woods, *Eckhart's Way*, (Wilmington, DE: Michael Glazier, 1986), p. 125.

ecstatic experience of God unveiled, had by a "person in Christ"—but Paul is surely describing his own mystical experience:

> I know a man in Christ
> who fourteen years ago
> was caught up
> to the third heaven.
> Whether it was in the body or out of the body
> I do not know....
> —was caught up
> to paradise.
> He heard inexpressible things,
> things that man is not permitted to tell.
>
> *—2 Corinthians 12:2-4*

St. Paul never met Christ in his mortal body; but Paul knew Christ through visions, mystically, in Christ' glorified body. Christ became for Paul his deepest point of being; "For to me, to live is Christ" (Philippians 1:21). Paul did not puzzle together a doctrine, like a man fiddling with riddles; Paul's soaring theology is mystical theology, a fruit of his deep experiences and transformation in Christ, the inner enlightenment of the Holy Spirit.

St. Paul's mystical theology grew in solitude. He spent years after his conversion experiencing inwardly the depths of Christ. Here is but the briefest sampling of the magnificent truths contemplatively realized by Paul—truths which have been relished by twenty centuries of Christians:

The Church as the Mystical Body of Christ: "Instead, speaking the truth in love, we will in all things grow up together into him who is the Head, that is, Christ" (Ephesians 4:15).

The participation of Christians in Christ's own Mysteries, including His redemptive suffering: "I want to know Christ and the power of his resurrection and the fellowship of sharing in his sufferings, becoming like him in his death" (Philippians 3:10).

The mysticism of faith: "Now we see but a poor reflection as in a mirror; then we shall see face to face" (1 Corinthians 13:12).

The Real Presence of Christ in the Eucharist: "Is not the cup of thanksgiving for which we give thanks a participation in the blood of Christ? And is not the bread that we break, a participation in the body of Christ?" (1 Corinthians 10:16).

We must try to appreciate how astonishingly original these insights are, how utterly underivative. There is nothing in Paul's Hebrew or Greek milieu that can account for his grand vision of Christ. His mystical instruction by the Inner Christ is obvious.

Sacred Tradition

As Christ's Apostles died one by one (each refusing at the point of the sword to renounce Christ), a post-Apostolic church continued its mission of testifying to the revealed Mysteries and transmitting Christ's transforming grace through the sacraments.[13] "From everyone who has been given much, much will be demanded" (Luke 12:48). The post-Apostolic church had been given much. They had been given the gospels of the God-man, records of His deeds and sayings; the life and teaching of the Apostles; sundry traditions of Christian worship, sacrament, and prayer; and mystical understanding handed on by the Apostles and their immediate successors. They were also given a promise:

> The Counselor, the Holy Spirit,
> whom the Father will send in My name,
> will teach you all things and will remind you
> of everything I have said to you.
>
> —*John 14:26*

Heartened by this promise of divine assistance, the early Fathers of the Church set about distilling from this wide orchard of gifts a single cup—a cup of the seen and unseen, of what is above and what is below: a Creed. At Councils they articulated the doctrines of the Trinity, the *Logos,* the divine-human natures of Christ, the meaning of His Mysteries, and the Virgin Mary as *Theotokos* ("Mother of God").

---

[13] The Apostle John was the exception according to tradition. He was not martyred, though attempts on his life were made.

To discern these truths, the Church Fathers pondered scripture as clarified by sacred tradition. What was their method? Was it sheer logic applied to scripture? Cultural convention? Linguistic guesswork? No: God did not suffer to incarnate only to leave the interpretation of His revelation to these limited instruments. Rather, the Church Fathers were led to discern the foundational doctrines of Christianity by mystical theology, by transformative graces fruitful of intuitive spiritual understanding.

The Mystical Theology of the Church Fathers

"Facts," observed Aldous Huxley, "are ventriloquists' dummies." They can be made to rant absurdities, or to proclaim wisdom, depending upon the knee on which they sit. Even facts in scripture. Take the superlative Fact, "God is love" (1 John 4:8). On the knee of one person, "God is love" can gabble vague nonsense; but on the knee of another, it fills the air with music. The apostle Peter made this very point, in cautioning the earliest Christians against ways that Paul's letters were being twisted by gnostics and others:

> His letters contain some things that are hard to understand, which ignorant and unstable people distort, as they do the other Scriptures, to their own destruction.
>
> —*2 Peter 3:16*

The Fathers of the Church had more than the sheer data of scripture and tradition to assist their understanding of truth; they were aided by the Spirit of Truth working in their souls, inspiring their mystical theology. In this way, the Fathers converted the data of revelation into an elixir-cup which enlivens the Church even today.

According to Christianity's detractors, this was not the case. The Creed and adjunct doctrines were not soulfully discerned, but graven by political machinations, with autocrats such as the Emperor Constantine carving creeds by pressure and fiat.

But such trivialization of Patristic doctrine is not shared by thoughtful historians, or by anyone who carefully reads the Church Fathers, and studies their lives. Who can read Augustine, Origen, Dionysius the Areopagite, Athanasius, Evagrius of Pontus, Gregory of Nyssa, and Bernard of Clairvaux (the actual shapers of Christian thought) and mistake their lofty mystical theology for Machiavellian angling, pandering to potentates? It is absurd. Consider these representative passages from early Christian teachers. Are these the thoughts of pawns of political intrigue?

> Trinity!!! Higher than any being,
> any divinity, any goodness!
> Guide of Christians in the wisdom of heaven!
> Lead us up beyond unknowing and light,
> up to the farthest, highest peak
> of mystic scripture, where the mysteries of God's Word
> lie simple, absolute and unchangeable
> in the brilliant darkness of a hidden silence.
>
> —*Dionysius the Areopagite,* The Mystical Theology

> For this purpose, then,
> the incorporeal and incorruptible and immaterial
> Word of God
> entered our world.
>
> In one sense, He was not far from it before,
> for no part of creation
> had ever been without Him Who,
> while ever abiding in union with the Father,
> yet fills all things that are.
> But now He entered the world in a new way,
> stooping to our level in His love
> *and Self-revealing to us.*[14]
>
> —*St. Athanasius*

Professor Andrew Louth of Oxford University, in his acclaimed *The Origins of the Christian Mystical Tradition,* estimates truly the

---

[14] St. Athanasius, *On the Incarnation,* trans. and ed. by Sister Penelope Lawson, C.S.M.V., (New York, NY: Macmillan Publishing, 1981), p. 13.

contributions of the Church Fathers. It was their mystical insight, Louth affirms, not political wrangling, which had the final word in the Creeds. Louth summarizes: "The basic doctrines of the Trinity and Incarnation, worked out in these centuries, are mystical doctrines formulated dogmatically."[15]

And in every age since the Patristic period, God has advanced the Church's treasury of Christ through her mystics, with particularly opulent contributions made by the Rhineland mystics (Eckhart, Suso, Tauler) and Discalced Carmelites (Teresa of Avila, John of the Cross, Elizabeth of the Trinity). "Christian mysticism in every age up to our own....has built up and continues to build up Christianity in its most essential element"[16] (John Paul II).

A Puzzling Gap

As springtime approaches, stores begin to feature racks of flower and vegetable seed-packets for gardening. But imagine coming across an odd display of this kind, featuring packets of unnamed flowers and vegetables, covered with images that give no clear indication of what they contain. One packet has a photo of tilled soil without vegetation. Another has a little green sprout, too young to carry a bloom. A third, just a close-up of a gardener. No depictions of flowers or vegetables, or how they will look in maturity.

This is comparable to what we see—or better, don't see—of the apostles in the four Gospels. We don't see them in bloom. Think of the last moments of Mark's gospel. Just six verses before the Gospel's conclusion, we read: "Later Jesus appeared to the Eleven as they were eating; he rebuked them for their lack of faith and their stubborn refusal to believe those who had seen him after he had risen" (Mark 16:14).

Matthew's gospel ends similarly. Peter's very last words recorded here are his wincing, "I don't know the man!" (Matthew 26:74). And

---

[15] Andrew Louth, *The Origin of the Christian Mystical Tradition, From Plato to Denys,* (New York, NY: Oxford University Press, 1983), p. xi.

[16] John Paul II, *Crossing the Threshold of Hope,* Vittorio Messori, ed., (New York, NY: Alfred A. Knopf, 1995).

consider the end of Luke's gospel. On the third day after the Christ's burial, the women who were taking spices to the tomb are met by angels who announce "He is risen"; when they rush to the Apostles to tell them the good news "they did not believe the women, because their words seemed to them like nonsense" (Luke 24:11). That same day Jesus draws near two apostles as they walk to Emmanus, but they do not recognize Him. He says to them, "How foolish you are! And slow of heart to believe all that the prophets have spoken!" (Luke 24:25)

The point is: we really do not get a clear picture of how the mature spiritual life looks by examining the Apostles in the Gospels.[17] More significantly, we do not get a clear picture of the Apostles' inner journey to maturity in Christ, to which they surely did come.

Some have speculated that the Spirit's enlightening descent on them at Pentecost miraculously transformed them in a flash. Perhaps. But how does that clarify the spiritual journey for the rest of us? It clarifies it as poorly as the explanation of a stork arriving with a baby clarifies conception.

But what of Paul, the mystic? Doesn't he document the inner journey in his many epistles? Not really. Though Paul's writings brim with mystic insight, he left no substantive record of his inner journey to union with Christ. What can be our conclusion except that there is a significant Christian knowledge not explicitly detailed in the Gospels?

It may be protested that Christ's life is the perfect revelation of the spiritual journey. It is. Christ gives us the exact master template of the journey from the unitive state to our final estate in the Trinity in the procession of His Mysteries: from union with God (his hidden years in Nazareth, onward) through His ascended glory in the Father.

And yet, let us recall that Christ's incarnation began in an egoless unitive state with the Father—ours does not. Our coming to the unitive state is the fruit of a spiritual journey. As Christ did not take that journey but was born into it, we do not have a map to it in his life.

Yet Christ's Spirit has not left the Church without guidance on this first great leg of the journey, but has inspired "light on" prayer in the

[17] Christ affirmed the bravery of the Apostles on other occasions: "You are those who have continued with me in my trials…" (Luke 22:28).

mystics so that they might clarify it for their sisters and brothers. Christ promised such knowledge to the Church:

> I have much more to say to you,
> more than you can now bear.
> But when the Spirit of truth comes,
> he will guide you into all truth.
>
> —*John 16:12*

In Chapter Nine we will study John of the Cross' map of the journey. Here is a capsulation of its major milestones:

> Reformation of life ("active night of the senses")
> Aridities ("passive night of the senses")
> Illumination (the ego's steady orientation to God)
> Dark night of the soul (the dissolving of the ego by grace)
> Union with God (God as the new divine center of self)

What hints of these milestones we find in scripture have been most clearly and coherently illumined in the writings of the Christian mystics, who recognize their significance by their experiential, intuitive knowledge of the journey. That their writings have closed the gap of understanding concerning the whole Way of Christ demonstrates once again that mysticism is central to Christianity, not peripheral to it.

Imagine a breeze blowing through an open window of a composer's study. A complex music score left on her desk scatters on the floor. Returning to her study after a break, she finds her score in disarray. This is an inconvenience, but not a problem. The composer easily re-assembles the score, as the music within her knows the music outside her.

In a similar way, the Christian mystic's insight is related to scripture. The Spirit-tuned nature of the mystic readily discerns the Spirit-inspired nature of the Gospels, with the assurance of the maestro discerning the right flow of a musical score. "In other words," wrote contemplative Aelreid Squire, "it is the man who lives a certain kind of life who is in a position to understand the doctrine. There are some kinds of knowledge to which experience is the only key."[18] Although

[18] Aelred Squire, *Asking the Fathers,* (Westminister, MD: Christian Classics, 1993), p. 3.

this applies to all Christians who know the ways of grace, it especially applies to the mystics and contemplatives whose charism has been to help us understand the ways of the journey.

The Relation of Mysticism to Religion

For twenty centuries, religion and mysticism have interfused in the Catholic religion. What is religion? It is God's communication to humanity. Such a communication makes sense, given the nature of God. God is Love, and Love communicates. Love's revelation to humanity through Christ is the religion of Christ. The truths that the Church proposes and her sacramental rites are the religion that she has received from Christ. By these—his truth and his sacraments—Christ extends his Life on earth through all time. "The Church is not only a social organization but also and principally a Living Mystical Body"[19] (Thomas Merton).

If the Church proposed no truths (dogmas) and offered no communication of grace, she would betray the trust of Christ who asked her teach, worship, and transform—the backbone of religion. What is the Church to say to those who ask, "What did Christ teach? Who was He? How may we receive His life in us? What is His Way?"

Is she to demur: "We have no truth-claims to share with you. We can give you no guidance. He did not teach us how to worship. As for His grace, it is gone with him, we cannot communicate it"? That would be madness—for he said to the Church on the eve of His Ascension:

> Therefore go and make disciples
> of all nations,
> baptizing them...
> and teaching them to obey everything
> that I have commanded you.
> And surely I am with you always,
> to the very end of the age.
>
> —*Matthew 28:19-20*

[19] Thomas Merton, *The Living Bread,* (London: Burns & Oats, 1956), p. 16.

So the Church continues to proclaim the truth He revealed and transmit grace He continues to pour forth in the sacraments—in brief, the Church continues to present Christ's religion. Mystical transformation is not opposed to this religion, but is catalyzed by it, as soul-transformation is fostered by both sacrament and truth. As vine and trellis, mysticism and religion have ever been twined in Catholicism. To protect this divine synergy, the Church has endeavored to avoid two errors.

The Error of Christianity Without Mysticism

As few years ago, while paging through a book by a popular fundamentalist Christian, I found a bulletized list of activities he believed scripture forbade to Christians. The list went something like this:

- crystal ball reading
- horoscopes
- spells
- oujii boards
- astral projection
- *mysticism*

As we see, there are forms of Christianity that are hostile to the mystical features of Christianity. They insist on religion without mysticism. Such churches teach that human nature is utterly depraved, and is never truly united to Christ or transformed into a participation in Christ, but remains sinful to the core even in heaven. But an ecumenical Council of the Catholic Church rejected this error, affirming with the Apostles that through Christ we have become "partakers of the divine nature" (2 Peter 1:4), so are truly transformed in Christ.

Some churches teach that the Eucharist is a symbol only, and not Christ himself, and so dispense with the great mystical means of transformation Christ bequeathed to the Church. Others condemn the prayer of interior silence as inviting diabolical influences. They exclude any doctrine that cannot be found explicitly in scripture, and so reject the "light on" prayer of the mystics as usurping bible truth.

The egregious error of religion without mysticism is avoided by Catholicism's integral approach to knowledge (epistemology), its practice of a *Holism of Knowledge*.[20]

---

[20] Certainly there has been resistance to forms of authentic mystical theology by influential prelates of the Church, especially in certain eras. Yet the mystical character of the whole Catholic doctrine, and its sacramental system, has perdured.

Some theologies exclude or marginalize mysticism and philosophy, affirming that vital truths can only be found in the Bible. In contrast, the Catholic faith is illumined by both mysticism and philosophy, as well as other non-biblical sources; these, too, may offer profound insight into God and the human condition. This is the *Holism of Knowledge.*

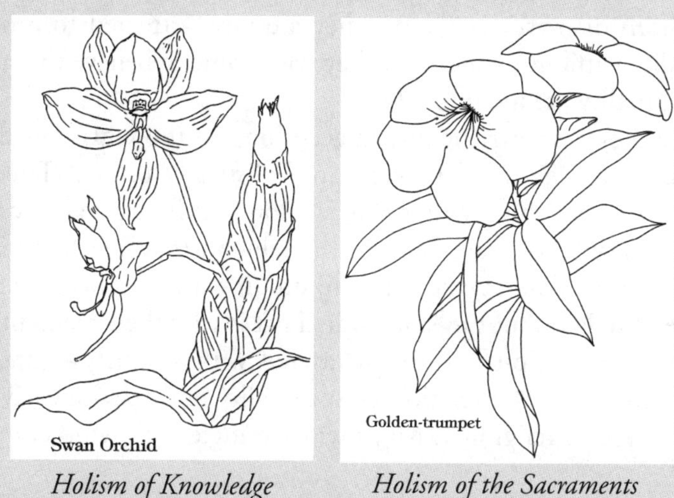

Holism of Knowledge *Holism of the Sacraments*

Affinity: The *Holism of the Sacraments* (Chapter Fifteen)

Concerning mystical knowledge in particular:

The Sacraments invite grace, God's Life in us, and so foster "light on" prayer in the mystics, whose theology so deeply imbues Catholic knowledge and doctrine. As well, the Sacraments foster in all the faithful an intuitive receptivity to the divine Mysteries which the Church perennially proclaims. In this way, the *Holism of the Sacraments* supports the *Holism of Knowledge.*

Mysticism Without Religion

A second error is a mysticism without religion. "I'm spiritual," many like to say, "but not religious."

To be spiritual, they believe, means seeking enrichment of soul by diverse experiences of the Sacred, especially healing and enlivening contact with nature, and meditation that aspires to know the Spirit within. These seekers often equate spirituality with transformation—with inner growth, the unfolding of potential. All these, of course, are true spiritual intuitions.

Some of these seekers grew up Catholic, but were never able to see its mystical depths. Others grew up in churches that teach a Christianity shorn of mysticism. Now they are now attracted to a mystical spirituality without religion, for they have come to believe that religion and spirituality are incompatible.

May they discover the gospel according to the Christian mystics, in which mysticism and religion are holistically united! The Christian mystics cherished the gifts of religion and flourished under their regime and, in turn, gave back to the religion that had fostered their transformation. The mystics came to union with God because of their practice of religion, not in spite of it. That is why the statement, "I am spiritual, not religious"—though uttered with sincerity—fundamentally misconceives the relation of spirituality and religion. Mysticism twines with true religion as May breezes mingle with wind chimes.

Light to the Magisterium and to the Faithful

Christianity without mysticism, and mysticism without religion are nearly opposite errors. The Church begs the help of the Holy Spirit to steer clear of both.

As said, on the eve of His Passion, Christ promised his Apostles that he would not leave them guideless, but would send His Spirit to shepherd their understanding, and that of the Church in all ages to come (John 16:13). Thus has His Spirit come as Light into the teaching office of the Church (her ongoing *magisterium*)—and into all Christians.

Both kinds of enlightenment are necessary. For what if the Holy Spirit only gave Light to individuals, and not to the Church's magisterium? There would be endless confusions over true and false private "revelations" in the Church, and endless factions, myriad conflicting mysticisms, each group claiming the true Light. And the magisterium of the Church, effete and unenlightened, could offer no discerning word on what was true and what was false.

Some have removed themselves from the Church, and started alternative organizations claiming to be pure mystical Christianity. A famous leader of one such esoteric organization told a rapt audience of his disciples that "in order to establish an occult foundation for the future union of spirituality and the intellect, Christian Rosencreutz sent his 'most intimate pupil and friend' Gautama Buddha to Mars"![21]

On the other hand: What if the Holy Spirit only gave Light to the Church's magisterium, not to the faithful? This would be a worse error, as the point of Christianity is individual growth in the Light. By sending Light to both the magisterium and the faithful, the Spirit continues to nurture a holistic give-and-take between the magisterium and the faithful. "Mysticism has everything to do with reality—the reality of God and the reality of man"[22] (Ruth Burrows).

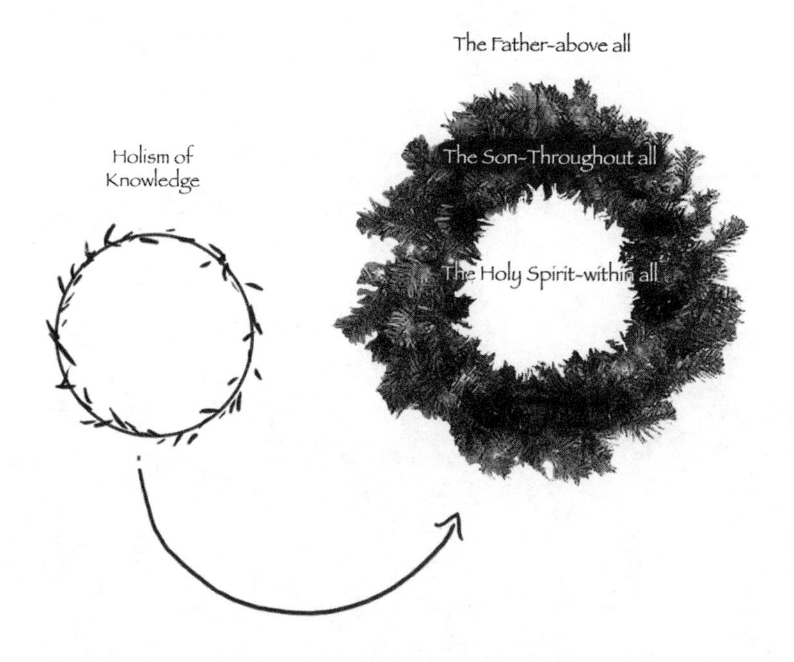

[21] "Those Darn Jesuits Are At It Again," *Gnosis Magazine*, Winter 1998, pp. 72-73.

[22] Ruth Burrows, *Ascent to Love: The Spiritual Teaching of St. John of the Cross*, (London: Darton, Longman, and Todd, 1987), p. 100.

CHAPTER 7

The Ego: Truly Orientated to God

"The truly religious understanding of man is not in terms of reward and punishment, but in terms of wholeness and division"[1]

—*John Main*

The diva Caterina Gabrielli was invited by Queen Catherine the Great to sing an opera before her court. Though honored by the invitation, Gabrielli did not hesitate to advise the Queen of her standard fee: five thousand ducats.

The Queen was aghast. "Five thousand ducats! That's ridiculous! That's an outrageously large sum! I'll have you know that none of my field marshals receive five thousand ducats!"

"In that case," Gabrielli replied matter-of-factly, "your Majesty has only to engage one of your field marshals to sing the opera."

Gabrielli received her 5,000 ducats.

✧ ✧ ✧ ✧

Though the coin of the realm differs radically from dimension to dimension, from heavy clinking ducats to the finest energies of the soul, life teaches us there is no receiving without giving. To know God

---

[1] John Main, *The Essential Teaching: An Introduction to Christian Meditation,* (London: Medio Media, 1994), tape 1.

and life in God, we must give ourselves wholly. "Love the Lord your God with all your heart and with all your soul and with all your mind and with all your strength" (Mark 12:30).

This calls for a radical conversion of the ego because the ego is naturally a will for itself, and does not easily see that its highest good is to know and love God. Yet to try to convince the ego of this by ordinary persuasion is like trying to convince a mirror in your house that it should be a window. The ego needs a different kind of convincing, beyond words. A divine convincing. So God, in the right season, sends special conversion graces upon the ego to lure it to the divine milieu.

If the magic takes hold and the ego sees the Light, it will endeavor with its extraordinary energy to be true to God by turning from itself toward God, submitting itself to God's will. It will try with all its might to cease to view itself as the ultimate center of self, and to recognize Spirit as its true center.

The ego was not meant to be our permanent center of self, but one season of self in a procession of seasons leading to full transformation into Christ. The ego is simply our first center of self, its first vital center of will or choice. God creates the principle of ego in us as an energy for our maturation. Yet because the ego is an energy of choice—not an automatism—it is an ambivalent power. Badly oriented, it is the only source of evil in the world, the ruiner of individual lives and the scourge of nations in the destructive grip of megalomaniacal dictators.

Well-oriented, the ego is an energy that can win the heart of Almighty God, coaxing Him to inhabit and rule the self's finest dimensions. On reaching maturity in God, the ego surrenders sublimely to God who accepts its sacrificial love and dissolves it, to become Himself the self's abiding center. "When a person surrenders and abandons his own self, God enters"[2] *(Theologia Germanica).*

As we reflect on the ego in this chapter, let us keep in mind a principle from an earlier one. The ego is not the whole of self or consciousness, but rather it is the first center of will or choice in consciousness. Consciousness is our specific mode of human knowing, chiefly defined

---

[2] *The Theologia Germanica of Martin Luther,* trans. Bengt Hoffman, (New York, NY: Paulist Press, 1980), p. 90.

by a profound sense of I and you, subject and object. Right now, look at an object in your surroundings. You do not naturally experience, "I am that," but feel in a subject-object relation to it. That is a true feeling, because you are not that, you are you. But the reflexive cause of your distinct sense of self is much, much more than just the ego: it is the self-reflexive nature of consciousness itself. Should your ego be dissolved by God and were you to come to egoless union with God, you would not cease to feel "I am I" because self-consciousness is much more than just the ego, and would go right on after the ego's dissolution. Nor would you feel in the unitive state "I am God," because God does not replace consciousness in the unitive state, but becomes its deepest point of reference. Consciousness includes more than just the ego; its profound self-reflexion also includes (but is not limited to) emotions, thoughts, and body-awareness.

We must clarify one more point at the onset of our reflections. Because God is the cause of our being, He is the ground of our being, present in us right now as our true center of consciousness. But God is not Himself consciousness. Think of a star. We see it through the earth's atmosphere but the star is not of the earth's atmosphere. It is beyond it. So God is within the self, but not the self. This dimension of God has truly been called the Beyond within. "He is the cause and deep center of your being"[3] *(The Book of Privy Counsel)*. You can experience this Beyond within right now. Close your eyes, go out to God in silent, receptive prayer. You sense a Presence within you that is not you. That is the Beyond within, God within.

So we see that there are really two centers in us before God dissolves the ego to create the unitive state. The ego is one center and God is the other, the Beyond within. To prepare ourselves to receive the grace of union, our task of the moment is to attune the one center (ego) to the other—God. "Your purpose is to pursue that life which dwells deep within your inmost center"[4] (Madame Guyon).

---

[3] William Johnston, ed., *The Cloud of Unknowing*, p. 150.

[4] Madame Guyon, *Union with God*, (USA: Christian Books, 1981), p. 21.

The Wrongly Oriented Ego

"We are more troublesome to ourselves than anyone else is," observed St. Francis de Sales. Tellingly, the German word for *sin* signifies "separation." The wrongly-oriented ego separates us from Life. In this way, the self-centered ego replays the old story of Genesis: the desire to be our own god, rather than subject to reality's God. You "will be like God," is the perennial, foundational lie (Genesis 3:4). The folly of egocentricity is futile. Trying to find a way to happiness and meaning with a selfish ego is like trying to open a formidable lock with a key snipped from tin foil. The narrow ego blocks us from the Wreath Enchanted.

Ignoring its true good in God, the wrongly oriented ego seeks meaning and happiness on a very superficial level. Treasuring its self-images as its very life, it strains to promote them publicly, figuring that if it can get the world to believe in these images, it can believe in them too. When these images appear to be affirmed by the world, the ego exults, hypnotized by what we have called the Feverish Feeling of Life.

But every self-picture the ego raises for the world's admiration has a target on its back. Does it want the world to think it is materially successful, owner of world's latest status symbol car? That same day that image will be shaken when a sleeker, even more expensive car slides up to it at a traffic light. Is its conceit in its genius? It will lose an argument this afternoon, and replay the argument all evening. Does it pride itself on physical attractiveness? Soon everywhere it looks, it will notice a younger generation getting all the attention.

Because a target is painted on the back of each of its self-images, the wrongly oriented ego spends as much time protecting itself as it does promoting itself. It is more or less overstrained all the time. The disordered ego is wearied, autointoxicated, vapidly repetitive. This was glimpsed by Dylan Thomas who, after hours of arguing and drinking at a smoky London pub, suddenly stopped in mid-sentence. "Someone is boring me," he muttered. "And I think it's me."

So acutely did a sense of futility and emptiness overcome the noted tennis player Boris Becker that suicide appeared to him the only way out:

> I had won Wimbledon twice before, once as the youngest player. I was rich, I had all the material possessions I needed: money, cars, women, everything....I know that this is a cliché. It's the old song of the movie and pop stars who commit suicide. They have everything, and yet they are so unhappy....I had no inner peace. I was a puppet on a string.[5]

Becker's candor is rare. Most are desperate to hide their unhappiness, as its admission risks the world's ultimate negation: the label "failure." The self-centered ego quickly masters the art of the artificial smile and the happy patter that goes with it. But tacking a sign, SWIMMING POOL near a swamp does not turn it into a resort. And neither does the forced smile on the face of a person who is living apart from the Spirit of Truth make for a happy life.

As frustration builds, the ego seeks relief by passing off its pain to others in the form of rudeness, impatience, even cruelty. We have called this principle the bewitching baton. This desperation limits its capacity for empathy; it comes to care little about who receives the bewitching baton it craves to pass, and the pain it mechanically spreads. It is, after all, only "letting off some steam"—one of its favorite phrases. And one of its saddest deceptions, as it continues to hurt itself and others.

The Practical Secret of Purgatory

The above sketch of the misdirected ego is not, of course, about our next door neighbor. It is about us, you and me, anytime we have allowed our ego to be its own god, apart from reality's God.

In our spiritual journey to union with God, we will be challenged to sidestep the well-camouflaged traps of the wrongly oriented ego to be true to Life. We will face a myriad of other challenges, ones that will tax the resources of our spirit to their limit. Dr. M. Scott Peck proposes a thought-experiment related to this, in a passage from *The Denial of the Soul*. It brings out a profound truth about life on earth:

---

[5] Alister E. McGrath, *Intellectuals Don't Need God & Other Modern Myths,* (Grand Rapids, MI: Zondervan Publishing House, 1993), p. 15.

> I defy you in your imagination to concoct a more ideal environment for learning than this life on earth. It is a life filled with vicissitudes and existential suffering, but as Benjamin Franklin said, "Those things that hurt, instruct." Many have referred to earth as a vale of tears. Keats, however, went deeper, when he called it "The vale of soul-making."[6]

To earnestly seek to be true to God in daily life is to literally pass through dimensions of purgatory while still alive, says Catholic doctrine. And on the other side of this purgatory is union with God beyond ego, to be lived in this life.

I suspect that for many people the concept of purgatory is abstract, ethereal, nebulous, maybe even comical, quite unrelated to daily life. It is a very misunderstood Catholic doctrine, and often cited by those who think the Church has no mystical theology, but fritters its time over trivialities—such as purgatory. But when the nature of purgatory is deeply grasped, serious truth-seekers find it a most holistic doctrine: compelling, realistic, and remarkably relevant to daily living.

According to its principle, those who die in a state of grace but have not yet fully given themselves to God in love, pass through a process after death which opens them fully to God, who is Love. Present after death to absolute Love, they find the vision intolerable, painful, oppressive, as their refusal to be true to love before death has alienated them from it. Now they must withstand its Light to pass into it, to be transformed into Christ.

Christ said, "I tell you, you will never get out until you have paid the last penny" (Luke 12:59). The soul will remain outside the Light until it has paid its dues to Love. "Purgation, then, consists in the reordering of love in accordance with the will of God"[7] (Jaroslav Pelikan).

Few know that the Church teaches that ideally purgatory is not passed through after death, but now. John of the Cross taught that

---

[6] M. Scott Peck, *Denial of the Soul: Spiritual and Medical Perspectives on Euthanasia and Mortality,* (CA: Three Rivers Press, 1998), p. 151.

[7] Jaroslav Pelikan, *Jesus Through the Centuries: His Place in the History of Culture,* (New Haven, CT: Yale University Press, 1985), p. 129.

our spiritual journey to union with God passes, here and now, straight through purgatory. When God dissolves the surrendered ego to become the self's new center, a painful "dark night of the spirit" ensues, says John, which is none other than a dimension of purgatory, here and now.[8] "During this purgatory charity is rooted more and more in the depths of the soul, and ends by destroying all unregulated love of self."[9]

If we would experience the egoless union of Christ's hidden years, we must pass through purgatory in this lifetime. Purgatory is a multi-dimensional reality. A profound dimension of it, as said, is the dark night of the spirit. And yet it includes other purifications that lead to that dark night. Practically speaking then, every time we refuse the glitter of the wrongly-oriented ego and adhere to God, we pass through a bit of purgatory. Think of a practical example. When you have refused to answer rudeness with rudeness, to honor God and to interrupt the cycle of pain (the bewitching baton), you passed through a bit of purgatory, Lightward. "There is literally not a moment when I am not given a choice between God and self"[10] (Ruth Burrows). We now see the holistic character of a true conception of purgatory, as it offers a spiritual context to the existential challenges of life.

Misconceiving the Ego

Are you familiar with any of the these ideas?

1. *The ego is an illusion, like a dream—it is a thought-construct that can be seen through and dissolved by enlightened insight.*
2. *The ego is essentially ignorant, misguided, and illusion-producing.*
3. *When one is rid of the ego through enlightenment, the "True Self" that remains is God.*

---

[8] *The Collected Works of St. John of the Cross,* trans. Kieran Kavanaugh O.C.D. and Otilio Rodriguez, O.C.D., (Washington, DC: ICS Publications, 1991), p. 375.

[9] Reginald Garrigou-Lagrange, O.P., *Life Everlasting And the Immensity of the Soul,* trans. Rev. Patrick Cummings, O.S.B., (Rockford, IL: Tan Books and Publishers, 1991), p. 32.

[10] Ruth Burrows, *Fire Upon the Earth,* (Denville, NJ: Dimension Books, 1981), p. 32.

According to Christianity, all three are misconceptions of the ego and the nature of ego-loss in God.

Truth be told, many of these wrong views have come into the field of contemporary spirituality by an uncritical acceptance of yogic and Buddhist critiques of the ego. Certainly, the warnings of Eastern sages against the dangers of egoism are well-pointed. The wrongly oriented ego, which is egoism, is the chief cause of human suffering. The East's traditional exposé of the trickiness and persistence of egotism has been a bracing antidote against the West's secular celebration of the ego.

Though Christianity, holistically conceived, must deeply appreciate this contribution, it cannot uncritically accept the East's views on ego and self. So let us review elements of those views.[11]

1. *The ego is an illusion, like a dream—it is a thought-construct that can be seen through and dissolved by enlightened insight.*

The ego is not a thought or a concept or an illusion, any more than poor eyesight is an illusion. Just as poor eyesight comes from a real eye, and is the effect of a real physiological dynamic, so the ego is a real function in the psyche. Like eyesight, ego can function well or poorly. Either way, the ego is not simply a concept or thought. The ego is a created energy, very real, given to us by God for our growth in Him.

Esoteric teachings that view the ego as an illusion believe it can be ended by getting a clear insight into its illusory character. It is true that insight can help us understand the tricks of the wrongly-oriented ego, and so help us rightly orient it to its highest good in God. But since the ego is not a delusive thought but a real energy, insight *per se* cannot end the ego and bring about the unitive state beyond it.

A story makes this point by analogy. During World War II, in occupied Holland, the Germans tried to deceive the British by building a phony airfield. They constructed it with an eye to detail, and almost entirely from wood, including wooden trucks, wooden airplanes, and wooden gun placements. But Allied photographers saw through the

---

[11] For an excellent study in comparative mysticism, see William Johnston, *The Mysticism of the Cloud of Unknowing,* (New York, NY: Fordham University Press, 2000).

scheme and informed the Royal British Air Force. Early one morning a single RAF plane flew across the Channel, circled the "airfield" once—and dropped a large wooden "bomb." But the bomb did not much physically alter the mock airfield because it was constructed of the same material as the airfield.

Likewise, human insight can only alter the way we think partially and temporarily because insight is part of thinking, not higher than it. As the ego is really not a thought, but a created power, it can only be ended with a power greater than it: God's grace. That is why holistic Christianity believes that both right views and grace are necessary for transformation in God—especially the grace of the Eucharistic Christ.

2. *The ego is essentially ignorant, misguided, and illusion-producing.*

The ego is not intrinsically misguided. It can be sorely mistaken about what is in its own good, and even diabolically rationalize evil, but its basic thrust—desiring what is good for itself—is essentially innocent, if limited. Moreover, the rightly-oriented ego is an excellent energy for good. The ego chooses its own character. It has license to embrace false values, or may exercise its liberty in virtue. The rightly-oriented ego has been ordained by its Creator to be that specific vitality in us that pursues God—and finally wins Him! Who would say that an energy that can capture the heart of Almighty God is an illusion?

Christianity's acknowledgment of the ego as a creation of God and not an illusion is an element of its holistic view of the human person, which does not estrange any true self-element from the human composite.

3. *When one is rid of ego through enlightenment, the "True Self" that remains is God.*

While Christian mysticism agrees that the ending of the ego is a high blessing for the psyche, it denies the view—found in prominent forms of Hinduism—that egolessness reveals God as the True Self. The

Hindu view is based on the idea that the Self, consciousness without ego, is God. The *Aitareya Upanishad* says, "And this Self, who is pure consciousness, is Brahman [the Absolute]. He is God, all gods."[12] But with all due respect to these sages and their admirable thirst for the Absolute, we must insist that consciousness, however purified and subtilized, is a created reality and so is not God, who is Uncreated Reality. God, who is Knowing without a knower, is entirely beyond the most exalted consciousness.

Thus, the testimony of the Christian mystics who have come to the egoless unitive state has never been, "I am God"—rather, "I now experience God as my deepest Center." In fact, because God is not consciousness, and God wants to give Himself completely, the Christian journey does not stop at the unitive state (egoless union with God), but continues by grace to the further Mysteries of Christ. We are to be transformed through Christ's Mysteries not only beyond the ego, but finally (after death) wholly beyond human knowing to divine knowing in the light and love of the Trinity.

Why Even the Good Ego Must Be Dissolved

In Chapter 9, we will trace five phases of the spiritual journey beyond the ego to union with God. We will find that at a certain point in this journey, the God-focused ego achieves a kind of self-made union with God. The Christian mystics have called this the Illuminative Way. But the Illuminative Way is not our final union with God. For our own good, God finally ends this self-made union, dissolving the God-focused ego of the Illuminative Way to create the union He wants with the self, which is an egoless union by which the divine infuses and superintends the subtlest energies of the soul.

Details of this process await development in Chapter 9, but by way of prologue, let us consider a question here: What is insufficient about the union of the righted, good ego with God, that God would finally dissolve it in favor of egoless union?

---

[12] Swami Prabhavananda and Frederick Manchester, trans., *The Upanishads,* (New York, NY: New American Library, 1975), p. 62.

In the first place, even though the mature ego adheres to God with deep abiding, it can still be shaken from its attachment to God. Spiritual progress can still be shipwrecked by foolishness, impetuosity, and cowardice.

Second, while prayer may come easy to the mature God-focused ego, it still essentially consists of one center, the ego, gazing into another center, God within. As this separation of centers limits the experience of contemplation, God wants to dissolve it to bring about in the soul a richer, deeper, more recollected contemplation. Because God is the ground of our being below the ego, as it were, when the ego is dissolved we have open access to this ground, and contemplation becomes new-dimensional.

The last reason is fairly complex, but one that we need to study if we are to appreciate the marvel of God's dissolving our ego, to become our new center.

How We May Come to "Pray Without Ceasing"

Imagine looking at a vase. As you do, not only does the thought naturally occur to you, "This is a vase," but another impression occurs on a mostly unconscious level: the affirmation "*I* see this vase." Try it.

In this way, every time you and I have a thought about something, we unconsciously and silently affirm the self. What is the relation of this phenomenon to the ego? To egoic consciousness, every perception refers back to itself, confirming its position as a self-center. This dynamic may be so depicted:

KNOWING WITH AN EGO CENTER

"Vase" <————————> *ego-center ("I* see") ¦ God-center

Notice that seeing the vase subtly reinforces the egosense: "*I* see." Look to the right side of the diagram. Notice that the God-center is not involved in the perception, only the ego. In this way, the ego-center keeps us in a relatively shallow mode of experiencing being. It blocks the act of knowing from passing to the depths of our being—the God-center, the ground of our being.

But after God dissolves the ego, a new way of knowing is experienced. Since the ego is gone, the reflexive mechanism of knowing is not blocked by the ego-center, and so bends on the God-center, putting us unconsciously in touch with God, subtly irradiating our ordinary knowing with the presence of God.

KNOWING IN AN EGOLESS CONSCIOUSNESS

"Vase" <——————————————————>*God-center*

egoless self ("I see")

Our self-reflexive knowing bends on the God-center, not the ego. Let me suggest an analogy. Think of a winter day in New England and a pond in a snowy woods. The pond is frozen. You find a small stone and toss it toward the center of the pond. It bounces a number of times and then slides a distance.

If it were springtime, the same stone would have plunged into the pond and be drawn to its depths. The frozen pond is like the self with an ego center. The tossed stone is like the act of knowing (in the earlier example, the perception of the vase). Blocked by the ego, the act of knowing does not penetrate the depths, but stops at the ego as if the pond were frozen. Every act of thinking and knowing reflexively affirms the ego, the relatively shallow 'I,' and doesn't touch the God-center.

But God's dissolving the ego in transforming union is like dissolving the ice. This dissolution radically changes the act of knowing, unconsciously linking each act of knowing to our God-center. Now, without conscious effort on our part, God participates in our every act of knowing. God becomes the silent background to all our understanding. Because of this, in the egoless condition we are in state of constant, effortless, silent prayer. "Whether I sweep, or work, or pray, everything seems good and delightful to me because I see my Master everywhere!"[13] (Elizabeth of the Trinity).

---

[13] M.M. Philipon, O.P., ed., *Sister Elizabeth of the Trinity: Spiritual Writings, Letters, Retreats, and Unpublished Notes,* (New York, NY: P.J. Kenedy & Sons, 1962), p. 42.

The self-lake, as it were, has been opened up, so that the stone—the act of self-reflexion—doesn't bounce along the surface but plunges toward the deep, toward the ground of our being, God.

Hence, in the unitive state there is an ongoing but largely unconscious practice of the presence of God, because now the God-center participates in our ordinary acts of knowing. This is one of the mystic meanings of St. Paul's words, "Pray continually" (1 Thessalonians 5:17).

CHAPTER 8

The Mind-Body Partnership

"Christ has ties to everything..."[1]
—*Emile Mersch, S.J.*

Imagine an ancient city networked with a clever aqueduct system that carries pure water to all its parts. But this grand unity nearly proves to be its undoing, as saboteurs are caught just before introducing poison into one part of the waterway. The poison would have spread quickly to all points.

Like that aqueduct, our psycho-biological system is unified. Introduce a factor into one part and its effects ramify throughout. Our interconnections conduce to healing or harm depending on what flows through them. The *Holism of the Mind-Body Partnership* describes these skeins of unity, and reveals how we can coax them to work for us, not against us—for the aim of being true to life, to God, moment by moment.

May I anticipate an initial difficulty in your relating to the material that follows? Having just finished a chapter on how God aims to transform the subtlest energies of the soul to divine union, you may be disconcerted by this chapter's physiological accent—its references, for example, to the hypothalamus and norepinephrine and adrenaline. Your consternation and resistance are healthy. Intuition tells you that science and religion ought not be glibly mixed. God cannot be puzzled

[1] Emile Mersch, S.J., *The Theology of the Mystical Body,* trans. Cyril Vollert, S.J., (St. Louis, MO: B. Herder Book Co., 1952), p. 23.

out by science; the soul, the essential mystery of the human person, transcends the probing of every empirical instrument.

But perhaps a maxim from Jacques Maritain, cited earlier, can help again here: "Distinguish to unite." Mysticism, theology, philosophy, science, art, and other media of knowledge, each is a distinct way of knowing, each contributes in its own way to our knowledge of reality. The Catholic way, we have seen, is to welcome each truth into a *Holism of Knowledge,* with certain truths superintending others in an interwoven whole. So, though science cannot speak to the deepest dimensions of the human person, its knowledge ought not be trivialized, but integrated into a multi-dimensional vision of reality, human and divine.

Ancient Seeds

We have seen that the Mind-Body Partnership is perfectly congenial with Christianity, which understands human nature as a soulful unity of body and mind. Catholic philosophers have for centuries made this point by cautioning against the *angelistic fallacy.* This fallacy attributes to human beings traits that are properly attributed to angels. Metaphysically conceptualized, angels do not truly have bodies, though scripture and art depict them so. (Philosophers say that angels create the appearance of bodies to delight their beholders.) An angel is a fantastic partless presence of insight and love. In contrast, human nature is a soulful unity of matter and spirit, body and mind, a vital conjunction of elements. To ignore the integral reality of the human person is to abet the angelistic fallacy, and that will not do: a bloodless, denatured, abstract analysis of the human person disserves a truly holistic Christianity.

An analogy speaks to the importance of this integral vision. Some years ago in the pyramids of Egypt, ancient seeds were discovered that had lain dormant for untold centuries. When they were planted and watered, they sprouted green.

There are ancient seeds within us too, but of a different sort, and they too have a hidden vitality. The biological heritage of our bodies is primeval, 400 million years old, part of an unbroken chain of life that began in the sea.

Looking through your eyes right now are 400 million years of evolutionary development—three million years of human evolution. The protective mechanisms, by which these early seeds of life survived, the factors by which they flourished, are still entwined in our genes, though refracted through human consciousness. When Christian holism meditates on the human condition, can it ignore these powerful primeval ties?

It is often assumed that Catholicism's theory of human origins is anti-evolutionist. Not so. In light of the data of astrophysics and of the paleontological record, Catholic theology (which strives for a holistic understanding) surely does not imagine that Genesis' six days of creation describe six twenty-four hour periods![2] (Tellingly, the Hebrew word for "day" in Genesis, *yom,* can mean any extended period of time—epochs even.) Cardinal Charles Journet wrote many years ago of God's creative role in evolution:

> God's omnipresence…having created the universe, uses the energies of the universe to make it gradually improve upon itself, lower orders being raised right up to where the higher orders start…[3]

What are the implications of evolution for human nature today, and our spiritual quest?

The Fight-or-Flight Mechanism

In *The Heart's Code,* Dr. Paul Pearsall reviews research on the evolution of the human brain, and discusses the role that fear and defensiveness played in our evolution:

---

[2] Science flourished in the West not in spite of Christianity but in large measure because of it. See Vincent Carroll and David Shiflett, *Christianity on Trial: Arguments Against Anti-Religious Bigotry,* (San Francisco, CA: Encounter Books, 2002), pp. 54-58.

[3] Charles Journet, *The Meaning of Evil,* trans. Michael Barry, (New York, NY: P.J. Kenedy & Sons, 1961), p. 132.

> The brain is self-protective and territorial. Its code is "I, me, mine." A natural pessimist, it evolved to expect and anticipate the worst as a form of self-defense left over from our primitive ancestors' necessary constant vigilance for outside threats.[4]

Pearsall agrees with other researches who affirm that

> the brain has an evolutionary bias towards pessimism, and that unhappy vigilant negativism helped our ancestors maintain an environmentally 'ready to defend' posture in order to survive in a hostile environment...[T]he pessimistic brain, by dwelling on unpleasant possibilities, is "better prepared for the unexpected."[5]

This tendency toward pessimism raises questions: Has the evolutionary servant of life—the brain's vigilance, its defensiveness—absurdly become our taskmaster? Are we unnecessarily overstrained today by miscues from a brain that was shaped in a tooth-and-claw milieu? Does anxiety needlessly and overmuch govern the brain's reactions?

Primitive man inherited the danger-sensitive mechanisms of earlier animal forms of life. We are physiologically endowed with much the same system as animals to deal with stress: the complex fight/flight response that equips them to fight or flee at the sign of danger. The likeness of our stress-biology to that of animals was recognized by Walter Cannon some 90 years ago at Harvard University. His experiments demonstrated that when confronted with threat, physical or emotional, the body reacts with a rise in blood pressure, heart rate, muscle tension, and respiratory rate, mirroring the fight/flight response of our evolutionary kin.

With birds and beasts we share the master-switch of the flight/flight mechanism: the hypothalamus. Place your index finger on the bridge of your nose; straight back from that point, deep in the folds of your brain, is the hypothalamus.

---

[4] Paul P. Pearsall, *The Heart's Code,* (New York, NY: Random House, 1999), p. 25.

[5] *Ibid.*

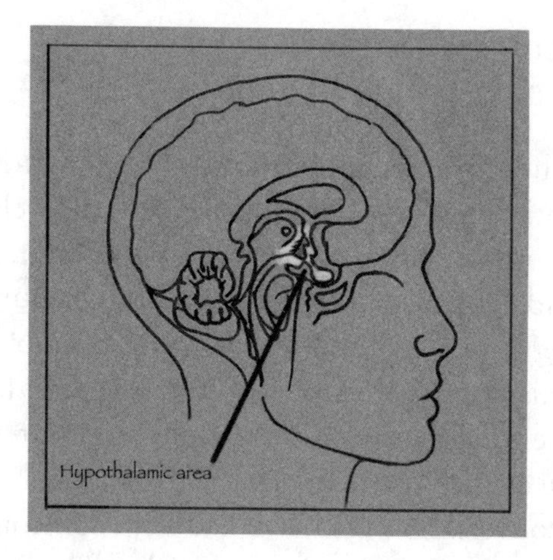

As with other forms of life, when we perceive danger our hypothalamus hyper-excites our sympathetic nervous system which pours fiery hormones (adrenaline and noradrenaline, or epinephrine and norepinephrine) through our interlinked system, increasing our heart rate, blood pressure, and metabolic rate. The fight/flight mechanism also steps up our breathing and suffuses our arms and legs with extra blood for aggressive or defensive action.

This mechanism is set off in animals at the perception of physical threat. So, too, it is with us. But the perception of *psychological threat* also triggers fight/flight in us. For example, any sense that we have been shortchanged or insulted, wronged or slighted, sets it off. Any expectation of social embarrassment or harsh scrutiny can also trip this switch, subjecting us to much the same tumultuous chemistry that anticipates tooth-and-claw threat: rapid respiration, increased heart rate, a system flooded with inflammatory agents.

Chronic activation of this response can cause hypertension, a weakened immune system, stomach ulcers, skin problems, and digestive difficulties. Stress may also be a factor in the induction and growth of cancer. "It appears," writes Kenneth Pelletier, M.D., of Stanford University, "psychophysical events can reduce immunological competence at a critical time and allow a mutant cell to thrive and grow."[6]

---

[6] Pelletier, *op cit.*, p. 178.

The Fight/Flight Response Abets the Wrongly-Oriented Ego

In addition to the physical implications of the fight/flight response, there are existential ones. We might say that stress chemistry is the milieu of the wrongly-oriented ego—its natural habitat. Spotting waves of adrenaline and noradrenaline gushing through our inner system, the wrongly-oriented ego virtually shouts, "Surf's up!" The ego uses fight/flight chemistry to feel its own phantasmagoric life. It loves the false thrills of resentment, arrogance, self-pity, and bitterness—feelings supported by the caustic chemistry of fight/flight.

Think of a conversation you have had with someone who became unduly defensive as you spoke. Instead of his listening thoughtfully and responding reasonably, he became reactionary, stubborn, and contentious. The fight/flight response was speaking through him—400 million years survival instinct, refracted through egoism. He was in no physical danger but, because he felt his ego affronted, his whole system mechanically reacted with counter-productive defensiveness.

Our response also differs from that of animals in recovery time. Swiftly the animal's "neurophysiological stress response subsides and its body rebounds into a state of deep relaxation and ultimately back to homeostasis," explains Dr. Pelletier.[7] Not so with us. After an argument or a tense situation, we may continue to have stressed-produced imaginations for hours, even days, triggering the influx of the same volatile chemistry produced by the original event.

Consider again the defensive conversationalist. Days after your conversation with him, he replayed it in his imagination over and over, trying to justify himself, mesmerized by fight/flight chemistry into further self-righteousness and resentment.

Unlike animals that respond to immediate danger picked up by their senses, human beings may artificially activate the fight/flight response at will, by a perverse use of our sophisticated powers of memory and imagination. For example, a man may cultivate the unhealthy thrill of self-pity by mentally stacking episodes of personal frustration

[7] *Ibid.*, p. 69.

and failure. A woman may revel in the sadistic excitement of pride by recalling the humiliation of her rivals.

Both are manipulating memory and imagination to sluice into their systems fight/flight chemistry to achieve what we have called the *Feverish Feeling of Life.* "We live in a world of unreality and dreams. To give up our imaginary position as the center…is to awaken to what is real and eternal, to see the true light and hear the true silence"[8] (Simone Weil).

> Each of us has to look into our dark world, recognize the forces which bind us, the blind instincts, the compulsions which, though they give us the illusion of power, freedom, and adulthood, ensnare us. We have to fight our way free; renounce the Dark Powers, learn to judge and act from our centre. Only then are we human and personal. This work of self-knowledge is absolutely essential.[9]
>
> —*Sr. Ruth Burrows*

First and Second Movements

It happened just before World War II, in Italy. Benito Mussolini was determined to rally his countrymen to a fever-pitch of Fascist nationalism. He decided that a series of propaganda films about the imperial power of ancient Rome would serve this. He chose his son, Victorio, an amateur filmmaker, to direct them.

Italian dignitaries gathered on premier night to view Victorio's flickering vision of the empire. The screen filled with Roman gladiators, speeding chariots, white marbled columns, toga-clad citizens, and telephone poles. Yes, Victorio had failed to shoot around the telephone poles. As the soldiers raised their arms to salute Caesar, Mussolini's

---

[8] Simone Weil, *Waiting for God,* trans. Emma Craufurd, (New York, NY: Harper & Row, 1951), p. 158.

[9] Ruth Burrows, *Guidelines to Mystical Prayer,* (Denville, NJ: Dimension Books, 1981), p. 25.

guests must have been hard pressed to control their laughter at another anachronism: Rome's legions were wearing wristwatches.

Like Victorio, the ego beguiled by the fight/flight response is an inept inner director. It has a knack for showing us exactly the wrong image at the worst time. If we make a mistake during the day, the ego-director instantly projects on our mental screen ten other things that we have recently done wrong. If we are facing a critical moment of truth and are most in need of calm intelligence, the ego may screen upsetting scenarios, fear-fretted moments of defeat and hopelessness—vexing us from our true good. If we have been criticized and need patience and thoughtfulness to handle the complaint, the wounded ego—revved up by fight/flight chemistry—flashes before our inner eye the faults of the one who brought the complaint, and a petty battle plan.

Today, you and I can practice standing back from these reckless reactions and doing something new, something truly pleasant:

1. Detect mechanical reactions in ourselves, in thoughts and moods.
2. Let go of reactions that are counter-productive.

Along these lines, the Christian contemplative tradition has perennially distinguished between "first movements" of the will and "second movements." First movements (what we have been calling "mechanical reactions") are not sinful *per se,* for every sort of feeling may visit us unbeckoned. It is only when we persistently seek a spurious feeling of life in them, that they become second movements, separating us from true life. "Whoever loves true prayer and yet becomes angry or resentful is his own enemy. He is like a man who wants to see clearly and yet inflicts damage on his own eyes"[10] (Evagrios).

Rationalizations

Novelist Aldous Huxley observed, "What you take to be the captain of your soul may just be its noisiest passenger." The fight/flight ego is

[10] *The Philokalia,* vol. I, trans. G.E.H. Palmer, Philip Sherrard, Kallistos Ware, (Boston, MA: Faber and Faber, 1979), p. 63.

not the true captain of our soul; it does not represent its best energies. It is a blustering stowaway using uproarious chemistry to usurp the prerogatives of the true captain. It haughtily commands, "You have a right to let off some steam! Go on, get really angry! Show them who's boss!" That is the "fight" half of mechanical reactivity; the "flight" half is silent resentment and frustration, debilitating social embarrassment, implosive self-pity and bitterness.

We can practice the following exercise to get a better understanding of the "fight" response in us. The next time it arises, we can notice its clever rationalizations. For example, resentment insists that its rumblings within us prove we are independent thinkers. A feeling of stubbornness will urge us to continue in our hardness: "You are a maverick to be reckoned with!" it tells us. Likewise, petty irritation will flatter us that we are uncompromising perfectionists who "Tell it like it is!"

But the truth is opposite: boiling inner chemistry is as common as boiling oatmeal. There is nothing special or individualistic about it. Not only is the attack-response we feel a generic human reaction (as its basic chemistry is shared by everyone), but it is a generic biological one: the birds in the trees and the squirrels on the ground are activated by the same hypothalamic discharges. So there is no independent thinking in it at all. On the contrary, such a response evinces mediocrity and slavery to external conditions. True individualism is far more subtle.

Dr. Benson's Discovery

The fight/flight response efficiently served the crude life and death decisions of primordial creatures, which jumped into holes at the flash of a predator's incisors, or lunged ahead, tooth and claw. Yet we have seen that in the human milieu, the response is as much a curse as a blessing. In *Mind As Slayer, Mind as Healer,* Dr. Pelletier goes so far as to say that our "neurophysiological responses for dealing with stress have become anachronistic."[11] They are glaringly incompatible with the unique subtleties and requirements of human relationship: a

[11] Pelletier, *op cit.,* p. 69.

Crackerjack-box toy compass guiding a complex satellite.

This invites the question: Is it possible that our Creator, foreknowing the direction evolution would take, providentially set within our frame a further function beyond the fight/flight response? A latent function that would help us adapt the older mechanism to our specific human situation?

It would seem so. This hidden function was first identified by Dr. Herbert Benson of the Harvard Medical School in the early 1970s, during his scientific studies of the physiological and psychological effects of meditation. He termed it the *Relaxation Response* to contrast it to the fight/flight response, as the dynamics of the Relaxation Response were exactly opposite those of the fight/flight response.

In the late 1960s and early 1970s, a number of medical researchers became interested in reports of the positive effects of meditation on physical and psychological health. At Harvard, Dr. Benson and his colleagues applied an empirical methodology to its study. Scientifically monitoring the vital signs of persons meditating, researchers noticed that their blood pressure dropped to healthy levels, heart and breathing rates slowed, muscles became less tense, stress was relieved. Dr. Benson later studied people at prayer (as distinct from meditation), and discovered that praying also evokes the Relaxation Response.

How does it work? Benson found that the Response interrupts the fight/flight cycle. It introduces an opposing, involuntary dynamic that causes a reduction in the excitement of the sympathetic nervous system. The Response stops the anxiety cycle by blocking the action of fear-stimulating hormones on the sympathetic nervous system.[12] Furthermore, it "tends to break up some of the inappropriate 'loops' of thinking formed in the 'wiring' of your brain," he wrote.[13] Uninterrupted, the anxiety-loop tends to continue firing off like a long pack of tightly twined firecrackers.

---

[12] Herbert Benson, *The Relaxation Response,* with Miriam Z. Klipper, (New York, NY: Avon, 1975), pp. xvi-xvii.

[13] Herbert Benson, M.D., *Beyond the Relaxation Response: How to Harness the Healing Power of Your Personal Beliefs,* (New York, NY: Berkley Publishing Group, 1994), pp. 97-99.

Since peaceful sleep may invite serenity similar to that of contemplative practices, it was hypothesized that meditation and prayer simply mimicked sleep, producing effects comparable to a relaxing nap. But research disproved this. Dr. Pelletier notes that it is "empirically verified that the meditative process relieves nervous-system stress more efficiently than dreaming or sleeping."[14]

Some researchers were concerned, though, that regularly evoking the Response might produce unintended consequences such as complacency, inefficiency, or lack of energy. But the opposite proved true. Pelletier writes:

> This research would seem to indicate that [those who evoke the Relaxation Response] had a higher level of arousal when it was appropriate, and perhaps a greater potential range of response when such response was warranted.[15]

> This enables the individual to be more reactive to his environment, while at the same time allowing him to recover more swiftly once the stressful situation has passed.[16]

Dr. Benson summarizes: "Practicing the relaxation response on your own is simple. Once you're comfortable with it, you can use it to cope better with stresses from road rage to performance anxiety."[17]

The Calming Breath

The Relaxation Response is not only evoked through prayer and meditation, but in many other ways. For example, traditional wisdom was right to recommend slow, deep breathing to invite calmness. It effectively elicits the Relaxation Response, says Dr. Benson.

---

[14] Pelleteir, *op cit.*, p. 212.

[15] *Ibid.*, p. 204.

[16] *Ibid.*, p. 203.

[17] "Brain Check," by Herbert Benson, M.D., Julie Corliss and Geoffrey Cowley, *Newsweek,* September 27, 2004, p. 47.

Judith Lasater, Ph.D., writes in *Relax and Renew:*

> Our physical and mental states are reflected in the breath. In fact, there is no more reliable measurement of stress than the rate and quality of the breath. Under stressful conditions, the breath is shallow, rapid, and jagged. To change these qualities, and therefore, relieve stress, all you need to do is bring your attention to your breath.[18]

Right now, take a slow deep breath. Exhale naturally. Become aware of the calm, mending forces that are streaming through your being. You have elicited the Relaxation Response.

We might use this healing breath to elicit the Relaxation Response in the following situations:

- During an intense conversation
- While waiting at a stop light
- When someone cuts you off in traffic
- Whenever you think of someone you do not like
- Whenever you think you have too much to do in too little time[19]

Please take another deep breath. Notice how the Relaxation Response naturally draws your awareness out of your head and down into your body, into its quiet, simple sense of being.

This is one dimension of true spiritual work: to pull our attention back from the hypnotism of stress chemistry, back to a serene, simple sense of being. We have to do this again and again: come back to quiet being, uncommanded by the calculations of egoism.

Imagine the following situation. A husband arrives home late for dinner. He hugs his wife, earnestly apologizing to her and their children that he had been stuck in heavy traffic. She is upset; she had prepared a special dinner, and the children have been getting cranky waiting to eat. She is tempted to speak sharply to him in front of the children—her

---

[18] Judith Lasater, *Relax and Renew: Restful Yoga for Stressful Times,* (Berkeley, CA: Rodmell Press, 1995), p. 209.

[19] *Ibid.,* p. 211.

"fight" chemistry is in high gear. But she knows his being late tonight was not his fault, and speaking harshly to him would not be right for her, or good for the children. Still in her husband's arms, she takes a few deep breaths to help calm herself, quieting the mechanical forces that urge her to speak caustically—gives her husband a kiss, and asks the kids to help her serve dinner.

Is that ideal? Yes. But as Christians we ought to aim high, as we have the Spirit as the will within our will, and Christ as the sacred heart within our heart. To be true to life is our aim, and we ought to employ whatever facilitates this, including the healing breath to evoke the Relaxation Response. "If anyone considers himself religious and yet does not keep a tight reign on his tongue, he deceives himself and his religion is worthless" (James 1:26).

The Song of the Body

Take one more slow, deep breath, and exhale leisurely. Feel serenity renewed in your body. Now, in this relaxed state, practice the Self-Release Prayer:

1. Let go of any agitated thoughts.
2. Do not fill in the interior silence that opens up, but allow God's quietude to reign in it.
3. Relax into the sense of God's peace.

The Self-Release Prayer vitally complements the healing breath to invite the Relaxation Response. We can combine them as often as we wish in order to return to a sense of God's presence in the now moment, and relate to life from that true inner reference point.[20]

Even if we begin by practicing the Self-Release Prayer and the healing breath separately, we may soon find that the practice of one naturally evokes the other; that they call to one another, solicit one another, as sea gulls call to one another over a stretch of coast.

---

[20] Certainly the Self-Release Prayer also invites graces that are unquantifiable, ones that transcend the empirical benefits of the Relaxation Response.

Moreover, after a season of their practice, we may find that anytime our bodies are deeply relaxed (as during a leisurely stroll), our quietude spontaneously initiates either the Self-Release Prayer or the healing breath or both. That is further proof of the unitary character of our being, and its aptitude for the circulation of true life. These interlacing life-forces are an expression of "the song of the body," as Vanda Scaravelli has expressed it. She adds: "This song, if you care to listen, is beauty."[21]

Another way to evoke the Relaxation Response in daily life is through short prayers and affirmations. Imagine yourself on your lunch hour, walking to a cafe. The prettiness of the sunlight on the leaves of sidewalk trees suddenly awakens you to the divine presence. You are moved to silently, mentally repeat the affirmation, "Christ is here…Christ is here…Christ is here," perhaps harmonizing it with your breath. Through the affirmation "Christ is here," you delight in Christ's omnipresence as the creative *Logos*, the secret beauty of the world.

You continue your affirmation as you walk along, seeking communion with Christ for its own sake, the delight of being with Love. And you have also evoked the Relaxation Response which will help you to be true to life throughout the day, avoiding counter-productive mechanical reactions.

A Modest but Vital Holism

Another luminous observation from Huxley goes to the heart of our subject. He starts by affirming with the New Testament,

> Perfect love drives out fear.
>
> —*1 John 4:18*

---

[21] Vanda Scaravelli, *Awakening the Spine,* (San Francisco, CA: HarperSanFrancisco, 1991), p. 8.

He then turns the words around, to find further illumination:

> Love casts out fear; but conversely fear casts out love. And not only love. Fear also casts out intelligence, casts out goodness, casts out all thought of beauty and truth…For in the end fear casts out even a man's humanity.[22]

Huxley is describing in existential terms the tragic effects of the stress miscue we have been considering. The ego, mesmerized by the fight/flight response, casts out beauty, truth, goodness, gentleness—the best of our humanity.

Note how the *Holism of the Mind-Body Partnership* has supplied us with a helpful context for Huxley's insight. Still, at first glance, this holism is not as obviously sublime as the others in our study. Patently impressive are the *Holism of the Christ-Logos* and the *Holism of the Mystical Body*, with their grand vistas encompassing worlds seen and unseen. Relative to them, the *Holism of the Mind-Body* may seem marginally significant to the Christian vision. If they are verdant branches of the holoarchical Wreath, then the *Holism of the Mind-Body Partnership* seems a tiny sprig.

But let us take a closer look. If the *Holism of the Mind-Body Partnership* supports insight and kindness, and so assists our desire to respond truly to life moment by moment, it goes to the heart of Christianity. "If I…have not love, I am only a resounding gong or a clanging cymbal" (I Corinthians 13:1).

Consider the *Holism of the Mystical Body.* Though I may belong to the Church, the Mystical Body of Christ, which is a jewel set in space and time, and a diadem beyond space and time, if I am ungenerous in love, I alienate myself from the soul of the Church. "When the evening comes, you will be examined in love" (John of the Cross).[23]

As the *Holism of the Mind-Body Partnership* helps us be more generous in love, it draws the sap of the *Holism of the Mystical Body* to us, and that of other holisms.

---

[22] Aldous Huxley, *Ape and Essence,* (Chicago, IL: Ivan R. Dee, Publisher, 1948), p. 51.

[23] *The Collected Works of St. John of the Cross,* trans. Kieran Kavanaugh O.C.D., and Otilio Rodriguez, O.C.D., (Washington, DC: ICS Publications, 1991), p. 90.

Mind, body, and spirit are interactive elements of our being. To artfully enlist the aid of each of these elements for the others to be true to the Holy Spirit—that is the *Holism of the Mind-Body Partnership.*

Holism of the Mind-Body Partnership

Holism of the Unitive State

Affinity: the *Holism of the Unitive State* (Chapter Ten)

The unitive state comes about by our willing what God wills. But as we are not angels, disembodied beings, but are embodied souls, our will is affected by powerful psycho-biological forces. An understanding of the Mind-Body Partnership can help us understand these forces, so that we may be true to life, and so invite union with God.

Prayer

To review this chapter's key points:

- Much of human behavior is unconsciously commandeered by ancient automatic responses.
- The wrongly-oriented ego is often abetted by fight/flight chemistry.
- Awareness of these mechanisms (and their rationalizations) helps free us from their blind domination.
- Evoking the Relaxation Response modifies the fight/flight response, reducing stress and mechanical reactivity.

We have studied practices that evoke the Relaxation Response on the spot: the calming breath, the Self-Release Prayer, and affirmations.

But we can also enduringly integrate the Relaxation Response into our mind-body system by periods of daily prayer. Dr. Benson offers basic guidelines to prayer in his now classic books, *The Relaxation Response* and *Beyond the Relaxation Response:*

- Sit in a comfortable position.
- Close your eyes and relax your muscles
- Focus on your breathing. Breathe slowly and naturally.
- Select a word, prayer, or phrase, such as the number "one." Then repeat it silently...
- When outside thoughts intrude during the meditation, disregard them by saying, "Oh, well," and return to the word or prayer you've selected. It is essential always to maintain a passive, relaxed style in dealing with any interruptions.[24]

Benson's suggestion that we chose a single word or a short phrase for prayer comes not only from his empirical studies, but from his study of the world's mystical literature, including the Christian classic, *The Cloud of Unknowing.*

Its author, an anonymous contemplative of medieval times, asked his reader to approach God with a heart uplifted by a very short prayer or a single prayer-word, for such prayer "pierces the ears of Almighty God more than does any long psalm unmindfully mumbled through the teeth."[25]

Please choose now a single prayer word or phrase, one that signifies your love for God. Perhaps one of these: peace, one, Supreme, Christ, Mother, Father. Or use a phrase such as "Reveal Thyself" or *Maranatha* (Aramaic, meaning *Come, Lord*—Revelation 22:17). Discover creatively, intuitively what word or phrase opens your heart to God.

[24] Benson, *Beyond the Relaxation Response, op cit.*, p. 96-97.

[25] Robert Way, ed., *The Cloud of Unknowing and The Letter of Private Direction,* (Wheathampstead, England: Anthony Clarke, 1986), pp. 60-61.

Once you have chosen a word or phrase, devote ten minutes to the following prayer.

Sit comfortably.

Put your hands on your lap: palms down or palms up, or fingertips lightly touching, but do not lock fingers together, as this may distract you. Close your eyes, and begin to repeat your word. You may want to harmonize it with your in-going and out-going breath.

Ignore other thoughts as they arise. Let the prayer-word conduct you into the Stillness. If distracting thoughts arise, relax away from them by your prayer-word. As Stillness arises, *simply be,* without thinking about your being, and *let God be,* without thinking about God. From the unknown in yourself, go out in a simple, loving movement to God who exists beyond the world of thought as Ultimate Mystery.

A Canticle of Silence

Pray in the above manner ten to fifteen minutes a day for the first week, and about twenty minutes each day thereafter. Be regular, be patient. "Whoever flees prayer flees all that is good"[26] (John of the Cross).

Of course, the implications of prayer ride far beyond its eliciting the Relaxation Response. This is not to belittle the Response. It is only to note that prayer is, first and last, an expression of love for God, a communion sought for its own sake. The graces that visit the soul in prayer are certainly not quantifiable according to the methodology of laboratory science.

In addition to our using the type of prayer described above, we can commune with God through the Self-Release Prayer. As you know, the Self-Release Prayer can be practiced even for a moment or two, with eyes open, right in the middle of daily activity. But now we shall find that it can also be prayed with eyes closed and in a sustained manner.

Sit comfortably. Relax away from self-concern, from self-focused thinking, and become receptive to your Creator. As thoughts arise, do not think about them, do not add to them, but let them pass by. The Self-Release Prayer is not meditation, which proceeds by thinking

[26] Kavanaugh and Rodriguez, *op cit.,* p. 97.

and imagination; instead, the Self-Release Prayer endeavors a wordless openness to God.[27] It invites the gentle whisper of the divine presence made known to the Hebrew prophet, Elijah:

> The Lord said,
> "Go out and stand on the mountain
> in the presence of the Lord, for the Lord
> is about to pass by."
>
> Then a great and powerful wind
> tore the mountains apart
> and shattered the rocks before the Lord,
> but the Lord was not in the wind.
>
> After the wind there was an earthquake,
> but the Lord was not in the earthquake....
>
> After the earthquake.....
> came a
> gentle
> whisper.
>
> When Elijah heard it,
> he pulled his cloak over his face....
>
> —*1 Kings 19:11-13*

Listen for this silence. Abandon yourself to it. Its shades are more variegated than the shades of green in a verdant land; silence is both a night blooming flower, and a wistful blossom that dawn wears in her hair. "The Father spake one Word, which is his Son, and this Word he speaks always in eternal silence, and in silence must it be heard by the soul"[28] (John of the Cross).

---

[27] My reference to meditation concerns its definition in a Christian context; it has other meanings in other religious contexts.

[28] Kavanaugh and Rodriguez, *op cit.*, p. 97.

As you pray, do not condemn or justify thoughts. Just be aware of the Supreme, silently and patiently abiding before your God. Then suddenly, in the course of prayer, letting go of thoughts may begin to occur spontaneously. You find that you are no longer releasing thoughts as they arise, but that thought is falling away of itself. Thinking now appears like a distant waterfall, so far away from the wide pacific stillness you sense.

Fr. John Tauler, the medieval contemplative, wrote:

> If a man would prepare an empty place in the depths of his soul there can be no doubt that God must fill it at once....So you must be silent. Then God will be born in you, utter His Word in you and you shall hear it; but be very sure that if you speak, the word will have to be silent. The best way to serve the word is to keep silent and listen. If you go out, He will most surely come in; as much as you go out for Him, He will come in to you; no more, no less.[29]

By "word" Tauler does not mean an inspired idea, but the transforming divine presence.

Pray in this way for at least twenty-minutes a day. Some days prayer will be delicious, a guilded breeze—a ray of God who is bliss. Other days it will be a wilderness, a tangle of boredom and restlessness—a ray of God who is patience that weathers all conditions. "The whole Blessed Trinity dwells in us, the whole of that mystery which will be our vision in heaven. Let it be our cloister"[30] (Elizabeth of the Trinity).

---

[29] John Tauler, *Spiritual Conferences,* trans. and ed. by Eric Colledge and Sister M. Jane, (Rockford, Illinois: Tan Books and Publishers, Inc, 1978), p. 157.

[30] M.M. Philipon, O.P., ed, *Sister Elizabeth of the Trinity: Spiritual Writings, Letters, Retreats, and Unpublished Notes,* (New York, NY: P.J. Kenedy & Sons, 1962), p. 54.

CHAPTER 9

The Path to Union With God According to the Mystics

"It is only a purified love that can attain God...."[1]

—*Andrew Louth*

In his *Autobiography,* Ben Franklin tells of an encounter with the remarkable minister, George Whitfield, known throughout the American colonies for his entrancing homilies. As Franklin listened to this true lover of God, he was unexpectedly moved:

> I perceived he intended to finish with a collection and I silently resolved he should get nothing from me. I had in my pocket a handful of copper money; three or four silver dollars and five pistoles in gold. As he proceeded, I began to soften...and...concluded to give the coppers. Another stroke of his oratory made me ashamed of that...and determined me to give the silver. But he finished so admirably that I emptied my pocket wholly into the collection, gold and all.[2]

---

[1] Andrew Louth, *The Origin of the Christian Mystical Tradition, From Plato to Denys,* (New York, NY: Oxford University Press, 1983), p. 186.

[2] Ben Franklin, *The Autobiography of Benjamin Franklin,* Kenneth Silverman, ed., (New York, NY: Penguin Books, 1986), p. 118.

This is an apt analogy of our journey to God. As our journey begins, we give God a copper of love. Then, as He opens our hearts further to Him, we are moved to give Him the silver of devotion. Then, in the unitive state, the soul gives God the gold of surrender.

✧ ✧ ✧ ✧

In this chapter we will study how the soul comes to the good life—to union with God. Our guide will be John of the Cross. Because John was graced by God with "light-on prayer," he was able to map out this journey with exceeding clarity.

As said, our coming to the unitive state is tantamount to Christ's recapitulating the Mystery of His hidden life in us. "The life of grace, in making us children of the Father, makes us also brethren of Christ, who must become like Him in all things to deserve the name"[3] (Jean Danielou, S.J.).

Our Journey to the Unitive State Begins with Conversion

Greg Parsons, the co-author of *New England Waterfalls—A Guide to More than 200 Cascades and Waterfalls,* was delighted by his first visit to a waterfall somewhere in Maine as a boy of five or six with his grandfather. Years later, when Parsons wanted to return to it, his grandparents couldn't remember which falls he had in mind. But Parsons eventually found it: Snow Falls, a small 25-foot cascade on the Little Androscoggin River. "The second I visited it I recognized it, even though I was only 5 years old the first time I saw it."[4]

Just as Parsons could not forget the little waterfall of his boyhood, so a conversion experience in God has an indelible effect. In this experience, God has not only disclosed His presence, He has sensitized the soul to it, drawing it to His divine depths. From these depths, God may now solicit the soul as it matures, as it now recognizes His familiar touch.

---

[3] Jean Danielou, *God and the Ways of Knowing,* trans. Walter Roberts, (New York, NY: Meridian Books, 1957), p. 229.

[4] http://www.newenglandwaterfalls.com/salemnewsarticle.php.

"When I was sixteen," writes Ruth Burrows, "my inmost depths were smitten by a 'realization' of the reality of God. There is nothing to be said of that 'moment' other than that it turned me upside down. I knew that *there* was the only Answer for me; life had no meaning except that Unutterable."[5]

A conversion experience sparks our spiritual quest in earnest—or for some, gives the quest an entirely new vivacity and direction. The grace of conversion comes out of the blue as a dancing benediction. The Spirit dazzles the soul's hearth by a sudden crackling, upleaping flame. It makes us want to honor this luminosity in all we do—to make God the ongoing reference point of our soul.

An Incomparable Guide to the Journey

Think of the poignant, comic sight of nesting baby birds when their mother has returned with a bit of food. Their trill peeping for attention is non-stop, and they are all mouth, turned straight up.

If the conversion grace sent from God has truly taken root, this is how we feel—crying for God, all mouth, eager for the next feeding.

We feel the urge for something to do—something to draw closer to this wonderful God who has personally summoned us. We want to honor the divine, to know God more deeply, to become the kind of person God wants us to be. "Laziness is love's opposite"[6] (M. Scott Peck, M.D.).

The doctrine of John of the Cross supplies us with a clear vision of how to walk with God, as we seek to be true to the grace of our conversion. We discover in John of the Cross "a man of rare wisdom, clear-sighted, closely united to God and knowing himself called to communicate to others the 'science of love'"[7] (Ruth Burrows).

---

[5] http://www.priestsandpeople.co.uk/cgi-bin/archive_db.cgi?priestsppl-00026.

[6] M. Scott Peck, *Denial of the Soul: Spiritual and Medical Perspectives on Euthanasia and Mortality,* (CA: Three Rivers Press, 1998), p. 271.

[7] Ruth Burrows, *Ascent to Love: The Spiritual Teaching of St. John of the Cross,* (London: Darton, Longman, and Todd, 1987), p. 16.

"There is certainly no one to whom we can turn with greater confidence for guidance in the developments in the life of prayer which may now occur to us"[8] (Aelred Squire).

Ironically, John wrote five hundred years ago, "Love to be unknown by yourself and others."[9] But John's doctrine of truth is irrepressible. It verifies itself to all lovers of God. Hence the immortality of his words, which are transparent to the divinity behind them.

Not only did the Catholic Church canonize John (recognize him as a saint), but it conferred on him the title "doctor" of the faith—the "doctor of mystical love," some have called him. The title "doctor" has enormous significance in Catholicism. Rarely conferred, it is the Church's official recognition that a saint's doctrine has superlatively deepened the Church's understanding of God. In two thousand years, the Church has recognized only about fifty doctors of the faith: the appointment of only twenty-five doctors every thousand years.

That the Church conferred this title upon John is a sign of her highest trust in his doctrine of prayer. It not only speaks to the authenticity of John's doctrine, but confirms the Church's mystical profundity.

In *Ascent of Mount Carmel,* the *Dark Night of the Soul, The Spiritual Canticle,* and *The Living Flame of Love,* and *Counsels of Light and Love,* our Doctor has charted the Way of the soul's progressive intimacy with God, from its earliest steps on the path, to its transformation into Christ in the Trinity.

The Active Night of the Senses

Our conversion-experience inspires us to abide in this dear God who has revealed Himself. Now we get down to business, endeavoring to reform our life to honor God and draw close to Him. This Reformation is called by John the *Active Night of the Senses.*[10] This is a time for disciplined living for the love of God.

---

[8] Aelred Squire, *Asking the Fathers,* (Westminister, MD: Christian Classics, 1993), p. 192.

[9] *The Collected Works of St. John of the Cross,* trans. Kieran Kavanaugh O.C.D., and Otilio Rodriguez, O.C.D., (Washington, DC: ICS Publications, 1991), p. 95.

[10] *Ibid,* p.147-148.

But God is working too—tunneling from the other side of the mountain. Frankly, it is His power behind our pick as well. Yet we must work, must prove our sincerity, because

> These are the words of him who holds
> the seven stars in his right hand
> and walks among the
> seven gold lampstands:
> "I know your deeds,
> your hard work and your perseverance.
>
> —*Revelation 2:1*

The Active Night of the Senses is the first of five major phases in our journey to union; the next are—

2. **Passive Night of the Senses**: God withdraws the sensible spiritual delights He had lavished on us during our earliest days of growth, to test our mettle, to attune us to subtler apperception of His presence.
3. **Illuminative Way**: The ego is now well-oriented to God's will and has constructed a kind of self-made union with God—a good union, but not as deep or abiding a union as God would have us finally know.
4. **Dark Night of the Soul**: God dissolves the ego, undoing our self-constructed union with Him to make way for a perfect union.
5. **Unitive Revelation**: Peace at last, union with God, as God draws together the elements of our being around Himself who is our new non-egoic center.

This chapter will trace the first four phases; the next chapter will discuss their culmination in the unitive state.

Phase One of Our Journey: Reformation

What does our Reformation consist in? (We will use "Reformation" from now on to indicate John's Active Night of the Senses).

To understand this, we must first understand the essence of union with God—just what our goal is. John tells us it is a union of likeness with God.[11] It is not a likeness of being (for the self is not God), but a likeness in the will. This likeness consists of our attuning our will to God's will, to let go of whatever in our will contradicts God's.[12]

> The man who says, "I know him,"
> but does not do what he commands is a liar,
> and the truth is not in him.
>
> But if anyone obeys his word,
> God's love is truly made complete in him.
>
> This is how we know we are
> in him:
> Whoever claims to live in him
> must walk as Jesus did.
>
> —*1 John 2:3-6*

To look at Reformation from a holistic angle, the closer we adhere to God by conforming to His will, the closer we adhere to our own human depths, the mystery of what God created us to be, our true human essence. During an interview, theologian Edward Schillebeeckx was asked, "What is sin?" He replied simply: "Everything that goes against being human."[13] The unitive state which Reformation is conducting us toward is the true flowering of the human in God.

To search the word of the mystics on Reformation is to find unanimity on these elements: the practice of the Self-Release Prayer, a searching self-honesty in the Light, the practices of goodwill and *Resent Not Evil*, and communion with the Eucharistic Christ at Mass.

---

[11] *Ibid.*, p. 163.

[12] *Ibid.*, p. 164.

[13] Edward Schillebeeckx, *God is New Each Moment: In Conversation with Huub Oosterhis and Piet Hoogeveen,* trans. David Smith, (New York, NY: Seabury Press, 1983), p. 68.

Sayings of Light And Love

John of the Cross' short work, known today as *The Sayings of Light and Love,* is a uniquely practical guide to Reformation. It consists of 175 maxims of plainly spoken advice to earnest souls. The result is an uncompromising compendium of the essence of the Christian path. Here are a few maxims to whet your interest to read the entire collection, which illumines like a miniature sun:

1. "The humble are those who hide in their own nothingness and know how to abandon themselves to God."[14] To be as nothing in our own imagination is to glimpse eternity right now. To experience the profound, we need only refuse self-trivia.
2. "When evening comes, you will be examined in love. Learn to love as God desires to be loved and abandon your own way of acting."[15] A king had a specially made ring with a secret compartment. When he opened its little hidden door, the ring revealed two miniature portraits, facing each other, likenesses of the king himself and his beloved. The contemplative heart is like that ring.
3. "Blessed are they who, setting aside their own pleasure and inclination, consider things according to reason and justice before doing them."[16] "Objectivity" does not sound very spiritual, does it? But it is high participation in the Spirit. For it is seeing without defensive self-reference. Notice the next time you use your mind objectively in some situation, how the Light is gently pouring in.

---

[14] Kavanaugh and Rodriguez, *op cit.*, p. 97.

[15] *Ibid.*, p. 90.

[16] *Ibid.*, p. 89.

The Face of Love

The very first advice that John of the Cross gives to readers of his *Ascent of Mt. Carmel* on reforming their lives is this: "First, have habitual desire to imitate Christ in all your deeds by bringing your life into conformity with his. You must then study his life in order to know how to imitate him and behave in all events as he would."[17]

Certainly an important aspect of this imitation is our endeavoring to be a presence of love for others in their struggles great and small. This principle is crystallized in a phrase spoken in a memorable scene in the movie, *Dead Man Walking*—"the face of love."

The movie is based on a true story of a Catholic nun who befriends a tough-talking young man, a convicted killer who finally comes to see, with immense horror and contrition, the evil he has caused. As he walks with Sister Helen down the final mile to the death chamber, he collapses both under the weight of his guilt and his fear. "You know the truth," she says gently, "the truth has made you free. Christ is here."

Then she looks him in the eye and says, "Look. I want the last thing you see in this world to be a face of love. So you look at me, when they do this thing. You look at me: I'll be the face of love for you." As he faces death, he will find in her face the *alter Christus*—the face of merciful Christ.

On an August day in 1941, half-starved prisoners at Auschwitz were told that a prisoner had escaped, and that they would be punished: ten would be locked in the infamous starvation bunker, condemned to die slowly of malnourishment and dehydration.

As one man is picked, he cries out, "My wife, my children!" A fellow prisoner steps forward and says to the guard: "I am a Catholic priest. I have no family like this man. Allow me to take his place."

Hesitating at first, the guard finally agrees. Fr. Maximillian Maria Kolbe, a Polish Franciscan priest, is marched with nine other men to the starvation bunker, and died fourteen days later. The man whose life was spared by Kolbe's generosity enjoyed longevity, his family by his side into old age, and never forgot the face of that priest—the face of love. Each of us is called to be the face of Christ for the other. "Love each other as I have loved you" (John 15:12).

---

[17] *Ibid.*, p. 148.

But Christ added a further instruction: "Whatever you did for one of the least of these brothers of mine, you did for Me" (Matthew 25:40). So we are not only called to be the face of love for one another, but to see Christ's face in the face of our neighbor. "Christ gives him a face, unlimited importance and superiority...I must stand up with this other man, recognize my own features in his countenance, be responsible for myself and him"[18] (Hans Urs von Balthasar).

To express Christ from one's deepest subjectivity and to find the deepest subjectivity of another ("Thou") is to experience the reciprocity of *The Holism of the Face of Love.* By it, we realize the I-Thou relationship in Christ.

Holism of the Face of Love

Holism of the Mystical Body

Affinity: The *Holism of the Mystical Body* (Chapter Fourteen)

To be the face of love for each other, and to be touched by the face of Christ in our neighbor, is to be drawn into rapport with the whole Mystical Body. "Thus the man who gives a piece of bread without saying a word, if his way of giving is right, sometimes gives eternal life at the same

---

[18] Hans Urs von Balthasar, *Who Is A Christian?,* trans. John Cumming, (New York, NY: Newman Press, 1967), p. 94.

time. A gesture of this kind may possess a redemptive value far higher than many sermons"[19] (Simone Weil).

Reformation Brings Consolations

"Come near to God, and he will come near to you" (James 4:8). As our years of Reformation continue, He makes Himself known to us interiorly, vividly, sometimes overflowing our "interior senses" with delightful experiences of His presence.[20]

Perhaps we have a favorite outdoor place for prayer—a nearby lake. God will mingle its waters with Bethesda's, and its grasses with the green of Judea upon which Christ rested. Perhaps a certain piece of music particularly awakens our love for God; God will vibrate within that song as a hidden line of melody. And if we are inclined to meditate, to visualize the life of Christ, God will cause a seraph to press her wing against our brow, to vivify the colors of our reverie.

In sum, the Spirit enchants us during Reformation with many consolations, to lure us into the divine milieu. Just as a butterfly can read nectar through her feet, so the soul now treads ahead on the path with enamored steps.

God's ways in the soul during this phase reminds us of a method used by the ancient rabbis to inspire a love of learning in the young. On the first day of school, they would feed youngsters honey cakes shaped like letters of the alphabet so that the children would associate learning with sweetness.[21] So does God lure us toward union.

But John would have us remember that these sensible consolations are just God's opening gambit. Very soon, He will begin to wean us from what our interior senses can grasp of Him, to what they cannot—to a richer, subtler octave of Spirit. We must not be discouraged when this begins; for this is a time of testing and maturing love.

---

[19] Simone Weil, *The First and Last Notebooks,* trans. Richard Rees, (New York, NY: Oxford University Press, 1970), p. 216.

[20] Kavanaugh and Rodriguez, *op cit.*, pp. 85-86.

[21] Leo Rosten, ed., *Religions of America: Ferment and Faith in an Age of Crisis,* (New York, NY: Simon and Schuster, 1975), p. 143.

This weaning begins Phase Two of our journey: the Passive Night of the Senses. God will eventually cast a dark night over our interior senses, and previous consolations will turn to ashes in our mouth, as God moves us along toward ever-steeper realizations of Love.

Phase Two: The Passive Night of Senses

As God ceases to be present in a way we can sense, we experience an interior dryness, or spiritual "aridity."[22] Yesterday our soul bloomed with delight in God; today it is parched, a desert at noon. Meditation brings no joy. Our habitual ways of prayer seem pointless; we seem to be talking to ourselves. Favorite "props" of our spiritual life—pictures, devotions, personal rituals we had created to express love for God, little rites of incense and flowers, all once drenched with meaning—are now insipid. What is going on? Is God displeased with us? Has He left?

No, says John; on the contrary! God's call on our heart is as intense as ever; it is white hot. But a trial is at hand—God is testing our mettle and motivation. Are we only on the spiritual path for its enchantments, or to be deeply united to God, apart from all consolations and favors?[23] Will we persist without these rewards?

And something else is going on that is really quite marvelous. Imagine pushing a movie projector closer to a screen—the image begins to blur. Just so, God is drawing closer to our soul, but our inner eyes have not yet adjusted their focus, and find only an unrecognizable blur: the soul cries, "What is this? Where is God?"

God is ever closer.

If only the soul knew its great fortune—for this is the beginning of contemplation. Contemplation is God's mystical communication with the soul, but not on the thought-level, or feeling-level, or level of imagination—rather on the level of "pure spirit."[24] Thus, what the soul took as God's turning His back on it turns out to be an even more intimate communion: for God is Spirit, and His communion with the

---

[22] Kavanaugh and Rodriguez, *op cit.*, pp. 373-405.

[23] Kavanaugh and Rodriguez, *op cit.*, p. 362.

[24] *Ibid.*, p. 380.

soul now is purely spiritual. In giving the soul contemplation, God is giving Himself.

When beginners would come to Father John of the Cross and complain that they were unable to meditate as before, that their prayers lacked savor, he would first discern if their dryness was rooted in a personal fault. If not, he would know that these aridities signaled the onset of contemplation, and he would tell them how to proceed:

> When spiritual persons cannot meditate,
> they should learn to remain in God's presence
> with a loving attention and a tranquil intellect,
> even though they seem to themselves to be idle.
>
> For little by little and very soon
> the divine calm and peace
> with a wondrous, sublime knowledge of God,
> enveloped in divine love,
> will be infused into their souls.[25]

"But, Father, maybe I'm not trying hard enough. Maybe if I tried harder..."

No, he would say, your inability to meditate *is* the grace. Don't try to meditate now. "Otherwise the soul will be disquieted and drawn out of its peaceful contentment to distaste and repugnance."[26]

John would tell this friend of God that she must walk in faith now—by faith she will now apperceive God in silence, beyond the old consolations. John might finally leave her with this word: Think that God is saying to your soul, "Learn to be empty of all things—interiorly and exteriorly—and you will behold that I am God."[27]

The prayer of faith John describes is none other than our Self-Release Prayer, as this prayer especially cooperates with the grace of contemplation; recall the essence of Elizabeth of the Trinity's prayer:

---

[25] *Ibid.*, p. 199.

[26] *Ibid.*

[27] *Ibid.*

Go out of yourself
in order to adhere to God
by a very simple, wholly loving movement
which allows God to imprint Himself on you and
to transform the soul into Himself.

Expressing the paradoxical character of contemplation, Jacques Maritain wrote:

Contemplation is
a winged and supernatural thing,
free with the freedom of the Spirit of God,
more burning than the African sun
and more refreshing than the waters
of a rushing stream,
lighter than birds' down,
unseizable, escaping any human measure
and disconcerting every human notion,
happy to depose the mighty and exalt the lowly,
capable of all disguises, of all daring and all timidity,
chaste, fearless, luminous and nocturnal,
sweeter than honey and more barren than rock,
crucifying and beatifying (crucifying above all),
and sometimes all the more exalted
the less conspicuous it is.[28]

The High Mysticism of Faith

John of the Cross was the first to definitively elaborate the capital role of pure faith in the soul's passage to God-union. He was correcting an error rife in his times (which continues into ours) that identifies growth in the Spirit with sensations of bliss or fabulous visionary illuminations. But these sensations are our sensations, says John—they are not God's; for God is beyond self and its sensations. God's truest communication is

---

[28] Jacques Maritain, *The Peasant of the Garrone: An Old Layman Questions Himself About the Present Time,* trans. Michael Cuddihy and Elizabeth Hughes, (New York, NY: Holt, Rinehart and Winston, 1968), p. 229.

purely spiritual. To seek God in ever-greater interior sensations—such as bliss, celestial visions, and felicitating angelic voices—is to seek more of oneself; ironically God *per se* is left out of the picture." John writes:

> From my observations, Christ is little known by those who consider themselves his friends. For we see them going about seeking in him their own consolations and satisfactions, loving themselves very much, but not loving him very much.[29]

What then is the way? Bare faith in prayer, not sensational prayer. This is the guiding principle of John's entire mystical theology. The soul possesses a supra-intellectual, intuitive capacity for God—faith. This capacity is made for God alone. "He has also set eternity in the hearts of all men" (Ecclesiastes 3:11).

This is why the Blessed Sacrament, Holy Communion, becomes a special refuge at this time, for faith discerns it to be Christ really with us. The soul may not feel God in prayer, but it is certain that God is in this Sacrament, because God Himself promised it, and this objective certainty of God's presence is a great comfort: "This is My Body…This is My Blood" (Matthew 26: 26-28). Ruth Burrows comments:

> In our sacred liturgy we have the concrete certainty of divine encounter and action. We are grounded on objectivity rather than on the quicksands of our poor subjectivity.[30]

For the Mass, says Burrows,

> the great central act
> of our religion
> *is not of our devising, it is given us.*
> We do not have to make our worship;
> we enter into, claim as our own,
> a worship God himself has given us.[31]

---

[29] Kavanaugh and Rodriguez, *op cit.*, p. 173.

[30] Burrows, *op cit.*, p. 100.

[31] *Ibid.*, pp. 99-100.

Faith Is the Divine Life Itself

Listening to John's counsel, we do not now insist on meditating during prayer, but practice self-release in God, inviting the silence of contemplation. After a season, our experience of aridity changes; its clean austerity now appeals to us, like the night-washed air of a desert morning and its stark terrain. Aridity savors of an inner gaze turned away from self and opened upon the unknown, upon Ultimate Mystery. Thomas Merton writes: "One has begun to know the meaning of contemplation when he intuitively and spontaneously seeks the dark and unknown path of aridity in preference to every other way."[32]

Contemplation is a mysterious knowing, the mystery of faith. Imagine yourself on a road trip. You stop in a village new to you, nestled in the foothills of a great mountain. As you walk through the town, you are spellbound by the blossom-rich air. Wherever you walk, you meet the same invisible luster, like incense breathed from another world. What is that fragrance? Where is it coming from?

"It's the orange blossoms from the groves of those hills," a local tells you, pointing to the foothills. "The scent covers the valley every spring." Pure faith is like the fragrances hidden among those hills and dark-green bushes—its origin and nature is obscure, but its fragrance is unmistakably sublime: a sense of God's presence!

The mystics know the secret flower which exhales the fragrance of faith. That flower is God! The mystics know that faith unveiled is God Himself—that God has been hiding in us all along as the mystery of faith! Faith is not mere belief. Faith is a high mystical principle. Pause right now and apperceive within yourself: Do you sense faith? That is God in you!

Is it now clear why the beginning of contemplation, which is an infusion of faith, is such grand news? God is communicating Himself to the soul as this infusion of mystical faith. "And just as God is darkness to our intellect, so faith dazzles and blinds us. Only by means of faith, in divine light exceeding all understanding, does God manifest

[32] Thomas Merton, *Contemplative Prayer,* (Garden City, NY: Image Books, 1971), p. 89.

himself to the soul"[33] (John of the Cross). Faith is divine light exceeding all understanding. To put this in a Trinitarian perspective: "our" faith is really not ours at all, but Christ's Holy Spirit in us! And our intuition of faith is apperception of Christ's Spirit in us loving the Father!

Contemplation, then, is resting in Christ's Spirit, his perennial prayer in us and for us to the Father. "What is the essence of contemplative prayer? The way of pure faith. Nothing else. You do not have to feel it, but you have to practice it"[34] (Fr. Thomas Keating). By "practice," Fr. Keating means setting aside time each day for prayer—without regard for experiences. (In this tradition, the monastic Order of Discalced Carmelites sits for prayer an hour in the morning, and one in the evening.)

It is a sublime mystic truth that non-experience, paradoxically, is the highest mysticism. It tells us that God, and the heaven of the Trinity, are beyond our human mode of experience, utterly beyond self.

Phase Three: The Illuminative Way

To review: The grace of conversion is followed by sincere Reformation. In response to the now rightly-oriented ego's pursuit of Him, God rewards the soul's love by charming it into His deeper presence through irresistible consolations. But after a season God begins to wean the soul from consolations, and aridities ensue. This is the onset of infused contemplation: a general loving knowledge of God in prayer.

As the soul accustoms itself to it, it begins to savor this way of faith, this direct, dark communication of God. Through prayer, through disciplined living for the love of God, and through the Blessed Sacrament, the soul continues on the path.

Soon a new phase begins: the Illuminative Way. The good ego (which undertook Reformation in the first place and has perdured through all the trials of the path) finally gathers itself together like a carefully woven mesh of fine energies, in receptivity to whatever God would give it. The ego-center has formed a kind of self-created union

---

[33] Kavanaugh and Rodriguez, *op cit.*, p. 177.

[34] Thomas Keating, *Open Mind, Open Heart: The Contemplative Dimension of the Gospel,* (Amity, NY: Amity House, 1986), p. 11.

with the God-center: not an egoless union, but a union of sorts between the two centers.

The Illuminative Way finds the ego at its peak of nobility. Certainly the ego would never think of applying the word "noble" to itself, as it is now more keenly aware than ever of its weaknesses and imperfections. But it is now habitually turned away from self-centeredness, truly knowing God as its highest good, and is avid to follow the divine lead.

The ego has built itself into a little cottage for God's habitation, and God is touched. Yes, God knows he will have to disassemble it, and build His own house for the soul—a truly sturdy way station for the soul's further travels toward Him. "Unless the Lord builds the house, its builders labor in vain" (Psalms 127:1). Yes, in vain, but not without touching the divine Heart.

Just as the ocean wave is most beautiful in its singing white summit as it abandons itself forward to its consumption, so the good ego—now a knight of faith, true to its Sovereign—rushes to its end.

The Fourth Phase: The Dark Night of the Soul

Only God knows when we have done all we can on our side to invite divine union. Then like an eagle swooping down upon its prey, God snatches the ego away, and it is never seen again. A little feather from God's wing is left behind, which will become the limitless downy ground of our being.

The ego can never be dissolved by human effort. No spiritual self-help program can dissolve it. The ending of the ego is sheer grace, a work of God. The lock of the soul is melted off by lightning, not turned by a key from a human hand.

And yet, this stroke of grace surely does not feel like a grace, but the utter absence of grace: the Dark Night of the Soul.

It is not the ego's absence that pains the self; it is God's absence, for God indeed seems to be gone—completely gone! Think of it: for all these years it was the ego that had a hold on God, a focus on God, an experience of God—and now that the ego is gone, there seems to be nothing in self that can grasp God, locate God, so God seems nowhere to be found.

It is a harrowing, lampless experience. A void, a grave and meaningless darkness, has usurped the Light.[35] But what is really going on is quite different, says John; the Light is not gone but is ever brighter in the soul. The soul is experiencing a "dark ray of contemplation."

God's Light is now darkness to the inner senses of the soul, which never have really appreciated God's refined presence. The Light is also now darkness because it blinds the more refined capacities of the soul. Now these capacities suffer directly a ray of God, unblocked by the wall of ego. They recoil, just as one's physical eyes are pained at a sudden and intense light.

The soul is Light-flooded, it is a pavilion of Light, but it senses nothing of its good fortune. It is distraught at what it feels to be the loss of God. But God is closer than ever. The soul's union with God is at hand, for the ego is gone and God is the self's new Center. One must only patiently and faithfully allow the elements of self to reconfigure around this new Center. When this divine work is finished, the soul will be God's, and will know it in the unitive revelation. Claudel writes:

> Like an artist bent over his crucible, God bends over this flaming basin where, not satisfied with having wrought the human soul, He returns it to the flame! It is a delicate operation, partaking at once of the engineer, the gardener and the scientist.[36]
>
> —*Paul Claudel*

Staying in the Center

John also tells us what we must do; we must be passive to this great work, suffer it, yield to it—walk now in bare faith. Jules Monchanin

---

[35] Ruth Burrows suggests in *The Ascent to Love: The Spiritual Teaching of St. John of the Cross,* that while some undergo the dark night as St. John describes it, as an acute suffering, others will experience it differently, including as a "long drawn out greyness in which in nothing happens and it seems inconceivable that anything will happen—ever" (p. 109). See Chapter Ten of Burrow's *Ascent to Love* for this important distinction.

[36] Paul Claudel, *I Believe in God,* Agnes du Sarment, ed., trans. Helen Weaver, (USA: Holt, Rinehart and Winston, 1963), p. 248.

advised: "Fidelity to the monotonous walking in a calcined desert is the act of faith that God asks."[37]

The ending of the ego sets in motion an enormous psychological dynamism. Try to imagine it: the self-elements that had been organized and held comfortably together by the ego are now released from the old center and so are now adrift. By God's grace they are being re-configured around Spirit as their new center. This re-configuration will not happen overnight. For a season much internally will be in flux—profound psychological forces are astir. How is one to respond to this?

According to contemplative tradition, the master principle is: God is doing the work of re-organizing the psyche, not us. Let Him do His work—do not try to do it for Him. Only He knows how to re-organize the finest energies of the soul—you and I do not. So this is what we must do: stay in the Center as much as possible, focus on the Stillpoint, and refuse to be carried off by the psychological turmoil.

John calls the procession of thoughts and emotions that may distract us and upset us the "foxes."[38] Stay in the Center, and disband the foxes by not fighting them. Let go of them as they arise. To embroil yourself in conflict with them is to be drawn out of the peace of the Center into a useless mental battle—which you cannot win. Abandon yourself to the silent Center, even though it may appear to be a nothingness—because that "nothingness," truly seen, is God at the Center. "Our wings are lacking, but we always have strength enough to fall"[39] (Paul Claudel). To fall into the Center.

Time passes. God is doing a work in the soul, reorienting self-elements around its new Center. The revelation of the soul's union with God is slowly dawning, like a necklace of fire on the horizon.

---

[37] J.G. Weber, ed. and trans, *In Quest of the Absolute: The Life and Work of Jules Monchanin,* (Kalamazoo, MI: Cistercian Publications, 1977), p. 169.

[38] Kavanaugh and Rodriguez, *op cit.*, pp. 539-541.

[39] Paul Claudel, *Ways and Crossways,* trans. Fr. John O'Connor, (Freeport, NY: Books for Libraries, 1967), p. 192.

CHAPTER 10

The Song of the Grateful Soul

"Every day is a god, each day is a god, and holiness holds forth in time."
—*Annie Dillard*

On that September morning in 1882 when the Church proclaimed Francis of Assisi a saint, did not the birds sing just a bit louder? And that evening when Sister Moon rose brightly to guild the treetops in festivity, the wolves craned their necks with special dignity to raise a choir of howls to honor their friend Francis, and the angels replied in antiphony, back and forth, each enjoying the language of the other, honoring Francis who was bilingual, fluent in both.

The pope's letter canonizing Francis accented how amazingly Christlike his life was, "even in externals":

> By his numerous virtues, then, and above all by his austerity of life, this irreproachable man endeavored to reproduce in himself the image of Christ Jesus.
>
> But the finger of Providence was again visible in granting to him a likeness to the Divine Redeemer, even in externals.
>
> Thus, like Jesus Christ, it so happened that St. Francis was born in a stable; a little child as he was, his couch was of straw on the ground.

> And it is also related that, at that moment, the presence of angelic choirs, and melodies wafted through the air, completed this resemblance.
>
> Again, like Christ and His Apostles, Francis united with himself some chosen disciples, whom he sent to traverse the earth as messengers of Christian peace and eternal salvation.
>
> Bereft of all, mocked, cast off by his own, he had again this great point in common with Jesus Christ,—he would not have a corner wherein he might lay his head.
>
> As a last mark of resemblance, he received on his Calvary, Mt. Alvernus (by a miracle till then unheard of) the sacred stigmata, and was thus, so to speak, crucified.[1]

St. Francis was the first to receive the stigmata, further marking him as *alter Christus.* It happened this way:

In his last days, Francis spent forty days in prayerful seclusion on a mountain. There a seraph with six wings appeared, and between his brilliant pinions Francis saw the figure of the crucified Christ. In the words of St. Bonaventure, who was Francis' biographer—

> as the vision disappeared, it left his heart ablaze with eagerness and impressed upon his body a miraculous likeness. There and then the marks of nails began to appear in his hands and feet, just as he had seen them in the vision of the Man nailed to the Cross. His hands and feet appeared pierced through the center with nails.[2]

So extraordinary was Francis' unity with Christ that historian Jaroslav Pelikan observed in *Jesus Through the Centuries,* "followers of

---

[1] *Auspicato Concessum* (On St. Francis of Assisi), Encyclical of Pope Leo XIII promulgated on September 17, 1882.

[2] Jaroslav Pelikan, *Jesus Through the Centuries: His Place In the History of Culture,* (New Haven, CT: Yale University Press, 1985), p. 136.

Francis in subsequent generations evolved a special literary form, the double biography," as they believed, "it was possible to know more about either one by studying the life of the other."[3]

When the egoless center is in rapport with the Holy Spirit, a deeper, Christlike union with God (and within the human person) arises—the *Holism of the Unitive State.*

Holism of the Unitive State

Holism of the Beatific Vision

Affinity: The *Holism of the Beatific Vision* (Chapter Seventeen)

The *Holism of the Unitive State* is made possible by the soul's passage through purgatory before death. If purified in this life, the soul will rejoice in the Vision of God at death. But if the passage is not made this side of eternity, the soul—unadapted to the intensity of Love—will at first bear the Light only with difficulty, until light becomes Light. Thus the unitive state incomparably prepares the soul for heaven.

Two Modes of the Unitive Life

I recall St. Francis' life here not only for the joy of remembering this great man with you, but to renew a few points made earlier about the unitive state. As noted, one manner of the unitive life is quite ordinary in externals. We work, raise a family, live as a good neighbor. This

---

[3] *Ibid.*, p. 135.

mode corresponds to Jesus Christ's first thirty years—the Mystery of His hidden years in Nazareth, which were outwardly unremarkable. He worked as we work, and was a good son to Mary and Joseph.

The second mode of the unitive life is full of miracles, healing charisms, high mystical drama—even the ability to excite mass conversion of hearts. This reminds us of Francis' life, and the lives of other saints who fill the literature of Christian spirituality. This mode recapitulates in the soul the Mystery of Christ's public ministry, his dramatic, three-year public career.

It is more likely our unitive life (should God bring us to it) will recapitulate Christ's hidden life rather than his public ministry: no wonder-working, no astonishing mystical phenomena and visions, no dramatic martyrdom. The slow burn of the hidden years speaks more truly to our reality than the Vesuvius of Christ's public life—and that of Francis.

Rather than the picaresque life of the spiritual whirlwind, our unitive life will be a secret between us and God. And yet, it will be a whirlwind of sorts! There will be kids to love and worry over, a spouse to adore and grow with and grow old with, aging parents to love and care for, career ups and downs, neighborhood relationships, pleasant and taxing—and during it all, first and last, a vital and deep life with God.

In short, the good life: "I have come that they may have life, and have it to the full" (John 10:10). We will have a true participation in Christ's union with his Father, with its joys and thorns—even with its redemptive effect on the Mystical Body as a whole. With whichever mode of union God graces the soul, it will sing in thanksgiving to this good God.

The Soul Sings

I am the soul which has been delivered by grace to union with God![4] I know that I am more unlike God than a starfish is from a star, but when I look into myself, by His grace I cannot tell where His life begins in me and mine ends in Him. Where His love starts, and mine joins

[4] This song represents the unitive condition of countless souls who by love and grace have become one with Christ in this life.

it. Where His alabaster silence reigns, and mine twines with it. For His grace is like a mist which kneels in me before Him, and it obscures what is mine and what is His. So it is that He is always present to me now, for to reflect on myself is to find Him, though He is the source of my being, and not I His.

Just as an evergreen tree brought into a living room on Christmas Eve fills all rooms with its drifting savor, so union with God at the Center carries through all the dimensions of my being.

Before union, by three veils I was veiled from God: by the veil of my bigness, the veil of my hardness, and the veil of my cleverness. And by three veils was God veiled from me: by the veil of His littleness, the veil of His gentleness, and the veil of His simplicity. These veils are no more, by His grace.

It is His doing, not mine. Because for years I strove for union with Him, but my love had not the strength of wings. But then imagine an eagle lending the strength of his wings to a sparrow's pinions—that is exactly what happened!

> A competition is held between a giant
> and a little tailor to see which is the stronger.
> The giant throws a stone so high that
> it takes a very long time before it comes down again.
>
> The little tailor lets a bird fly
> and it does not come down at all.
>
> Anything without wings
> always comes down again in the end.[5]

Now that He has taken the ego away, He is my Center. But my journey to Him is only half-ridden. He now lives in me the Mystery of His Hidden Years—but greater Mysteries yet has He to live in me. I await His Passion, His Death, His Resurrection, and His Ascension in me! He is the sun of these seasons, and will cause their procession as He will.

---

[5] Simone Weil, *Waiting for God,* trans. Emma Craufurd, (New York, NY: Harper & Row Publishers, 1973), p. 195.

Christ's Hidden Life

Of His Hidden days I love to daydream, because they speak of His most beautiful quality—His humility: "I am gentle and humble in heart" (Matthew 11:29).

When the boy Jesus played with His friends, the children of Nazareth did not know they were playing with God—that their playmate Jesus who tossed them a ball was, in His *Logos* nature, causing the sun and all stellar worlds to fly through the sky.

His life was "hidden"—not like a gold vein hidden beneath a mountain, but like a wellspring that silently feeds wells.

Not like an actor obscured by a curtain, but like the nourishing morning dew which we do not notice.

Not like a dark comet yet beyond our view, but like the fragrant jasmine grove hidden behind a cobbled wall.

Not like a fire hiding in cold flint, but like an eager mother yet unknown to the child within her womb.

And He recapitulates His Hidden Life in me now.

His will was one with the Father, and now the Father holds my will.

I see clearly that I am not the true source of the unitive virtues, but they radiate from the Spirit at my center, like a flaxen mane radiates from the head of a lion. Counsel, fortitude, wisdom, love, joy, peace, patience, faithfulness, and self-control—these are inseparable from the God-Center, as fragrance is inseparable from the sandalwood tree.[6]

Have you ever recognized and rejoiced at the familiar footfalls of a loved one in a hall, whom you yet cannot see? So it is that when one of these virtues arise in me, I hear His footfalls.

The "Man of Being"

I am the soul in the unitive Way, and by grace I have been united to the source of Being at my deepest center!

---

[6] Isaiah 11:2 and Galatians 5:22-23

The man of being stands in awe before the wonderful plenum of being, with all its amazing variety and wealth and content, with all its diversity of levels and orders. The man of not-being dissolves this plenum into smaller and smaller parts until they finally merge indistinguishably into one another and vanish into not-being.[7]

The man of being affirms—and rejoices in every positive being. The man of not-being is afraid to affirm, or only affirms in order to contradict, in order, that is, to destroy some positive being.[8]

The man of being sometimes stops talking altogether, because he gets lost in contemplation and wonder. The man of not-being never stops talking, because that is his way of destroying or suspending or covering up or drowning his sense of amazement at being.[9]

The man of being is ultimately turned—turned, that is, in his inmost heart—in the direction of the fullness of being, and implicitly draws all being from that fullness. The man of not-being is ultimately turned...in the direction of absolute not-being.[10]

The man of being rejoices in the least bit of being and is deeply thankful for it. The man of not-being is almost incapable of thanking anybody or being thankful for anything.[11]

His "Other Selves"

Our Lord came as a Semite—but by grace He has shared His sonship with us, making us His other selves, so I am now the soul of Christ's

---

[7] Charles N. Malik, *The Wonder of Being,* (Waco, TX: Word Books, 1974), p. 109.

[8] *Ibid.*

[9] *Ibid.*

[10] *Ibid.*

[11] *Ibid.*, p. 112.

European humanity, His Asian humanity, His African humanity, His Latino humanity. The Messiah came as a Son of Israel, but in making us His other selves, I am now also a Christic daughter of the Most High. In His original humanity, He was unmarried, a mystic and a priest, given to solitary communion in the mountains.

He is still the soul of the priest who has come to the unitive state, in whom He relives His Priesthood. On coming to union with God, the priest John of the Cross sang:

> Mine are the heavens and mine is the earth.
> Mine are the nations, the just are mine,
> and mine the sinners.
> The angels are mine, and the Mother of God,
> and all things are mine;
> and God himself is mine and for me,
> because Christ is mine and all for me.
> What do you ask, then, and seek, my soul?
> Yours is all of this, and all is for you.[12]

I am too the unitive soul of the consecrated Sisters of the God-Man—of Teresa of Avila, Catherine of Siena, Therese of Lisieux, of Elizabeth of the Trinity. Because they were most humble, their souls were most vast—like great oceans, and as receptive. For are not the oceans, though vaster than the continents, even more obedient to the sun than they? An ocean is dark to its floor without complaint when the sun is not, and then becomes a perfect sheet of light when the sun is. So these God-exalted ones were perfectly docile to His will for them, whether for dark or light.

And I am the soul in God-union, too, of the ones given to marriage. For His first miracle was at a wedding—and when He saw the darting glances of love between the bride and the groom, His joy was such that it became a Sacrament.

---

[12] *The Collected Works of St. John of the Cross,* trans. Kieran Kavanaugh O.C.D., and Otilio Rodriguez, O.C.D., (Washington, DC: ICS Publications, 1991), p. 88.

> "My darling, what else is there to do?" reasoned the Irishman. "What other occupation is there for an active man on this earth, except to marry you?"[13]
>
> —*G.K. Chesterton*

Comely is the sight of a woman united to God, and a man united to Him, as these spouses embrace. God would take the egos of both to open up a divine space, a fragrant breezeway of love between them.

And though it is Christ alone who grants union, I am also the God-united soul of women and men of many faiths—those whose lips remain still when they might confess Him, but whose deeds worship Him robustly—like leaves fluttering brightly upon a still branch.

The unitive state is a secret between God and the soul, more beautiful in its hiddenness, like a letter from the beloved kept in a secret drawer. You have seen my face many times without recognizing it.

Untrammeled Silence Invites the Divine Touch

I come into being as the Spirit completes its renewal of the psyche around our Lord—my new Center.

Now alongside of practical thought, an interior, verdant silence, a mystic hymn is heard, gently radiating from the Center—it says wordlessly, *All is well.*

This untrammeled, exquisite silence is the breath of the Center. And just as a bird naturally draws its wings to his side after a flight, so the mind now returns to this receptive silence after flights of practical thought.

The flute of springtime pipes the pastels of cherry blossoms and the breeze of jasmine: I, the unitive soul, pipe the mirth of vivid stillness.

Yet this inner stillness does not impede practical thought, but only strengthens it, as the air of early October, which is full of cold sunshine, sharpens and clarifies.

---

[13] Robert Knille, ed., *As I Was Saying: A Chesterton Reader,* (Grand Rapids, MI: William B. Eerdmans Publishing Company, 1985), p. 122.

Memory and stillness are both needed; the unitive state is like the good oak that keeps seasoned circles of memory in its pith, but also tender leaves flashing in the sun.

And when I came upon the unitive way, my eyes were opened anew upon the everywhereness of Christ in creation—the Christ-Logos "through whom all things were made," the mystic Unknown of matter.

Before divine union I saw Christ in nature, but through the shutter of ego—but now that He has plucked the ego from me, I see Him clearer, as the trackless Figure behind all forms.

What of the shade tree at noon? Christ forms the shade which lays a veil of peace on your being.

What of the crimson sunset? It is the hearth-fire of Christ, beckoning all to His fireside and table as evening falls.

Behold, a flock of stars grazing on the Wreath of Being.

I revel in the benediction that steals through the woods, the innocence of the *Logos* breezing through nature. And I find the gardener's palace of fragrance is no less solid than the mason's palace of marble.

The Wider Cup

"From everyone who has been given much, much will be demanded" (Luke 12:48). Because God has strengthened me in uniting me to Himself, He expects much. As He has crafted for me a wider cup to hold a wider draught of joy, so too a deeper cup to bear a deeper draught of suffering. Long before union, when my cup was bitter, I emptied it into two other cups, but found after the pouring that my portion had doubled. Now when I must drink a bitter cup, I find that when it touches my lips they turn to His, and my throat to His throat, and my bitterness finally to His peace.

> Suffering has a power not only of purifying but of illuminating, and there are truths which one sees better through tears.[14]

A fire leaps through a pine forest, with one tree passing its flames to the next. If you saw one pine that did not pass on the destruction, would

[14] Jacques Maritain, *Notebooks,* trans. Joseph W. Evans, (Albany, NY: Magi Books, 1984), p. 120.

you not consider it a wonder? A person who does not pass on the pain of the world when it is handed to him or her is such a wonder.

My thanksgiving yearns to give back to God something of the love He has shown me. "The soul's aim is a love equal to God's" (John of the Cross). For the Lord of the universe has given *Himself* to be my deepest center! I am now in a state of ongoing contemplation—working, speaking, recreating, praying, loving, creating.

> The soul,
> like one who has been unshackled
> and released from a dungeon
> and who can enjoy the benefit of spaciousness
> and freedom, experiences great sweetness
> of peace and loving friendship with God
> *in a ready abundance of spiritual communication.*[15]
>
> —*John of the Cross*

My Way forward into the final Mysteries of Christ is lit by this "living flame of love," in the phrase of John of the Cross, which would give to God as well as it has received. But this is impossible—and since I cannot return as I have received from Him, the flame has nowhere to go, and so consumes me unto Him, like an burnt offering that finally burns its altar to ashes.

The Soul's Portion of the Mystery of the Passion

So it is that the Mystery of the Hidden Life which I live becomes at moments, by His grace, a little participation in His Passion, His redemptive suffering. And I have known spirits who invite Christ to do this through them in a such a way that their souls blended unto His, like the shadows of two friends embracing.

Father Damien was sent to the mission fields of Hawaii, to be a chaplain to the leper colony on Molokai. There he found that the lepers had neither proper medical nor spiritual care. He helped them

---

[15] Kavanaugh and Rodriguez, *op cit.*, p. 408.

construct houses, medicated their sores, and buried their dead. After two decades of caring for them, he himself contracted the disease. On a hot Sunday in 1885, he revealed his condition at Mass. He began his homily not with his usual "My brethren," but with "We lepers."[16]

The passion of such a one intermingles with His Passion. Damien did not view the story of His Passion outside himself, like a summer storm seen from the dry shelter of a porch.

And so it is finally with all souls, if by degrees: that their Way forward with the Son is bearing a portion of his bitter cup—though the Son of Love always insists on the deepest draught.

> If we died with him
> we will also live with him;
> if we endure,
> we will also reign with him.
>
> —*2 Timothy 2:11-12*

Lord, how could we praise You as beautiful if You had remained locked away in Your heaven—even though we knew it was You inspiring every beauty on earth, and though the eye of the unitive state gave us to see a thousand springs in a single spring because we found Your Cosmic Form in all things?

But now, because You came to us, and suffered a thousand winters in one day among us, our lips cannot stop repeating your name: *The Beautiful.* Your son, John of the Cross, sang:

> Reveal your presence,
> and may the vision of your beauty be my death.[17]

You began our union with You in beauty, and so You will end it: in a tempest of beauty we will not be able to stand, and so will fall, never to rise again—in Love.

---

[16] John Deedy, *A Book of Catholic Anecdotes,* (Allen, TX: Thomas More, 1997), p. 241.

[17] Kavanaugh and Rodriguez, *op cit.,* p. 510.

CHAPTER 11

Mystical Ecstasy: The Great Clue to Our Destiny in God

"The Christian, another Christ."[1]
—*Paul Claudel*

"Save me!" comes a wild cry from a half-submerged figure in the sea. Sailors rush about a storm-washed deck to find a lifeline.

With this scene, we have an illustration of the how the word "save" is used: it implies being saved *from* something—here, the cold cauldron of the ocean. "Christ saves"—but from what? What are we being saved from? From death? From suffering? From sin? From exactly what? The answer that the Christian mystics supply is astonishing.

✧ ✧ ✧ ✧

The mystics teach us that at each stage of our journey to God, God saves us in a distinct way from a specific limiting force that, at that stage of the journey, is blocking a fuller life in Him. Thus, in the first movement of our journey, God saves us from the wrongly-oriented ego.

---

[1] Paul Claudel, *Ways and Crossways,* trans. Fr. John O'Connor, (Freeport, NY: Books for Libraries, 1967), p. 70.

He does this by sending awakening conversion graces, which invite us to see that our highest good is in Him. As we lovingly respond, God leads us to divine intimacy, which results in our coming to the illuminative Way, the ego's single-hearted attachment to God, and then beyond the ego to the unitive state. But God still has more saving work in us to do. For though the unitive state is a state of Light, it is not fully transparent to the Light, in ways that we will explain presently. Thus begins the second movement to salvation.

This second and final Way God saves us is to deliver us beyond all self: for the medium of self, even the God-united egoless self, does not give us God as God is in Himself, but only God as God is in ourselves. The ultimate gift God wants to give us is to know Him as He knows Himself. Thus in the second movement of the journey, God saves us from our limited view of Him in ourselves, to God as God knows God: "Christian faith tells us that God alone, seen face to face, can satisfy this immeasurable desire"[2] (Reginald Garrigou-Lagrange). But how does God accomplish this? To understand how God saves us fully, let us seek, now, a clearer understanding of human consciousness.

The First Limitation of Human Consciousness

All of our daily thoughts and emotions are part-and-parcel of human consciousness. And obviously the knowledge of the world which is ours through consciousness is true as far as it goes, and certainly practically helpful. But in terms of our final destiny, two limitations of human consciousness must be overcome.

The first is that consciousness does not deliver to us the innermost experience of what we contact. We bite into an orange and experience its sweet tang. But the orange does not experience itself as sweet and tangy—the experience is ours. The point is simple and incontrovertible: what we experience is refracted through self or self-consciousness. We do not get the orange's experience, but our experience of tasting an

---

[2] Reginald Garrigou-Lagrange, *Life Everlasting: And the Immensity of the Soul,* trans. Rev. Patrick Cummings, O.S.B., (Rockford, IL: Tan Books and Publishers, 1991), p. 9.

orange. When we smell the rose, we do not get the rose's experience of the rose, but our experience of the rose.

Think of a good friend—focus on her personality. Notice that your knowledge of your friend unites you to the truth of her being to a certain degree. Your knowledge of her, delivered to you by the power of your consciousness, allows you to grasp in a certain way her inner life. But this grasp has its limits. To see this, let us continue with our thought experiment. Imagine a new approach to knowing your friend made possible by some strange magic. Imagine you are able to actually enter her innermost consciousness. You think what she thinks, you know what she knows, you feel what she feels. Then, after experiencing this radical, magical empathy, it fades, and you come back to yourself. Now you compare your amazingly complete inner knowledge of your friend to your outer knowledge of her, knowledge mediated by consciousness.[3]

When you compare the two, two things become clear. On the one hand, you see that your natural, self-mediated knowledge is indeed true. The qualities you have admired in your friend for years are really hers, as you have verified them from the inside-out. On the other hand, you have experienced a world of difference between knowing her magically from the inside-out, from knowing her from the outside-in: from the relation of your consciousness to hers.

This truth has enormous consequences for our experience of God. While our consciousness does indeed allow true and significant contact with God, it also blocks our knowledge of God's deepest interiority—God as God knows God. Even our coming to the unitive state does not bring this kind of interior knowledge. Certainly it brings us deeply into contact with God and establishes a deeper intimacy with Him than we had before. But it does not give us God's knowing of God.

You see, in bringing us to the unitive state, God has radically transformed self-consciousness, but God has not ended self-consciousness.

---

[3] Strictly speaking, you could not compare the two, because the hypothetical, absolute union with your friend would preclude memory of the event. When you came back to yourself, you would remember nothing of this radical identification. In this respect our thought-experiment is limited, but it is still helpful.

The ego is gone, but the rest of self-consciousness remains. And self-consciousness is still in a subject-object relationship with God. In the *Divine Comedy,* Beatrice, who is Dante's guide up the divine mountain to the summit of God, says to Dante, "You see that reason's wings are short."[4] Consciousness, too, has short wings; of itself, it cannot attain God as God knows God. For even as our consciousness limits what we can know about each other, it limits what we can know about God. A life-long contemplative said along these lines: "Prayer and experience are not God, though they belong to our relationship to him."[5]

But will it be this way forever? Even in eternity, will we never know God truly and directly, but only imperfectly and obliquely? It would be maddening, would it not, to be blocked from fully knowing God forever. Will not God send His "deeper magic still" (in C.S. Lewis' phrase) to deliver us our heart's true aim? Otherwise, it were as if God has created us as His treasure chest, apparently meant to contain Him fully, to possess and encompass all the jewels and gems of His Being—but then buried this chest empty in a glorious Mountain of His divine jewels and gems! Oh yes, we—His treasure chest—can feel His divine treasure pressing upon us from all sides, but can only experience it from the outside-in! We do not possess Him! Dark, lonely, sealed, we lie empty of Him in this gleaming Mountain of His Being, the Treasure of His Presence crushing maddeningly upon us from all sides.

Surely, God would not do that to us! God will not withhold His true Presence from us for all eternity! Writes philosopher Peter Kreeft: "If we say we love someone, we are interested in knowing everything we can about him or her. The same is true of our love of God."[6] God knows we will not be satisfied with knowing Him from the outside—and will not frustrate forever our passion to know His inner Life.

---

[4] Dante Alighieri, *The Divine Comedy, Pardiso,* trans. Charles S. Singleton, Canto II, (Princeton, NJ: Princeton University Press, 1975), p. 19.

[5] Aelred Squire, *Asking the Fathers,* (Westminister, MD: Christian Classics, 1993), p. 177.

[6] Peter Kreeft, *A Summa of the Summa: The Essential Philosophical Passages of St. Thomas Aquinas' Summa Theologia Edited and Explained for Beginners,* (San Francisco, CA: Ignatius Press, 1990), p. 440.

An Impediment to Knowing God Fully

Before studying the solution to this deprivation of God, we must recognize another hurdle, also seemingly unleapable, to our knowing God as God knows God. For even if we could know God from the inside-out, how could our knowing then reach out to delight in all that God is, for God is the All, an Infinity of goodness, peace, freedom, and love?

A wag once quipped that for any map to be perfectly accurate, it would have to be exactly as big as the country it depicted. This gets at a daunting truth: a true knowing of God would be divinely capacious. To embrace God in true knowing, we would have to have arms to gird Infinity, and know the love of a God-sized Heart.

Where are we to get such arms and such a heart? To appreciate this challenge we must acknowledge that we poorly conceive God's transcendence of the human. "'For my thoughts are not your thoughts, neither are your ways my ways,' declares the LORD" (Isaiah 55:8).

I am convinced that our tendency is to imagine God as more or less some Superman, a certain number of degrees above normative humanity. But this is entirely false. God's uncreated Existence is, ontologically, wholly different from our created being.

We should think on that Knowing which knows the worlds into existence. We should ponder that Love which is so sublime that it permitted its Immensity to be crucified by the atoms it created. We should revel in the dizzying fact that all worlds are as a mote orbiting the moon of a mote, relative to this Almighty God. Once the mystic Julian of Norwich of fourteenth-century England received a visionary revelation, a "showing" that spoke to this point. She was shown a nut-sized version of the entire cosmos—

> [Christ] showed me a little thing, the size of a hazelnut, lying in the palm of my hand. It was as round as a ball, as it seemed to me. I looked at it with the eyes of my understanding and thought, "What can this be?"
>
> My question was answered in general terms in this fashion: "It is everything that is made." I marveled how this could be, for it seemed to me that it might suddenly fall into nothingness, it was so small.

To that, the Spirit said to Julian—

> "It lasts....because God loves it. And in this fashion all things have their being by the grace of God."[7]

This is God the Holy, "edged with intolerable radiancy."[8]

So even if the barrier of reflexive human consciousness were to fall, how would God be fathomed as the Absolute? "It would be madness," writes Jacques Maritain, "to endeavor to attain by our own powers" the precincts of God.[9]

Another Thought Experiment

Imagine coming home one day and being greeted by your dog. But today is different. Instead of his excited barking as you turn the key, silence. When you open the door, your dog calmly says with perfect articulation, "How are you?"

Somehow taking this magic in stride, you answer him, then sit with a cup of tea and talk together. He listens to you with full understanding, nods his head empathically, and interjects thoughtful comments like: "I'm glad you told your boss how you felt about the extra paperwork."

For your dog to so communicate with you, his power of knowing would have to be miraculously raised to a human level. That is because to truly know someone, one has to share her nature, participate in her level of being—experience the same dimension of life that she occupies. That is why only human beings can truly communicate with each other, and deeply know each other. Our pets, of course, are dear to us, and they know us in a certain manner, but not with full human understanding. We humans know each other because we inhabit a distinctly human dimension of thoughts and words and self-consciousness.

---

[7] Ronda De Sola Chervin, *Prayers of the Women Mystics,* (Ann Arbor, MI: Servant Publications, 1992), p. 70.

[8] Percy Bysshe Shelley, *Shelley: Poems,* selected by Isabel Quigly, (New York, NY: Viking Penquin Books, 1985), from "Queen Mab," p. 31.

[9] Jacques Maritain, *The Degrees of Knowledge,* trans. Bernard Wall, (New York, NY: Charles Scribner's Sons, 1938), p. 419.

This delivers us to an incredible, but unavoidable conclusion: Just as your dog could only be raised to your human feelings and thoughts through magic, so for us to really know God, you and I will have to be raised by divine magic to God's own level. To really know God—not from the outside-in but from the inside-out—God will have to raise us by grace to a full participation in divine nature. This is the fulfillment of the Way, the Way of Christ's Mysteries: by recapitulating His Mysteries in us, Christ transforms us into Himself. As Christ, the Son, knows and loves his Father in heaven, we will know heaven with His identical knowing and loving, as our souls will be transformed into Him by His grace. "We will be just like him, for we will see him as he is" (1 John 3:2).

"Whosoever wants to know must wait until he becomes what he knows"[10] *(Theologia Germanica)*. Anything less than being raised to God's level will not afford us a true knowledge of God. In heaven we will know the Trinity exactly as Christ knows the Trinity, having been transformed into Him. And why would God want to give us anything less than His complete Life? Will He say, "You can know half of me, but that's all"?

"Please, more!" we say, following Abraham's lead, who begged and bargained with God to save a doomed city (Genesis 18:22-32).

We say: "How about seventy-five percent, Lord—let us know seventy-five percent of your Being!"

"No more than seventy-five."

"Eighty, Lord?"

"No more than eighty percent of Me."

"Please: ninety-nine!"

"You shall know ninety-nine percent of Me, but no more."

"A hundred! A hundred! A hundred!"

> Come, you who are blessed by my Father; take your inheritance, the kingdom prepared for you since the creation of the world
>
> —*Matthew 25:34*

Mystical Ecstasy

"With man this is impossible, but with God all things are possible" (Matthew 19:26). Mystical theology confirms this! God will make possible what

[10] *The Theologia Germanica of Martin Luther*, trans. Bengt Hoffman, (New York, NY: Paulist Press, 1980), p. 85.

is humanly impossible: for us to know and experience God in heaven with the complete fullness of Christ's knowing and experiencing the Trinity.

By "light-on" prayer, the Christian mystics clarified for us the first movement of the journey, to the unitive state. So will they now clarify for us the journey's second and final movement to the fullness of Trinitarian knowing beyond all self, by describing to us the condition of mystical ecstasy.

Though the word *ecstasy* is commonly used to mean great delight, this definition does not approach its sublime meaning in the mystic's vocabulary. Ecstasy is liberation from self to a wholly other kind of knowing. Ecstasy is a miraculous grace by which God stops the psychological self, completely suspends self-consciousness, and substitutes Christ's divine knowing for the self's limited knowing.

This is not just suspension of the ego—that would simply be the condition of the unitive state. No, it is more than that. By the grace of ecstasy, God suspends *all* self-consciousness, to reveal a divine knowing of God. Before exploring the features and implications of ecstasy, let us hear a description of it by St. Bernard, borne of his own experience:

> Blessed and holy, I would say,
> is he to whom it has been given
> to experience such a thing
> in this mortal life at rare intervals or even once,
> and this suddenly and scarcely
> for the space of a single moment.
>
> In a certain manner to lose yourself
> as though you were not,
> and to be utterly unconscious of yourself
> and to be emptied
> and, as it were, brought to nothing,
> this pertains to heavenly intercourse.[11]

---

[11] *Saint Bernard on the Love of God,* trans. Terrence L. Connolly, S.J., (Techny, IL: Mission Press, 1943), p. 37.

St. Bernard was mystically "brought to nothing"—and yet discovered in this condition Life itself! For beyond self is the Life of the eternal Son who alone knows the Father. Ecstasy uncovers the true principle of Christ's saying: "Whoever finds his life will lose it, and whoever loses his life for my sake will find it" (Matthew 10:39). When the self is not, as in the grace of ecstasy, the Son is revealed—God as God is in Himself, not in ourselves. Johannes Tauler, medieval mystic of the Rhineland, wrote of ecstasy:

> It is absorbed in God,
> and now all equality and inequality disappear.
> In this abyss the soul loses itself,
> and knows nothing of God or of itself,
> of likeness to Him or difference from Him,
> or of anything whatsoever.
> It is immersed in the unity of God and has
> lost all distinctions.[12]

Ecstasy, as Tauler describes it, is a timeless episode beyond self, but not yet a permanent state; the mystic returns from ecstasy to self-consciousness. And yet the great lesson of ecstasy is clear. Since God can temporarily suspend self to reveal His own knowing, He can do it permanently—God can permanently transform the soul beyond self into Christ. Our final estate is in Christ, not in ourselves, for Christ alone knows the Father. "Father, I want those you have given me to be with me where I am, and see my glory, the glory you have given me...before the creation of the world" (John 17:24).

Ecstasy reveals how God overcomes the two impediments to divine knowing discussed earlier. First, ecstasy demonstrates that God can suspend all self-consciousness: this dissolves the subject-object division, with the self becoming naught, and God becoming All-in-all. Second, ecstasy replaces our usual knowing through consciousness with a Christic knowing of God—an absolute, immeasurable divine knowing.

Think of an eagle's nest way up in the mountains. Only from the height of this nest can we see another eagle's nest at the same

---

[12] John Tauler, O.P., *Spiritual Conferences,* trans. and ed. Eric Colledge and Sister M. Jane, O.P. (Rockford, IL: Tan Books and Publishers, 1973), p. 167.

height. Only from the transcendent height of the Son in the Trinity can the Father be really seen. And that is how God solves the second impediment: by completely transforming us into the Son. "No one knows the Son except the Father, and no one knows the Father except the Son and those to whom the Son chooses to reveal him" (Matthew 11:27).

In the Son Vast we meet the Father Vast through the Spirit Vast. This is the very secret of heaven. "Perfectly to know the Father we must be the Son"[13] (Mesiter Eckhart). Teresa of Avila writes of her ecstatic experience in *The Interior Castle* (Chapter 5)—

> the soul really seems to have left the body;
> on the other hand, it is clear
> that the person is not dead,
> though for a few moments he cannot
> even himself be sure if the soul is in the body or not.
>
> He feels as if he has been in another world...
> and has been shown a fresh light there,
> so much unlike any to be found in this life that,
> if he had been imagining it, and similar things,
> all his life long, it would have been impossible for him to obtain any idea of them...
>
> It is a fact that, as quickly as a bullet
> leaves a gun when the trigger is pulled,
> there begins within the soul a flight
> (I know no other name to give it) which, though no sound is made, is so clearly a movement
> that it cannot possibly be due to fancy....
> Great things are revealed to it.[14]

---

[13] *Wandering Joy: Meister Eckhart's Mystical Philosophy,* trans. Riner Schurmann, (Great Barrington, MA: Lindisfarne Books, 2001), p. 55.

[14] Thomas Dubay, S.M., *Fire Within: St. Teresa of Avila, St. John of the Cross, and the Gospel—on Prayer,* (San Francisco, CA: Ignatius Press, 1989).

Scala/Art Resource, NY

The Ecstasy of Saint Teresa by Gian Lorenzo Bernini

Though is a rare grace, we see now that ecstasy is not a fantastic spiritual curio. Rather, it is a grand presaging of our final destiny in God. The mystical theology of the saints, which knows ecstasy, is a divine gift to the whole Church, as it anticipates our permanent transubstantiation into Christ, our final estate.

"You May Also Be Where I Am Going"

Still, our initial amazement and soaring joy at hearing the wonderful truth of ecstasy, may suddenly be darkened by a natural fear: If the grace of ecstasy tells us that heaven is a transcendent condition beyond self, that our soul will be transfigured beyond self into Christ, what will become of me? Where will *I* be in heaven?

To begin with, the saints' experience of ecstasy proves that the suspension of consciousness is not annihilation. On the contrary, the ecstatic mystics report only Life triumphant beyond self. Beyond self the divine Christ IS, and that is Life itself. "And if I go and prepare a place for you, I will come back and take you to be with me that you may also be where I am going" (John 14:3).

We usually think of life after death. But once a noted composer, intuiting the truth of the matter, was given to see differently. He saw that earthly existence, though good in itself, was shrunken compared to heaven. He thereupon composed a symphony titled, *Death—then Life*. Thomas Merton, too, seems to have tasted of ecstatic Life. He wrote in *The New Seeds of Contemplation* of the "perfect contemplation in which the soul vanishes out of itself":

> What happens is that the separate entity that is you apparently disappears and nothing seems to be left but a pure freedom indistinguishable from infinite Freedom, love identified with Love. Not two loves, one waiting for the other, striving for the other, seeking for the other, but Love Loving in Freedom.[15]

---

[15] Thomas Merton, *New Seeds of Contemplation,* (New York, NY: New Directions Book, 1972), p. 283.

In selfless ecstasy we have a clue to the final meaning of salvation. What we are ultimately saved from is self—not just saved from the limitations of the ego, but from the limitations of all self, for God is only known truly beyond the limited subject-object knowing of consciousness, by our complete transubstantiation into Him.

Please do not misunderstand this point. Christianity does not say that this transfigured condition is the ideal human state here and now, before the death of the body. No. Self-consciousness is the natural context of human life, and the unitive state—mature human existence—is God-united consciousness, not a condition beyond self. But at death, the context of existence changes, to put it mildly. Now the soul's appointed destiny is fulfilled by a transformation beyond consciousness into the divine Son Vast who alone knows the Father Vast.

> There is a Persian story of a lover who sought his beloved. He knocked at her door and was asked, "Who is there?" "It is I," he said, and was told there was no one within for him. He tried again and failed, but, at the third time, he answered the beloved's question with "It is thou," and the door opened.[16]

The Final Mysteries of Christ

In Chapter Five we discussed the first three of Christ's Mysteries: His hidden years, public years, and Eucharist. As Christ relives them in us, His Spirit advances us to greater degrees of wholeness, human and divine. "Christ is the way. We must be raised up from his humanity to his Trinity"[17] (Jules Monchanin).

Because the final Mysteries of Christ pertain to the revelation of God beyond self, we saved them for this chapter. To understand them, we first needed to reflect on the limits of the self's ability to know God and the explosive truth of mystical ecstasy. We found that our hearts

---

[16] Martin C. Darcy, S.J., *Of God and Man: Thoughts on Faith and Morals,* (Notre Dame, IN: University of Notre Dame Press, 1964), p. 61.

[17] J.G. Weber, ed. and trans, *In Quest of the Absolute: The Life and Work of Jules Monchanin,* (Kalamazoo, MI: Cistercian Publications, 1977), p. 180.

will be satisfied with nothing less than to know God as God knows God—to know the Father as the Son does in the Spirit. Nothing less will do as our heaven.

As ecstasy is a rare grace experienced by only a few in this life, but has so much significance for the spiritual journey, it would seem important that God make its truth known to all in some way, so we might know the final truth of the journey. Only in the ending of self may God be known in Himself. But how? How might God publicly reveal this truth to all?

God has already done this. He has revealed this truth publicly and definitively—in Christ's crucifixion. What the mystics laconically conveyed to the Church by their reports of ecstasy, the Mystery of Christ's death on the cross dramatized for all the ages. How Christ did this is our present subject.

The Mystery of Christ's Passion and Death

The Mystery of Christ's passion begins in the Garden of Gethsemane, where Christ goes to pray after his last supper. Christ sweats blood as he prays aloud:

> Father, if you are willing,
> take this cup from me;
> yet not my will, but yours be done.
>
> —*Luke 22:42*

The kind of suffering which Christ undergoes in the Garden and on the cross is essentially two-fold. His body suffers the most dreadful human affliction, in solidarity with all human suffering. It is as if He has chosen to give a face to all anonymous suffering—so that we would see His face, God's face, in every face in the darkened boxcars of Auschwitz, in every starving villager ignored by a dictator, in every frightened child and grieving widower, in every elderly face forgotten in a nursing home.

How different is this God from the deist's God, that detached, immobile cosmic Spectator! God-in-Christ does not make Himself a transcendent presence beyond this world, but as a little tree rooted on a hill, open to all tearing elements, one with all the beautiful, vulnerable things of the world. (Here we find the *Holism of the Face of Love*—Christ in the suffering and in those who care for them.)

Christ cries from the cross: "My God, my God, why have you forsaken me?" (Matthew 27:46). This is babble to the soldiers, but prayer to the Jewish onlookers, who are astonished to hear in His cry the first wingbeat of Psalm 22. He has quoted a phrase from the scriptures:

> My God, my God, why hast thou forsaken me?…
> My strength is dried up like a potsherd;
> And my tongue cleaveth to my jaws;
> And thou hast brought me into the dust of death.
> For dogs have compassed me:
>
> A company of evil-doers has enclosed me;
> They pierced my hands and my feet.

Another Kind of Suffering

Yet a suffering befell Christ on the cross that was of a wholly other order than the sheer physical horror that was inflicted on His body. To understand this other suffering, we must recall an earlier point: the unimaginably dreadful price that the Son paid to cross the infinite abyss between the Uncreated Trinity and the created world to incarnate as Jesus Christ. Having known the heavenly bliss of the Father (His *doxa,* glory) before incarnating, Christ experienced His coming into the coil of consciousness as a horrific burden, as its assumption excluded the experience of heaven's bliss.

The Cross reverses this. Christ must pass from human consciousness back to His divine Knowing. But there is an absolute Void between the two, they are incommensurate. Christ's human knowing as Jesus is not His Logos Knowing as the Trinitarian Son. This passage back is so dire—from human knowing to divine knowing—a transition that passes through an absolute Void between the created universe and the uncreated God, that only God can withstand it.

On the cross, as His physical body dies, Christ relinquishes His mode of human consciousness to pass to his divine Knowing, as the eternal *Logos* of the Trinity. This movement is from Christ's created human consciousness to uncreated divine Knowing.

As these modes of knowing are utterly different, of entirely different dimensions, Christ passes for a instant through an excruciating Void between the human and the Divine—hence His cry, "Father, why have you forsaken Me?" (Matthew 27:46). The self of the God-Man has ended, and with it ends his self-knowing of the Father. What a horrible Void Christ enters! His whole humanity was for the Father. Now with the death of self, Christ's self-knowing of the Father is gone! It is a state of desolation we cannot imagine, this absolute Void between the created and the uncreated, and one which prompts Christ's cry: "Father, why have you forsaken Me?"

But this is not Christ's end. Though the self-mode of Christ's knowing of the Father has dissolved, Christ is the man-*God,* and his divine Knowing of the Father arises and perdures beyond this horrible Void. Recall that this divine knowing is the Son's original Knowing before His incarnation and even before worlds began.

In this way the Mystery of Christ's death yields to the Mystery of his Resurrection. In his passion, Christ demonstrates on the cross for the ages that death *of all self-limited knowing (not just the ending of ego)* is the condition for fully coming to the Father. Now in His Resurrection, he illustrates for all time by physically rising from the dead that beyond the death of self is the glorified, eternal Christ who alone knows the Father.

Though Christ's body was indeed miraculously healed and biologically resuscitated after his crucifixion, this biological restoration is not the great significance of Christ's rising from the dead. His physical rising is only an outer form of His deeper resurrection, which is the arising of his divine Logos Knowing that truly knows the Father, as only God fully knows God.

The Mystery of the Resurrection

"The Head and members are as one mystic person," said St. Thomas Aquinas.[18] Christ, the Head of the Mystical Body, recapitulates his life

---

[18] Charles Journet, *The Wisdom of Faith: An Introduction to Theology,* trans. R.F. Smith, (Westminister, MD: The Newman Press, 1952), p. 29.

in all his members unto eternal Life, including the Mysteries of his passion, death and resurrection.

The manner in which the Mystery of Christ's passion and death is recapitulated in us is two-fold. The first pertains to physical human suffering. Persecuted for years as an apostle of Christ, St. Paul was made to suffer in many ways. He wrote: "Now I rejoice in what was suffered for you, and I fill up in my flesh what is still lacking in regard to Christ's afflictions, for the sake of his body, which is the church" (Colossians 1:24). Paul united his own suffering to Christ's suffering, giving it redemptive significance. That is what Christ would have us all do: unite our suffering to his. To gaze at a crucifix in a season of suffering and prayerfully unite one's suffering to Christ is to find suffering existentially transformed in Him: "Come to me, all you who are weary and burdened, and I will give you rest" (Matthew 11:30). In this manner, as Pope John Paul the Great lay in his deathbed, he asked that the Liturgy of the third hour of Christ's Passion be read to him.

Bernadette Soubirous (1844-1879) also experienced the mystery of redemptive suffering. In her youth, she was vouchsafed at Lourdes a vision of the Virgin Mary. Later, during her stay in a convent, ill-health often compelled her to bed. A visiting nun came to her room one day and found her in bed. Sharply she asked Bernadette what she was doing.

"I am doing my job," Bernadette responded.

"Oh," asked the nun, "and what might that be?"

"My job," said Bernadette, "is to be ill."[19] That was Bernadette's work of the moment: to be non-resistant to suffering, to suffer in love with her crucified Lord. The redemptive graces released into the whole Body by such love bespeaks the *Holism of the Mystical Body.*

But there is a second way Christ's passion and death are recapitulated in us, even more profound. At the moment each of us dies, it is really Christ who dies for us, for he completes the radical transformation of soul beyond self which is the truth of our death. And then it is Christ alone who passes through the Void between the created and

[19] John Deedy, *A Book of Catholic Anecdotes,* (Allen, TX: Thomas More, 1997), p. 220.

the uncreated to eternal divine Sonship, our soul having been transfigured into Him. We could never of our own power make this passage through the Void that separates the human knowing of God from divine knowing. Only Christ the God-man can ford this Void, and our soul transubstantiated into Him. "If we have died with Him, we shall also live with Him" (2 Timothy 2:11).

In this way, Christ recapitulates his resurrection in us. Mystically understood, our resurrection will not be a far future event, but essentially occurs immediately after death. It will not be a biological resuscitation as it was with Christ (the outward sign of his true resurrection), but our resurrection is the transubstantiation of our soul into Christ who alone is "the Resurrection and the Life" (John 11:25). Since the human self can no more contain the Infinite God than a sunflower seed can contain the sun, death is necessary to end our limited mode of human knowing and make way for glorified knowing, Christ's knowing, which alone knows God. "All things die, but they die in God"[20] (Paul Claudel).

Christ completes the Mystery of his resurrection in us after death in a form hidden from the eyes of the world. "The mystery of Christ is ours also. What was accomplished by the Head must be accomplished also in the members: Incarnation, death, and resurrection"[21] (Henri de Lubac, S.J.). Just as Christ transformed bread and wine into himself at his last supper, so he transubstantiates us into himself and passes through the Void separating limited human understanding from God's knowing of God in the Trinity. "When the perfect comes, the imperfect will pass away" (1 Corinthians 13:10).

"God knows us and loves us! And he wants to dilate us to his fullness"[22] (Jules Monchanin). The mystic Angelus Silesius wrote—

---

[20] Paul Claudel, *I Believe in God,* Agnes du Sarment, ed., trans. Helen Weaver, (USA: Holt, Rinehart and Winston, 1963), p. 286.

[21] Henri de Lubac, *The Church: Paradox and Mystery,* (Staten Island, NY: Alba House, 1969), p. 37.

[22] J.G. Weber, ed. and trans, *In Quest of the Absolute: The Life and Work of Jules Monchanin,* (Kalamazoo, MI: Cistercian Publications, 1977), p. 115.

God, whose boundless love and joy
Are present everywhere;
He cannot come to visit you
Unless you are not there.[23]

We are "not there" in the Resurrection—only Christ is there, and we transubstantiated into Him. What could be more wonderful? There is one Resurrection, and it is Christ's.

The Mystery of Ascension

The Mystery of Christ's resurrection is followed by the Mystery of His ascension. The Son "was taken up to heaven," (Luke 24:51) into God's Trinitarian fullness:

> He was taken up before their very eyes,
> and a cloud hid him from their sight.
>
> They were looking intently up into the sky as he was going,
> when suddenly two men dressed in white
> stood beside them.
>
> "Men of Galilee," they said, "why do you stand here
> looking into the sky?
>
> —*Acts 9-11*

Just as the sun is more clearly seen as it sets, passing out of view, so Christ's divinity, his *Logos* nature, was more clearly seen by his apostles as he left their view in His glorified body. As he goes up to heaven they know that he is the sole Son who has come down from heaven—the Son who existed before all things existed, even before the clouds, sky, and sun into which He disappears.

Christ's disappearing from earthly view teaches us a great lesson about the heaven of the Trinity. Heaven is beyond all human knowing,

[23] Huston Smith, *The World's Religions, Our Great Wisdom Traditions,* (San Francisco, CA: HarperSanFrancisco, 1991), p. 262.

transcending the knowing of consciousness and that of the senses. An episode in the life of St. Catherine of Genoa hints of this truth. Returning to consciousness from ecstasy, she endeavored to set forth propositions about God, but ended each: "I blaspheme!"—acknowledging that nothing she could say in the language of consciousness could even faintly express life in God beyond consciousness.[24] Though ecstasy is not, strictly speaking, heaven itself, Catherine's remarks suggest heaven is untouchable by consciousness, and nothing of heaven can touch the brain.

> The divine circle of knowledge will finally be closed—but upon an Abyss.[25]
>
> —*Cardinal Charles Journet*

> What is at issue is the mystery of the uncreated one who is 'Light beyond all light.' How should we speak of this? *Silentium tibi laus,* 'Silence is thy praise'. All we can do is worship.[26]
>
> —*Fr. Yves Conger*

The Mystery of the ascension is the revelation of the unmanifest Father: Light beyond all light. The Father is the bliss-condition in which the Logos-Son dwells, even before creation, as in "the glory I had with you before the world began" (John 17:5). As Christ recapitulates this final Mystery in the soul, transubstantiating the soul into Himself, the Father is revealed as the final emparidised condition—through Christ, with Him, in Him. This is the revelation of the uncreated Whole, the *Holism of the Beatific Vision* (Chapter 17).

> But I, when I am lifted up from the earth, will draw all men to myself.
>
> —*John 12:32*

---

[24] Yves M. J. Congar, *The Lord and the Spirit,* trans. David Smith, (San Francisco, CA: Harper & Row Publishers, 1986), p. 2.

[25] Charles Journet, *The Dark Knowledge of God,* trans. James F. Anderson, (London: Sheed & Ward, 1948), p. 119.

[26] *Ibid.*

CHAPTER 12

The Bread of the Mystics: The Eucharistic Christ

"Jesus found a way by which he could ascend to Heaven and yet remain on earth."[1]
—*St. John Vianney*

Catholic Churches have a curious furnishing that, though plain and inconsequential in appearance, is a dramatic piece of mystical teaching. It is a sink called the *sacrarium,* which may be found in the sacristy, a room adjacent to the altar area.

In appearance, the sacrarium resembles, more or less, a common household sink. However, a handyman examining it closely would be puzzled because the drain completely bypasses the conventional plumbing system and feeds directly to the earth.

That is because it is used for one purpose: as a basin to wash the vessels of the Mass, vessels which still contain particles of the Blessed Sacrament after the consecrated bread and wine of Holy Communion have been distributed to the faithful. For two thousand years the Church has believed on the word of the Savior that the Mass makes present the Mystery of the Last Supper: that the bread and wine really become the Resurrected Christ. The Eucharist is truly Christ, not a

[1] Jill Haak Adels, *The Wisdom of the Saints: An Anthology,* (New York, NY: Oxford University Press, 1987), p. 82.

symbol of Christ. To receive Holy Communion is really to bring into our being Almighty God, by which the indwelling Christ advances His Mysteries in us.

That is why Catholic Churches are furnished with this curious little basin, the sacrarium. After Mass, the chalice which has for a few minutes borne Christ's Elixir-Blood and the dish which has borne His resurrected Body, are washed in this basin. Therefore, it carries the left-over particles of heaven directly into the earth, which is thereby also blessed.

The Poem Becomes Real

In the soul of the poet are born "phrases which toll with a pang in our hearts."[2] We are drawn to rest beneath the fronds of music in the poet's garden.

Christ is the primordial Poet. For He is the Incarnation of the *Logos,* the very creativity through whom all things came to be—all things which poets, His progeny, sing with delirious clarity. Ralph Waldo Emerson aptly called Christ "the Bard of the Holy Spirit." For Kahlil Gibran, Christ was the "Master Singer":

> Master, Master Singer,
> Your tears were like the showers of May,
> And your laughter like the waves of the white sea...
> You laughed for the marrow in their bones that
> was not yet ready for laughter;
> And you wept for their eyes that were yet dry.[3]

According to Aristotle's *Poetics,* the supreme poetic skill is "to be a master of metaphor. It is the one thing that cannot be learnt from others." Let me suggest that uniquely in the Mass, mastery of the

---

[2] A phrase about the Psalms, from *History of the Gregorian Chant* by Alison Hope. (Reproduced from the Oriens website: www.ozemail.com.au/~oriens).

[3] Kahlil Gibran, *Jesus The Son of Man: His Words and His Deeds as Told and Recorded by Those Who Knew Him,* (New York, NY: Alfred A. Knopf, 1995), p. 252.

metaphor attains its superlative degree: a symbol finally and completely attains the real. For on the altar, the symbols that Christ selected to represent Himself, bread and wine—actually pass from metaphorical figures to metaphysical reality, not only becoming real, but Reality Itself, the Lord of the universe.

Master, Master Singer!

Think of a painting of a rose—which suddenly startles you by gushing the lush fragrance of a real rose. Think of holding the photo of a lion—who overleaps his two-dimensional captivity and begins to roar. Think of a map in your hands—that unexpectedly gleams with rivers, frosts with snowcaps, burns with deserts.

All of this happens at every Mass, as symbols—bread and wine—all of a sudden cease to obey the laws of matter, in order to obey the words of Christ, "This is my body, This is my blood"—and thus really and substantially become Him under the appearance of bread and wine. The appearance of bread and wine continues for our senses, but the original substance of each, their ordinary created ground, is now gone—replaced by Christ Himself. In this wise, the poet Claudel suggested that just as an ancient star continues to show its light to us though it is long gone, so bread and wine continue to appear to our senses after consecration, even after they are long gone—having really become the eternal Christ.[4]

If you are twenty-five feet away from the Eucharist at that moment, you are twenty-five feet away from your Creator. If fifteen feet—then fifteen. Then suddenly, He who holds your destiny in His hands is now in your hands. And then in your very being—as He was in Mary. But now you are not giving birth to Him, but He to you.

It is not by accident that poets are drawn to the Mass. The Mass itself is the Great Poem—the poem that attains the real. The metaphorical becomes the metaphysical in the Mass. Ritual becomes Actual.

The Eucharistic Presence inverts the great flow of creation. It is the earth herself that grows from the mystic Wheat, and it is all space and time that draws sap from the cool vineyards of its mystic Wine. "The

---

[4] Paul Claudel, *Ways and Crossways,* trans. Fr. John O'Connor, (Freeport, NY: Books for Libraries, 1967), p. 61.

Catholic faith is the reconciliation both of mythology and philosophy. It is a story and in that sense one of a hundred stories; only it is a *true story.* It is a philosophy and in that sense one of a hundred philosophies; only it is a philosophy that is like life"[5] (G.K. Chesterton).

Miracles of the Eucharist

Innumerable mystical wonders have attended the Blessed Sacrament through the ages. Yet to speak of Eucharistic miracles is really to express a redundancy. One might as well say that of the four-layers of the sun, its outermost corona is very hot. The fact is, the sun is altogether hot. And the Eucharist itself, apart from any additional marvel, is altogether miraculous. For it is nothing less than God with us, the incarnate Christ, now under the species of consecrated bread and wine. In receiving the Eucharist, the faithful "receive the whole God-Man Who is in Heaven"[6] (Paul Claudel).

"The Blessed Sacrament is therefore the very heart of Christianity, since it contains Christ Himself, and since it is the chief means by which Christ mystically unites the faithful to Himself in one Body"[7] (Thomas Merton). One hundred people walk up to receive the Blessed Sacrament—only One Person returns to the pews. Is this not a wonder? For the ten minutes or fifteen minutes that it takes the consumed Eucharist to fully disintegrate in us, we are perfectly united to the One, the glorious Body of God. We are literally in heaven, even if consciousness and senses do not perceive it. Therefore, any Eucharistic marvel, in addition to its intrinsic wonder, is like an unexpected solar flare from the sun—just a reminder of the reposeful molten bounty within.

Two transformations occur at every Mass. First, bread and wine are transformed into the living Christ. "We believe that the fullness of God can take the form of a man—Jesus. Why should it be more difficult to

---

[5] G.K. Chesterton, *The Everlasting Man,* (London: Hodder and Stoughton, 1925), p. 283.

[6] Claudel, *op cit.,* p. 69.

[7] Thomas Merton, *The Living Bread,* (London: Burns & Oats, 1956), p. 11.

believe (on Jesus' word) that God can be fully present in another part of creation—bread and wine?"[8] (Alan Schreck). Second, when we consume the Sacrament, Christ transforms us into Himself. For a timeless span, our soul participates in the perfect Wholeness of Christ. "Christ the Redeemer, who assimilates Christians to Himself, is Christ in the greatest act of His love"[9] (Emile Mersch).

As frankincense frequently burned, though briefly, comes to permeate the walls of a temple, so the Eucharistic Christ faithfully received comes to permeate our reality. For Christ offers Himself to us "no longer for your *instruction* but for your *construction*"[10] (Paul Claudel).

Grace Defies Gravity

The true miracle of the Eucharist is, then, simply itself. Nevertheless, sundry and memorable wonders have followed the Blessed Sacrament for two thousand years, like a trailing zephyr of ginger and cinnamon following a spice caravan. Christ produces these external wonders to reveal that the Blessed Sacrament is not merely a symbol of Himself, but really is Himself. "And surely I am with you always, to the very end of the age" (Matthew 28:20).

In nineteenth-century France, two professors who had often heard acclaimed the saintliness of the priest John Vianney, decided to visit his parish. Committed to skepticism, they intended to debunk what they assumed to be fraud and nonsense. Arriving at the chapel, they found Father John saying Mass, and positioned themselves near the altar. When the priest raised the Blessed Sacrament before the kneeling throng, one of the professors remarked to the other, "How can rational beings adore their God in this little piece of bread?"

At that moment, Vianney looked penetratingly at the professor, and returned his gaze to the first communicant at the altar rail. The

---

[8] Alan Schreck, *Catholic and Christian, An Explanation of Commonly Misunderstood Catholic Beliefs,* (Ann Arbor, MI: Servant Books, 1984), p. 132.

[9] Michael L. Gaudoin-Parker, ed., *The Real Presence Through the Ages,* (Staten Island, NY: Alba House, 1993), p. 168.

[10] Claudel, *op cit.,* p. 70.

communion wafer levitated from the priest's fingers and ever so slowly drifted to the communicant's tongue. Before the professors' eyes, grace had defied gravity. The holy priest looked back at the professor with a glance that said, "Can a mere piece of bread from such a distance place itself of its own accord upon a person's tongue?" Some years later, one of the professors became a Dominican priest.

The Bread of the Mystics

Imagine Michelangelo contemplating a possible subject for his brush, but then frowning, not knowing how to make a start, daunted by his subject's sublimity—putting down his brush for this hour. Or Neruda's pen poised over a notebook, then withdrawn without a trace, as words for his theme remain vaporous. Or Bach withdrawing his fingers from a keyboard because he cannot find an outward vibration for the enrapturing music he is hearing within.

We find a similar dumb-struck hesitation among many contemplatives and mystics when they would write on the Blessed Sacrament. Its beauty and depth momentarily tie their tongues. "Yesterday I said I wanted to speak about the glory of the Blessed Sacrament—though no one can adequately do so"[11] (Johannes Tauler).

> When I am before the Blessed Sacrament I feel such a lively faith that I can't describe it.[12]
>
> —*Anthony Mary Claret*

"Its greatness is such that, to explain it adequately," said Emile Mersch, "we should have to make of survey of the whole Christian teaching; we should have to review all that touches on Christ and the gift of Christ to the Church, and all that, from one end to the other, this book is trying to express."[13] (Mersch is referring to a book of 663 pages.)

---

[11] *Johannes Tauler: Sermons,* trans. Maria Shrady, (New York, NY: Paulist Press, 1985), p. 109.

[12] Adels, *op cit.*, p. 81.

[13] Emile Mersch, S.J., *The Theology of the Mystical Body,* trans. Cyril Vollert, S.J., (St. Louis, MO: B. Herder Book Co., 1952), p. 580.

What causes this poignant stammering? First, the gift is so extraordinary—Christ with us, transforming us into Himself!—that one hardly knows how to speak of it with adequate gratitude.

Second, the knowing transmitted by the Eucharist is not of this world—it is a divine knowing which cannot be transposed into human language. Anyone who has tried to sing the song of the Eucharist finds that astonished silence is its first verse, and reposeful silence its last. And yet, words finally do come to the mystics about this *sacramentum unitatis,* the Sacrament of union. They sing:

> The Eucharist, the completion of the Incarnation.[14]
>
> —*Jules Monchanin*

And Teresa of Avila, writing autobiographically:

> The Lord represented Himself to her, just after she had received Communion, in the form of shining splendor, beauty, and majesty, as He was after His resurrection, and told her that now it was time that she considered as her own what belonged to Him and that He would take care of what was hers.[15]

And Blessed Julian of Norwich:

> The human mother will suckle us with her own milk, but our beloved Mother, Jesus, feeds us with himself and with the most tender courtesy does it by means of the Blessed Sacrament, the precious food of all true life.[16]

We Consume Him, And He Consumes Us

Thomas Merton summarizes an august theme among the mystics—even as we are consuming the Eucharist, it is consuming us: "While

---

[14] J.G. Weber, ed. and trans, *In Quest of the Absolute: The Life and Work of Jules Monchanin,* (Kalamazoo, MI: Cistercian Publications, 1977), p. 164.

[15] Teresa of Avila, *The Interior Castle,* trans. Kieran Kavanaugh, O.C.D.. and Otilio Rodriguez, O.C.D., (New York, NY: Paulist Press, 1979), p. 177.

[16] Gaudoin-Parker, *op cit.,* p. 113.

we 'eat' the substance of the true Body of Christ under sacramental species, we ourselves are eaten and absorbed by the Mystical Body of Christ"[17] (Thomas Merton).

Consider the divine ingenuity in this. By God making Himself substances we consume, bread and wine, He not only conveys His Real Presence, but reminds us of the truth of assimilation: even in nature, what is eaten is not annihilated but assumed into a higher form of life.

This happens superlatively in Holy Communion, for as we consume the Eucharist, It consumes us. According to the law of assimilation, as God consumes us we are not annihilated, but we are transformed and elevated into His very Being.

> Christ gave his flesh to be our soul's food and his blood to be our soul's drink. Such a marvel of love had never been heard of in previous times.... Although he gives us all that he has and all that he is, he also takes from us all that we have and all that we are...He consumes us right to the depths of our being.[18]
>
> —*Blessed John Ruusbroec*

In this *Holism of the Sacraments* (Chapter 15), the human person, who is a created whole—a unity of body and soul—is assimilated to the uncreated Whole, God. When we eat the Christic Bread, it consumes us; and when we drink the Wine, it drinks us.

Christ Is the True Priest of the Eucharist

Because Christ commanded his apostles to "do this in remembrance of me" (Luke 22: 19), the re-enactment of the Last Supper became the central rite of worship of early Christianity. Very early on only ministers approved by bishops, or the bishops themselves, could conduct the Eucharistic rite. Ignatius of Antioch wrote to the church at Smyrna in

---

[17] Merton, *The Living Bread,* p. 119.

[18] James A. Wiseman, *John Ruusbroec: The Spiritual Espousals and Other Works,* (New York, NY: Paulist Press, 1986), p. 208.

the early second century, "Let that be deemed a proper Eucharist which is administered either by the bishop or one to whom the bishop has entrusted it."[19]

Though an ordained clergy presides over the Eucharist, it is Christ, the "high priest" (Hebrews 8:1), who is the true Minister of sacrament. The priest is a functionary of Christ, a stand-in for Him. The power of transubstantiation (the transformation of the bread and wine into Christ) is really Christ's power. "I always feel a twinge of annoyance," writes Fr. Benedict Groeschel, "when I see in a college or a hotel a list of 'religious services' and observe the Mass listed at 9 AM. The Mass is not a religious service…something *we* do for God…"[20] The Mass is not "—in its essence—done by man at all."[21]

> Let me tell you, I've been a priest for forty years and I never conducted a "service" called the Mass. I was a "stand-in" for the High Priest, to use the word of the Church teaching, I was there functioning in *persona Christi*—in the person of Christ, the High Priest of the Epistle to the Hebrews. People do not come to Mass to receive my body and blood.… They come for communion with Christ.[22]

What Makes the Mass Different

Most Christian denominations (and those which call themselves "non-denominational") do not believe that the bread and wine actually become Christ, but that the bread and wine remain only symbols. But Catholic doctrine has affirmed the truth of the Eucharistic Christ for two thousand years, an understanding intrinsic to its mysticism and holism.

---

[19] Mike Aquilina, *The Fathers of the Church: An Introduction to the First Christian Teachers,* (Huntington, IN: Our Sunday Visitor, 1999), p. 63.

[20] Scott Hahn, *The Lamb's Supper: The Mass as Heaven on Earth,* (New York, NY: Doubleday, 1999), p. xiii

[21] *Ibid.*

[22] *Ibid.*

An abundance of New Testament sayings and episodes testify to the Eucharistic Christ. "I am the bread of life.... For my flesh is the real food, and my blood is real drink. Whoever eats my flesh and drinks my blood remains in me, and I in him" (John 6:48, 55-56).

Having sanctified bread and wine at the Last Supper, Christ said to the apostles, "Do this in remembrance of me" (Luke 22:19). Christ's use of the word "remembrance" is highly significant, given the Jewish idiom in which He pronounced it. In Jewish culture, "remembrance" does not so much mean to merely mentally recall, or to imagine again—but to re-*live.* "As an act of remembrance (*amanuensis*) the Eucharist not only recalls to mind what Jesus did but also effectively makes it present again."[23]

St. Paul writes of the Eucharistic Christ in his first letter to the Corinthians: "Is not the cup of thanksgiving for which we give thanks a participation in the blood of Christ? And is not the bread that we break, a participation in the body of Christ?" (10:16). And John recorded in *Revelation,* Christ's summoning us to His Mystical Supper: "Here I am! I stand at the door and knock. If anyone hears my voice and opens the door, I will come in and eat with him, and he with me" (3:20).

The Eucharist was certainly the central act of Christian worship in the early Church.[24] "To summarize a vast amount of literature," writes Alan Schreck of Franciscan University, "nearly every notable writing of the early Church that mentions the Eucharist either implies or directly states that the bread and wine of the Lord's Supper is truly the body and blood of Jesus Christ."[25] Notably these include the writings of Ignatius of Antioch (c. 110 AD, *Letter in the Smyrneans,* 7:1), Justin Martyr (c. 150 AD, *First Apology,* Ch. 66), Irenaeus of Lyons (c. 185 AD, *Against Heresies,* Book V, Ch. 2), Cyril of Jerusalem (c. 250 AD, *Mystagogical Catecheses*), and St. Augustine (c. 400 AD, *Sermon 272*).[26] Professor Schreck concludes:

---

[23] Richard P. McBrien, *Catholicism,* (New York, NY: HarperSanFrancisco, 1994), p. 822.

[24] Schreck, *op cit.,* p. 132.

[25] *Ibid.,* p. 131.

[26] *Ibid.*

> I can find no reliable early Christian writer who did not believe that the bread and wine of the Eucharist is the body and blood of Christ. Hence, the Catholic understanding of the Eucharist as truly the body and blood of Christ is supported by both the New Testament and primitive Christian church.[27]

Ignatius of Antioch (who learned the gospel from the Apostle John himself) strikingly described the Eucharist as "the medicine of immortality, and the sovereign remedy by which we escape death and live in Jesus Christ forever more."[28]

How the Eucharist Supports Contemplative Prayer

The Eucharist has innumerable lessons for us, including instruction in the character of prayer. We have the certitude of the word of Christ that each time we receive the Eucharist in faith, we are intimately united to Him. This union is essentially non-experiential (as it is so far beyond the reach of our consciousness), but no less real for its not producing a blissful experience. So too with prayer. Prayer can be a high contemplative communion with our Creator, and yet be essentially non-experiential. The absence of delight in prayer does not betoken a lack of unity with God, but may suggest an intimacy that exceeds comprehension.[29]

By confirming the high mysticism of non-experience, the Eucharist teaches us an important truth about contemplative prayer—and about the grand mysticism of bare faith. Whether our reception of the Eucharistic Christ brings experience or non-experience, it always conduces to our growth in Christ. "Each Holy Communion should intensify in us this grace and this indwelling. We should come away from it, our souls

---

[27] *Ibid.*

[28] Andrew Louth, ed., *Early Christian Writings, The Apostolic Fathers,* trans. Maxwell Stanforth, (London: Penguin Books, 1987), p. 66.

[29] Recall that this is an aspect of John of the Cross' doctrine of contemplation.

more open to, and more deeply penetrated by the Trinity" (Cardinal Charles Journet). Having received the Blessed Sacrament, we remain after Mass for awhile making a Thanksgiving—that is, sitting silently with Christ in prayer.

St. John Vianney (whom we met earlier in our story of a Eucharistic miracle) spoke of the lovely simplicity of prayer with the Eucharistic Christ:

> When I first came to Ars, there was a man who never passed the church without going in. In the morning on his way to work, and in the evening on his way home, he left his spade and pickaxe in the porch, and he spent a long time in adoration before the Blessed Sacrament.
>
> Oh! how I loved to see that! I asked him once what he said to Our Lord during the long visits he made Him. Do you know what he told me?
>
> "Eh, Monsieur le Curé, I say nothing to Him, I look at Him and He looks at me!" How beautiful, my children, how beautiful![30]

✧ ✧ ✧ ✧

Mary Josephine Ward (who co-founded, with her husband, the publishing house, Sheed & Ward) was especially devoted to the doctrine of the Real Presence. Her appreciation of the Eucharistic Christ was due in part to a story that had shocked her since youth, which she liked to retell for the point it dramatically illustrated. A woman had been attending a church of a Christian denomination which regarded the Eucharist as a symbol of Christ only. The bread and wine was said to be just bread and wine before and after communion, which was held to be merely a memorial ceremony.

During such a communion, she accidentally spilled some wine on

[30] Abbe' H. Convert, ed., *Eucharistic Meditations: Extracts from the Writings and Instructions of Saint John Vianney,* trans. Sr. Mary Benvenuta, O.P., (Trabuco Canyon, CA: Source Books & Anthony Clarke, 1993), p. 22.

her dress. The minister quickly consoled her, "Never mind, my dear, the new cleaning methods will get it out completely"—as if she had just got a bit of mustard on her outfit.

"Of course the woman became a Catholic immediately," said Mary Ward.[31]

The point of the story is not of Catholic triumphalism, but of an appreciation of the Church's fidelity to the truest wonder on earth, the Eucharistic Christ.

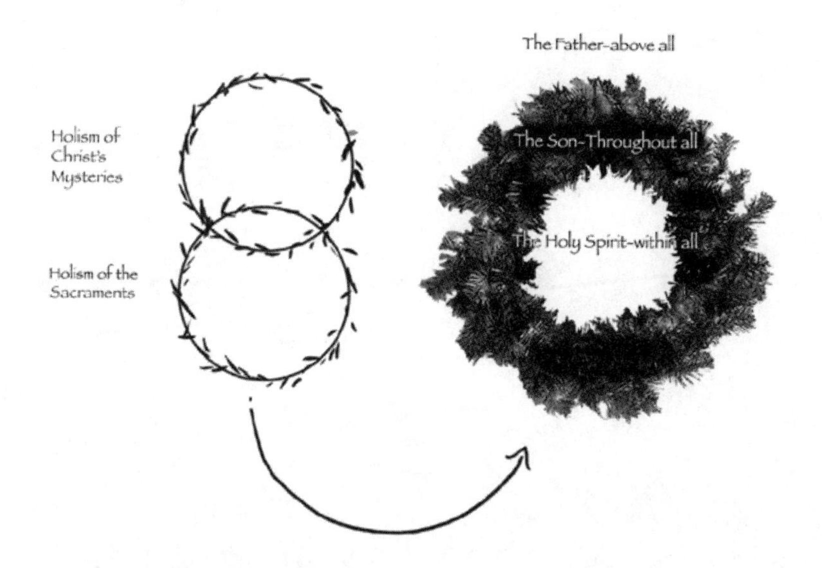

[31] John Deedy, *A Book of Catholic Anecdotes,* (Allen, TX: Thomas More, 1997), p. 250.

CHAPTER 13

The Adventure of Being: Philosophy in a Christian Key

"Only by reaching beyond the human can we succeed in becoming fully human. To refuse to do so condemns us to fall short of the human itself. To be a human person fully means to self-transcend toward the Infinite."[1]

—*W. Norris Clarke, S.J.*

As a child, Thomas Aquinas had a pressing question: "What is God?"[2] It was the question that dominated his mature student years and his adult life as well—and so passionate was he in asking it that its living Answer visited him not infrequently. For example, toward the end of the life of this great philosopher, as he was praying before the crucifix, a "voice spoke from the outstretched arms of the Crucified,"[3] asking him to choose any gift as his reward for a lifetime of consecrated love. Comments G.K. Chesterton on this incident, at first wryly, then penetratingly:

---

[1] W. Norris Clarke, S.J., *Person and Being,* (Milwaukee, WI: Marquette University Press, 1993), p. 108.

[2] Jacques Maritain, *The Peasant of the Garrone: An Old Layman Questions Himself About the Present Time,* trans. Michael Cuddihy and Elizabeth Hughes, (New York, NY: Holt, Rinehart and Winston, 1968), p. 128.

[3] G.K. Chesterton, *Saint Thomas Aquinas, "The Dumb Ox,"* (Garden City, NY: Image Books, 1956), p. 135.

> Nobody supposes that Thomas Aquinas…would ask for a thousand pounds, or the Crown of Sicily, or a present of rare Greek wine. But he might have asked for things he really wanted; and he was a man who could want things; as he wanted the lost manuscript of St. Chrysostom. He might have asked for the solution of an old difficulty; or the secret of a new science; or a flash of the inconceivable intuitive mind of the angels….[4]

But Thomas' answer was that of a contemplative: "I will have only Thyself."

By the end of his short life (he died at 49), he completed one hundred books, and sparked a philosophical tradition that for centuries to come literally filled libraries internationally and continues as a vigorous philosophy into our own time—a philosophy in a Christian key, or metaphysics.

Thomas Aquinas (1225-1274) was proclaimed the common Doctor of the Church, not only for his first-magnitude contribution to theology, but also for his foundational contribution to Christian philosophy. What is the difference between theology and philosophy? This is an enormous question, the subject of whole volumes. (Matthias Joseph Scheeben's *The Mysteries of Christianity* includes a perceptive study of the difference.[5]) Brief working definitions of the two will have to suffice.

Theology is the systematic elaboration of the truths of God's revelation in Sacred Scripture, tradition, and the teaching of the Church by reason illumined by faith. In contrast, philosophy explores reality by way of experience, intuition, and insight. Philosophy and theology are not mutually exclusive ways of knowing, said St. Thomas, but complementary ways to truth. In a phrase, Thomas taught the unity of truth, a principle called in these pages the *Holism of Knowledge.*

Many are surprised to learn that Christianity nourishes philosophy. If they associate philosophy with religion at all, they connect it with far Eastern religions of Taoism, Buddhism, Hinduism. Yet Christianity

---

[4] *Ibid.*

[5] Matthias Joseph Scheeben, *Mysteries of Christianity*, trans Cyril Vollert, S. J., (St. Louis, MO: B. Herder Book Co., 1964), pp. 733-761.

has always had a vital philosophical tradition, in addition to its biblical and theological deposit. The Apostolic Fathers did not despise philosophy to love scripture; Justin Martyr (d. 165), a Platonic philosopher in his youth, continued to wear the *pallium,* the cloak of the philosopher, after his Christian conversion.

Certain non-Catholic Christian churches reject philosophy, insisting that, apart from scripture, no profound truths about God and human existence can be found. But Catholicism—even as it exalts scripture as God-breathed—is avid for other healing wisdom wherever it can be found, as it embraces a robust *Holism of Knowledge.* Catholicism "is characterized by a radical openness to all truth and to every value," writes Fr. Richard P. McBrien.[6] Just as Catholicism welcomes mystical understanding to suffuse its theology, so it invites philosophical insight to expand its vision.

A poet writing about the dusk of an October's day in New Hampshire will reveal insights into it that a meteorologist will not, and *vice versa.* They reveal the same reality from two angles. So too the Christian philosopher and theologian often ponder the same realities and arrive at complementary, mutually enriching insights into them. Below is a brief reflection on a few principles of Christian metaphysics, one approach to philosophy in a Christian key. Along the way we will touch on a few holistic connections between philosophy and spirituality. Francis Klauder goes so far as to say: "The purpose of Christian philosophy is to restore the mystical sense of a divine attraction that constantly draws the soul beyond itself to God, ontologically present to the spirit itself."[7]

The Luxuriance of Being

You remember it well; you were in your early twenties. It had been a harsh winter, and April had just started. It was still chilly and foggy when you arrived at the university for an early morning class in

[6] Richard P. McBrien, *Catholicism,* (Minneapolis, MN: Winston, 1980), p. 1173.

[7] Francis Klauder, *A Philosophy Rooted in Love: The Dominant Themes in the Perennial Philosophy of St. Thomas Aquinas,* (Lanham, MD: University Press of America, 1994). p. 208.

philosophy. After the hour and half lecture, you stepped outside to a surprise: springtime. It had sneaked up on you, as you had been for months so involved in your studies, but there it was, unmistakable, in that silken warm wind that met you as you left the building.

As you walked to your car you had some thoughts about the philosophy class. The professor had spent the whole period trying to prove to students that reality was just a mental construct, a social fabrication. That there was no way you could prove you existed, or the world existed—let alone the existence of God. You felt intuitively that there was something wrong with his argument, but could not pin it down—at once it sounded logical but absurd. A hall-of-mirrors. It made your mind spin, and your gut sick with nausea. The professor was not conducting an exploration of truth, but an autopsy of it.

But when that spring breeze touched your face as you left the building his whole lecture was suddenly overturned. The sumptuous clarity of the moment stopped you in your tracks. The breeze exists. You exist. These people walking around you, talking and laughing, are all exuberantly real.

The abstract idea that the world was unreal and true knowledge of anything was impossible was carried away in the spring air, and perished in the green fire of the grass at your feet.

What had just happened to you has a name in Christian metaphysics—the *intuition of being.* This intuition, not word-games, is the true beginning of all philosophy. Writes Francis Klauder in *The Wonder of Intelligence:*

> The universal, indisputable and absolute experience of human nature is the Consciousness of Reality. Every man can say *I Know That Something Exists.* In fact, every man making a judgment, every time he does so, proclaims his knowledge of reality. When I say for instance, "This is chalk," I am saying that this thing *Is,* that it is chalk, and that I know it.[8]

As in real life, philosophy in a Christian key starts with our nearest experience: I exist and the world exists. It starts with a metaphysical

---

[8] Francis Klauder, S.D.B., *The Wonder of Intelligence: A Study of Human Knowledge,* (North Quincy, MA: The Christopher Publishing House, 1973), p. 20.

realism that makes this simple, commonsensical affirmation: "We hold it a fact, in the first place, that there is reality, and that the human intellect is capable of knowing it, and that this is the very purpose of philosophy itself"[9] (Francis Klauder).

This is one way Christian philosophy serves us: as an antidote to other kinds of philosophy that deny even elemental truths, such as the possibility of knowledge. C.S. Lewis wrote: "Good philosophy must exist if for no other reason than because bad philosophy needs to be answered."[10] Bad philosophy is, for Lewis, mechanically skeptical and agnostic, anemically relativistic—unable to touch the real world, or speak of real virtue. The devolution of philosophy into a hall-of-mirrors, linguistic gamesmanship is especially sad when we remember the two Greek roots that compose the word: *phil* means love and *sophos,* wisdom. Philosophy should not devolve into abstract, smaller-than-life riddles, but should be one with life, like pine cones are one with the life of the branch.

The Wonder of Is

If you can read this chapter outdoors, or at least before a big open window, that would be ideal. For philosophy is about reality, not about words, and there is nothing like contact with the natural world to bring us back to reality—the reality of the world, ourselves, and God. "Now the end of philosophical studies is not for us to have learned philosophy. Just as physics is not about physics, but about nature, so also philosophy is not about philosophy but about reality…"[11] (E. Gilson).

The whole action of philosophy is to bathe the intelligence and the heart in the real. It begs us to open our eyes in wonder. It agrees with naturalist George Wherry that the outside of a mountain is good for the inside of a man.

---

[9] Klauder, *A Philosophy Rooted in Love, op cit.*, p. 4.

[10] C.S. Lewis, *The Weight of Glory and Other Addresses,* (New York, NY: Macmillan, 1980), p. 28.

[11] Etienne Gilson, *The Spirit of Medieval Philosophy* , trans. A.H.C. Downes, (Notre Dame, IN: University of Notre Dame Press, 1936), p. 93.

Now and then as you read, put the book down and just look around you; you will find that connections between what you are reading and the natural world will flow naturally back and forth, like birds calling to one another across a field.

Now take a look at those hills in the distance, and the tender blue sky and the clouds, and the two friends sitting there in the shade of that tree. Everything speaks of being, each in its own specific way.

But let us not think of the differences among the entities of the scene just yet. Let us focus on what all the elements of the scene share. We may have overlooked this subtle common factor, it is so obvious. Yet when we do see it, its wondrous reality will add a new dimension to every scene.

What Christian metaphysics would have us see now is the sheer existence, or ISNESS, of everything before us—including our being. The tree IS, you ARE, the sky IS, the little dog playing over there IS—we all share that implacably solid yet threadlike delicacy of PRESENT EXISTENCE. This ACT OF EXISTENCE—connoted by the little-big phrase, *to be*, is the unsung dynamic of each moment. "Being constitutes the very stuff of the universe and of all its differentiations; it is the secret heart of things"[12] (Cardinal Charles Journet).

At once we see that existence or ISNESS is one, in that all that is before us shares it, yet it is multiple, myriad, infinitely variegated, eminently rich. The tree exists, the sky exists, the bird exists, you exist, yet each *expresses existence* in a different way.

W. Norris Clarke, S.J., a great contemporary metaphysician, has a charming way of putting this. Clarke asks us to look around this field with him. See that horse? We may say that over there EXISTENCE is "horsey." And under our feet, EXISTENCE is grassy. Look over there, to that grove of trees—there EXISTENCE is elmy and evergreeney. And gliding in a flock overhead right now, EXISTENCE is sparrowy! What Clarke is accenting is that whatever we see is a certain vivacity of existence—a specific capacity for existence.

---

[12] Charles Journet, *The Dark Knowledge of God,* trans. James F. Anderson, (London: Sheed & Ward, 1948), p. 5.

The Savor of the Now

Gazing at the plenum of natural existence as it arises moment by moment, we are struck by its innocent flow. It flows without selfish motive, without mean resentment, without strained comparison, without contracted focus. All things in nature know God because of the uncontracted, radically unselfish character of the natural world.[13] Its flow of life is essentially spiritual. We yearn to join our souls to this innocent flow. *Soul-Seeing* can give us at least an analogous taste of it.

That is because Soul-Seeing, as discussed in Chapter Three, quiets for a time the self-reflective mechanism of the mind (though not the self-*reflexive* character of consciousness) that otherwise mechanically refers back to the ego and its thick self-imagery.[14] Soul-Seeing leaves self-focus behind in a simple, innocent gaze at the natural world.

To practice Soul-Seeing, take a stroll in a natural setting. Put your attention out of yourself. Do not think about what you are seeing, just see, listen, be aware.

Automatic self-reactions will continue to arise within your mind, commenting on what you are seeing. You see an old oak. Your mind will want to tell you all it knows about oaks—to instantly classify your experience into familiar categories. Quietly ignore your mechanical mini-encyclopedia, and just look afresh at the oak. Look at the sunlight on its branches. Look with your senses, not your mind.

Breathe in the scents, open your senses. Do not strain to concentrate on the moment, but just listen and look, ignoring the mind's commentary and resistance. Relax away from yourself. Let the setting reveal itself like a perfume of music. Listen without reference to the

---

[13] To describe nature as "unselfish" is not to deny that each part of nature instinctually seeks its good, but that its mode of knowing is sensory awareness, not subject-object consciousness. As subject-object consciousness is self, and the animal mode of knowing is not subject-object consciousness, animals are radically non-selfish or unselfish.

[14] The self-reflective mechanism of the mind is part of consciousness and can be modified. In contrast, the self-reflexive nature of consciousness is the very nature of self: its subject-object bending back on itself. This is not interrupted by Soul-Seeing, but is suspended by ecstasy, which is not our topic here. For a discussion of ecstasy, see Chapter Eleven.

past or future. Listen as you would to a song, for its own sake. In this innocent listening and seeing, the years fade and a freshness comes to the heart.

When self-focus is not, the sacred arises. "The secret of seeing is, then, the pearl of great price....It is always a gift and a total surprise"[15] (Annie Dillard).

A Convivium of Being

Now that we have seen that it is existence that magnificently unites all things and beings, let us turn to another aspect of reality, *essence.* Existence is *that* a thing is; essence is *what* a thing is—its specific nature, we might broadly say, as distinct from the nature of other existents, other things and beings.

Sitting outdoors now, you are vital with existence, as is the grass under your feet. But obviously you differ from the grass—you and it differ in essence. Think of the existence which manifests both as grass under your feet and the squirrel over there climbing that tree. Essence, understood in this way, is a certain restriction of the full amplitude of existence. Your being, your essence, expresses a certain amplitude or degree of existence, just as the essence of the grass expresses another degree—perhaps as the separate keys on a piano each express a degree of tonality.

Active Presence

Yet essence is not simply a restriction, but positively it is what metaphysics calls *active presence.* "From the very fact that something exists in act, it is active"[16] (W. Norris Clarke, S.J.). Moreover, it is interactive.

---

[15] Annie Dillard, *Pilgrim at Tinker Creek,* (New York, NY: HarperCollins, 1974), p. 35.

[16] Clarke, *op cit.,* p. 6.

"To be, it turns out, means to-be together."[17] This convivium of being is stated classically in the phrase, *Bonum est diffusivum*—the good is diffusive of itself. Wrote Fulton Sheen:

> All life is enthusiastic. It is the very nature of life to be enthusiastic, for all life tends to diffuse and communicate itself and even to overflow its perfections in order that others may share.... The old Greeks and scholastic philosophers used to express this truth in the principle "everything that is good tends to diffuse itself."
>
> In the plant kingdom there is not only a diffusion of matter but also of life; in other words, there is real fecundity. The oak is good and diffuses itself in the generation of the acorn...the flower is good and diffuses itself in its perfume; the plant is good and diffuses itself in other plants.[18]

The tree sighs oxygen, our next breath. The rose bush slakes itself on sunlight and water, and materializes yellow petals—which a little girl is gazing at now, which will turn into a sun in her dream tonight, which she will fingerpaint above a blue sea in kindergarten tomorrow morning—evoking a smile from her teacher. *Bonum est diffusivum.* There is a universe of subtle and overt variations on this. This morning on a walk around my neighborhood I took a route new to me, and saw a swing hanging from a tree limb. That was the first one I had seen in the whole neighborhood. Across the street I saw another one, inspired no doubt by the rigging up of the other. *Bonum est diffusivum.*

Unseen exchanges occur too. Researchers have determined that when we touch someone (or are within a few feet of someone), a measurable exchange of electromagnetic energy occurs, from our heart to his or her brain.[19]

---

[17] *Ibid.*, p. 23.

[18] Fulton Sheen, *Life of All the Living,* (New York, 1929), pp. 43-46.

[19] Doc Childre and Deborah Rozman, *Overcoming Emotional Chaos,* (San Diego, CA: Jodere Group, 2002), pp. 206-207.

Here metaphysics again shades into spirituality. The Holy Trinity is the First Good that diffuses Itself, as the Three Persons eternally and infinitely diffuse their good to each other in the Godhead even before creation. Then the good of the Trinity flows over, by God's design, into a created universe—Meister Eckhart likened this overflow to that of a cooking pot! In this way, *bonum est diffusivum* in the natural world mirrors the Trinity's cascading goodness. "No wonder, then, that self-communication is written into the very heart of all beings, as finite but positive images of their Source"[20] (W. Norris Clarke, S.J.).

When we see *bonum est diffusivum* in the natural world, may it remind us of the Trinity! The butterflies combing through that little garden in your front yard hint of the Triune One.

Waking Sleeping Beauty

Catholic philosophy then asks us to see in each nature or essence the exuberance of potency and act. Potency is what a thing or being may become; act (used in a metaphysical way) is the perfection of that potency as existence. At this moment, a human baby is being born in your town—and a certain number of miles away, a sprout of grass has just pushed its green tip above the earth to begin to dream in air and sun. Both the baby and the blade of grass are newborn, but each radically differs in potencies, according to its particular nature:

> Every thing acts according to its bent. There exists in it a permanent determining principle which lies at the source of its way of acting. This is called its nature...God has created a universe of natures and has endowed beings on every level, and they are as it were permanent sources of activity.[21]
>
> —*Cardinal Charles Journet*

Intrinsic to the infant's human essence are potencies of being absent in the seedling—especially conceptual intelligence and love—powers

---

[20] Clarke, *op cit.*, p. 12.

[21] Charles Journet, *The Meaning of Grace,* trans. A.V. Littledale, (New York, NY: P.J. Kenedy & Sons, 1960), p. 10.

that are destined to bloom as she grows in subjectivity and personal interiority, and also empathy and generosity. "Man exists only in dialogue with this neighbor. The infant is brought to consciousness of himself only by love, by the smile of his mother"[22] (Hans Urs von Balthasar).

A father and mother lean quietly over their daughter's crib. The smiling mother caresses her cheek, drawing her little one's gaze. Suddenly the baby smiles and her eyes widen. Here we have an essential dynamic of life—that we are awakened and deepened by our interacting with others. "Our intellectual consciousness starts off not yet in act, but potential, in the dark…It must be activated from without.…like the Sleeping Beauty"[23] (W. Norris Clarke).

The Good Is a Flourishing of Being

The metaphysics of potency and act, as we have briefly reflected on it, is an inlet upon the shore of ethics. Imagine a barren piece of land: no trees, dry and stony soil, parched grass stubble here and there. Now imagine someone had been given responsibility to cultivate this area: to seed it, plant flowers in it, water it regularly in dry spells—but shirked responsibility, and failed to cultivate it. A flourishing of life that ought to have arisen here—a garden—is absent.

Now imagine otherwise: that the garden was cultivated, and has come to fruition. A good that ought to be there, is. That illustrates the difference between good and evil, metaphysically conceived. Good is a flourishing of rightful being; evil is the suppression of rightful being.

Think of the infant in the above "sleeping beauty" scenario. But let us change the scene now, and imagine that her parents are quite different from the loving ones of our description. They are oddly indifferent to her. They do not activate her potentials by love. In fact, by their inattention and impatience, they neglect and even suppress her potentials, ones that ought to flourish under their care. As she grows, they criticize her inappropriately, making her nervously distrustful of others. A void

---

[22] Francis Klauder, S.D.B., *The Wonder of the Real: A Sketch in Basic Philosophy,* (North Quincy, MS: The Christopher Publishing House, 1979), p. 12.

[23] Clarke, *op cit.*, p. 45.

is left in her personality—distrust—where the good of trust ought to have flourished. Also, they rarely read to her and discourage her natural curiosity; so in place of another human good that ought to be there, an expanding intelligence, another void in her being is carved out.

This returns us to the metaphysical definition of evil (first proposed by Aristotle, and then renewed by St. Augustine and St. Thomas): evil is an unnatural void or vacuum in rightful being. "Evil is not a being, it is the lack of being, the privation of a due good"[24] (John F.X. Knasas). The parents' neglect of the child is evil.

To pause from our metaphysical inquiry for a moment to make a theological point: Christ said, "Apart from me you can do nothing" (John 15:5). Christ—speaking at that moment from his *Logos* nature, his divine nature—is making a point about evil. To act apart from God is to "do nothing," to introduce a nothingness, a void, into the order of creation where there ought to be flourishing being.

The Created Universe: Being-With-Nothingness

Notice, though, that a void in being is only evil if it is void of a "due good"—a good that ought to be there. An absence in being is not evil *per se;* only an unnatural absence in being. That a boulder does not have the fragrance of a little rose, or the rose the firmness of the boulder, does not suggest evil—because these missing vitalities are only natural to the one, not to the other. Evil is only an unnatural void in being that ought to be there—as a debilitating distrust in a child is a privation, and the action that caused it evil.

As we gaze upon the created universe we see that it is shot through with voids, latticed with non-existence—but these are not evils. Look at the squirrel as it loops its way across the lawn. It lacks the aerial motion of the bird overhead, and the bird lacks its nimble paws, yet neither of these absences in being is evil, for neither is a due being in each.

So each thing and being in the universe has distinctive powers, but lacks others. Each is relatively incomplete, restricted in being; it has

---

[24] John F.X. Knasas, ed., *Jacques Maritain: The Man and His Metaphysics,* (USA: American Maritain Association, 1988), p. 228.

being and existence, but it does not exist completely. Nothingness is intermingled with its positive being, we might say. In Jacques Maritain's phrase, the created universe is being-with-nothingness.

It is only natural to wonder: Is there some being that is complete, having none of these gaps, a being that lacks nothing—a being of perfect, unrestricted existence? Our intuition leaps to the possibility, even the necessity, of a unique reality, a Being without voids, a Whole Being, a being of Sheer Existence: in brief, a Being-without-nothingness—God. God is uncleft Existence, untinctured Goodness, the fullness of what it means To Be. Not being of act and potential, but Pure Act.

That is why St. Thomas' favorite philosophical name for God was the one that God revealed to Moses: I AM (*Yahweh,* in Hebrew). When Moses encounters God's presence in the burning bush, and hears his call to liberate the Hebrews from bondage in Egypt, Moses asks: "Who shall I say sent me?" The answer comes:

> Tell them…
> I AM
> has
> sent me to you.
>
> —*Exodus 3:14*

Our human "I am," the existence we experience in ourselves, is not fundamentally of our own making—we didn't create ourselves. But the Supreme "I AM"—God, Being-Without-Nothingness—has Existence of His own. God is the fountainhead of existence, from which all things borrow existence.[25]

If we were now to look upon *what is* from a standpoint of being—

> What we would see…
> would be the universe,
> its riches, its beauty, its being, and doubtless that is something!

---

[25] Strictly speaking, God includes and transcends Being. The "Father" transcends Being; the "Son" is Being.

It is something, but it is being which is
weak, limited, fugitive; philosophers call it contingent being…
It is borrowed being,
dependent on the Being *per se,* the Absolute.

Then, in the order of nature,
God is the great X
on whom the world depends.[26]

—*Cardinal Charles Journet*

The created universe is a Wreath of thronging vitalities suspended from the uncreated Absolute.

The Human Person

Whatever God creates must be less than God. Indeed, God creates by restricting being in some way, and can do so with infinite variation. Yet even the smallest restriction in being means an infinite abyss of difference between limited created being and the uncontained, uncreated God. Whatever God does create imitates a fraction of the unlimited divine essence. "He sees that His Infinite Essence can be imitated in an infinite number of ways"[27] (Francis Klauder).

From this measureless abundance God has created us, and so we reflect Him to some degree. Since God is the summit of communicable love, our human character reflects love—we are lovers by nature.

Each of us is a center of love and intelligence. For we naturally love the good, such as the good things of the earth and our good human companions. And this aptitude for the good shows that we have an in-built desire for God—as God is unrestricted Good.

We are also naturally curious and delight in knowledge of all sorts, for practical reasons and for its own sake: of friends, of all manner of natural phenomena, and of ourselves. This also speaks of our in-built desire for God, as God is unrestricted Truth.

---

[26] *Ibid.,* p. 8.

[27] Klauder, *The Wonder of the Real, op cit.,* p. 49.

Two Poles of Human Nature

We see there are two poles of human personhood. On the one hand we are drawn to relationship. From our earliest awakening to relationship through our mother's smile and our father's gentle embrace, we delight in friendships and love. Our aptitude for relationship proves that "to be is to be related."

Yet relationality is only half of the human story; the other is the mystery of interiority, of self-possession, of subjectivity. The deepest point of our subjectivity is God, who is the cause of our being. That cause is communicative Love. Since our subjectivity is ultimately rooted in God who is Love, "Love is not a passing pleasure or emotion but the very meaning of being alive"[28] (Jacques Maritain).

Our relationship to the world, to its intimacies and challenges, compels us to call upon our best interior resources, the deepest of these being our subjectivity rooted in Spirit. Desire to relate truly to others prompts a diving into our interior depths for energy and insight, and our desire to deepen our subjectivity prompts our deepening relationship to God, to discover that Being who is communicative Love.

The philosophy of atheism insists that the principle of God is heteronomous to self—that the idea of God is intrinsically alien to the self and dictatorial in relation to it. Atheism thus asserts that self-realization and true relationship to others can only be had by renouncing God.

But metaphysics suggests otherwise. It holds that God is not heteronomous to human being, but is our deepest center of being. Love of God does not therefore alienate us from self, but enhances self-understanding. Moreover, since this center is communicative Love, theism does not impair authentic relationship but is its true basis.

In sum, metaphysics shows that to love God is to unfold both poles of the human person: the subjective pole (our interiority) and the relational pole. Clarke crystallizes this point: "to be fully a person consists in living out to the full the alternating rhythm of self-possession and openness to others…for it is in the spark that passes from one of these

---

[28] *Ibid.*, p. 77.

poles to the other and back again that lies the secret of all authentic personal growth, creativity, life, and love."[29]

By our having taken a little excursion into metaphysical understanding, we can see that Clarke's insight is not a theological conclusion, but the fruit of philosophical insight. Yet notice how Clarke's idea holistically coincides with that of theological wisdom. Writes Cardinal Avery Dulles: "Christ as the living centre draws the members together and at the same time impels them to actualize their individuality to the utmost."[30] Here we have a resonance between theology and philosophy that bespeaks the *Holism of Knowledge* characteristic of Catholicism.

---

[29] *Ibid.*, p. 113.

[30] Avery Dulles, *The Catholicity of the Church*, (New York, NY: Oxford University Press, 1985), p. 42.

CHAPTER 14

The Mystical Body of Christ

"Of course when we talk of the 'Church', every Christian must realize that he is under discussion."[1]
—*Hans Urs von Balthasar*

Almustapha, the blessed protagonist of Kahlil Gibran's *The Prophet,* says of prayer: "Therefore, let your visit to that temple invisible be for naught but ecstasy and sweet communion."[2]

The Temple Invisible! Anyone who has ever prayed knows where this holy garden is. Anywhere the heart and mind lift to God, there is the Temple Invisible—the perennial truth of God's omnipresence and immediate accessibility.

But some would take this a step further. They hold that the Temple Invisible renders physical churches superfluous; indeed, to worship in a physical church building is to contradict God's everywhereness. To affirm God is there is to tacitly say God is not here. They protest that they do not have to "go to church" to enter the Temple Invisible; it is here now.

Christ's words, they point out, were twined with the whisperings of the woods and His breath with the sighing of the wind. The lilies he

[1] Hans Urs von Balthasar, *Who Is A Christian?,* trans. John Cumming, (New York, NY: Newman Press, 1968), p. 118.

[2] Kahlil Gibran, *The Prophet,* (New York, NY: Alfred A. Knopf, 1998), pp. 67-68.

spoke of were not in pots but in fields. Didn't He say, "The kingdom of heaven is among you"? And didn't the Christian mystic Meister Eckhart say: "Whoever truly possesses God in the right way, possesses him in all places: on the street, in any company, as well as in a church or a remote place"?

And didn't the Christian contemplative Brother Lawrence make famous "the practice of the presence of God" among white columns—but they were smooth white columns of birches, not the portico-columns of a stony temple. He heard the song of God not from organ music, but among the clamoring pots and pans as he worked in the monastery kitchen.

For those who speak thus, the Church has become a notable anti-metaphor—a monument against the Temple Invisible, a prime symbol of their alienation from organized religion.

Christ-in-Matter

How wonderful that they worship in the Temple Invisible, the everywhereness of God! But they are mistaken if they imagine that Christianity does not also walk the leafy lanes of this Temple. For what is the Temple Invisible except the omnipresent *Logos*—the universal Body of Christ? "In Him we live and move and have our being" (Acts 17:28). For while the Father is God beyond creation, and the Holy Spirit is God in creation, the Son, the *Logos,* is God throughout creation, the bright Axle of the circling seasons.

The *Logos* is like the great yule Tree, adorned with all stellar worlds, with every dancing brightness of nature. We live in a "God-bathed and God-permeated world," says Christian philosopher Dallas Willard.[3] We are sisters and brothers to all things, as in the singing of St. Francis of Assisi:

> Praise be thou, O Lord, for Sister Moon and the Stars,
> For that thou madest them clear, precious, and lovely.

---

[3] Dallas Willard, *The Divine Conspiracy, Rediscovering Our Hidden Life in God,* (San Francisco, CA: HarperSanFrancisco, 1998), p. 62.

Praised be thou, O Lord, for our Brother Wind,
For air and cloud and sunshine and every weather
Whereby thou givest thy creatures their sustenance.

Praised be thou, O Lord, for our Sister the Earth
That as a Mother sustaineth and feedeth us,
And after its kind bringeth forth fruit
And grass and many-colored flowers.[4]

But what of the earlier references to the life of Christ, that seemed to suggest He exclusively worshipped in the precincts of nature and soulful inwardness, alienated from the stony Temple? Certainly Jesus' parables are crowded with natural wonders: lilies, sparrows, wheat, sand and rock, waving harvests, flashing fish, figs, oil, lambs, fragrant vineyards, pearls. He was, course, luminously aware of the natural world—how could it be otherwise, as His cosmic Body was its ground and pavilion?

But He did not shun buildings of mortar where His Father's name was honored—worship-places where that Name rang in the very bricks, as when cymbals sing after their striking. In his boyhood Jesus remains in the Temple to speak of the Torah with the elders, after Mary and Joseph have left for home. When they finally find him there, he says, "Why were you searching for me? Didn't you know I had to be in my Father's house?" (Luke 2:49). Later in his mature years, Christ rebukes those who were profaning this house, so much did He love it (Matthew 21:13).

The Temple Visible

While Christ delighted in the sky-arched Temple Invisible, He Himself built a Temple Visible—a visible Church—as a necessary complement to the Temple Invisible, infusing His very Life into it. "I will build my church and the gates of Hades will not overcome it" (Matthew 16:18).

[4] Roy M. Gasnick, O.F.M., ed., *The Francis Book—800 Years with the Saint from Assisi,* (New York, NY: Macmillan Publishing, 1980), p. 104.

Of course, buildings are not the Church any more than the cover of your diary is your life. But where, then, do we see the Temple Visible, the visible Church of Christ?

- in the Eucharistic Christ
- in the whole sacramental order, especially the Mass
- in the baptized who live by grace and love
- in all the holy works of the Christian community, works of fraternal love and justice
- in the canonized saints of all times, in her choir of mystics, and the Blessed Virgin above them all
- in the Christian family, the domestic Church
- in the holy prayer and work of religious orders, in the monasteries, hermitages and cloisters
- we *hear* the Church in the Divine Office, her daily prayer
- in the voice of the ecumenical councils from age to age,
- in the daily teaching of the Church, that has proclaimed the Trinity and Christ's Mysteries since the Apostolic Age
- in the voice of the bishops in union with the Pope

But what of the earlier citations from Meister Eckhart and Brother Lawrence, which seemed to indicate their indifference to the visible Church? Taken out of context they do seem to indicate aloofness from it, but not in context.

Yes, Eckhart sang of the omnipresent divine, but that was but one page in his hymnal; he also acclaimed the sacramental Church, and especially the Eucharistic Christ. For however comely the wheat of nature, and however generous its swelling indigo vineyards, Eckhart knew that they cannot produce a single Eucharistic wafer and cup, which is food and drink of another world, entering this world during the Mass of the visible Church. He knew that the Eucharist enters our atmosphere less like a sprout pushing itself through soil, than like a meteor falling fast to earth.[5] Eckhart said that the Eucharistic Christ of the Mass possesses

> as does nothing else,
> the grace by which your bodily strength
> will be united and collected
> through the wonderful power
> of our Lord's bodily presence....
> as your body is strengthened by his Body
> ...wholly united, so that what is his becomes ours,
> all that is ours becomes his,
> our heart and his one heart,
> our body and his one Body.

The same is true of Brother Lawrence. From the happy glens of the Temple Invisible he always returned to the Inn of the Absolute, the visible Church, which hearth is lit by an ember plucked from the sun, and which board is set with bread and wine from beyond the sun. Lawrence's biographer tells us what joy the gift of the Eucharistic Christ brought him—how the holy friar was sundered with "happiness eating and drinking at the Lord's table."[6]

We have seen that to oppose the visible Church to the Temple Invisible is to create a false dichotomy, for they form a holistic unity. This unity is pictured well by Thomas Howard:

> To be Christian...is to hear the praises of God in the soughing of the west wind, the soft fall of surf on pebbles, and the song of the winter wren, the hermit thrush, or the white-throated sparrow

---

[5] That some of the theological propositions of Meister Eckhart were rejected as false by the Church does not mean that Eckhart was indifferent or hostile to the Church, as some assert. It has been my experience that those who would make Eckhart into a maverick mystic, only nominally connected to the visible Church, are unaware of his devotion to the Eucharistic Christ. That devotion makes all the difference, as it demonstrates Eckhart's commitment to a theology of Christ's grace, which makes his relation to the visible Church not nominal, but essential.

[6] Michael L. Gaudoin-Parker, ed., *The Real Presence Through the Ages,* (Staten Island, NY: Alba House, 1993), p. 135.

and even in the scream of jays and the cackle of crows. But the still point at the center of it all, for a Catholic, is the Eucharist.[7]

The Mystery of the Church

And yet, however grand the sacraments are, the Church is still more than a channel of the Sacraments. The visible Church is a dimension of the whole Church in her full integrity and amplitude. Writes Jacques Maritain:

> Many people too frequently see the Church
> only as a vast judicial administration charged
> with the duty of reminding them that God exists,
> and they look no further
> than its external apparatus.
>
> They do not know what the Church is.
> The Church is a mystery
> as profound as the Incarnation.[8]

What is this mystery? What is the Church? The Church is nothing less than Christ's own Mystical Body, which infinitude exceeds the reach of our senses. The whole star-fretted night may be likened to a glinting archway that leads forward upon its pathways.

> The Church is the body of the God-man,
> and all who enter it
> become members of the God-man
> so that, linked together in Him and through Him,
> they may share in the divine life
> and the divine glory of their head.[9]
>
> —*Matthias Joseph Scheeben*

---

[7] Thomas Howard, *On Being Catholic,* (San Francisco, CA: Ignatius Press, 1997), p. 78.

[8] Jacques Maritain, *The Peasant of the Garrone: An Old Layman Questions Himself about the Present Time,* trans. Michael Cuddihy and Elizabeth Hughes, (New York, NY: Holt, Rinehart and Winston, 1968), pp. 174-175.

[9] Matthias Joseph Scheeben, *Mysteries of Christianity,* trans. Cyril Vollert, S. J., (St. Louis, MO: B. Herder Book Co., 1964), p. 541.

We will now try to form some idea of the Church as the Mystical Body of Christ by considering how the Holy Spirit unites the Church of heaven and the Church of earth.

Perhaps you had the experience as a child of being taught the pattern of constellations on warm summer's night. "There it is," said your companion, "the Big Dipper. See it above the moon—to the right?" At first you did not see it, but just continued to gaze, and then it clicked into your perception: "I see it! I see it!"

Something similar happens when we take time to meditatively gaze upon the Hebrew scriptures and the New Testament together. A certain compelling pattern, a minute ago unseen, now becomes visible. It now constellates these books into one, as stars configure a cloudless night from east to west.

The *Shekinah*, The Light of God

We begin by noting that the Torah (the first five books of the Hebrew scriptures) says the divine was revealed to the Hebrews as a visible Mystic Light. Paging through the Hebrew scriptures, we find scores of references to the "glory of the LORD," the "pillar of fire," and the "glory cloud." All these are ultimately connected to the Hebrew word for the Light of God—the *Shekinah*. We will follow that Light now, as it cuts a path through the Hebrew scriptures into the New Testament.

Early in his walk with God, Moses sees a bush that is on fire but does not burn. "I will go over and see this strange sight" (Exodus 3:3). As if from within the bush, the *Shekinah*, the Light of God, speaks to him: "I am the God of your father...the God of Abraham, the God of Isaac, and the God of Jacob." The Light calls Moses to lead the Hebrews from Pharaoh's captivity.

During the Hebrews' escape, the Light appears again to defend them against Egypt's armies. It manifests as an awful pillar of Fire, which blocks the Pharaoh's chariots.

> The Egyptians pursued them, and all Pharaoh's horses and chariots and horsemen followed them....During the last watch of the

> night the LORD looked down from the pillar of fire and cloud at the Egyptian army and threw it into confusion.
>
> —*Exodus 14:23-24*

Having made their speedy escape, the Hebrews are commanded by God to set up a tabernacle, a tent of thanksgiving and worship—a kind of portable temple, wherein the Light descends to bless and fortify. Moses had received the Ten Commandments at Mt. Sinai, which were placed in a box or ark. Since it is above the ark that the *Shekinah* now manifests, the Ark of the Covenant is installed in that tabernacle. Here the exhausted people of Israel are heartened by the Light:

> For the cloud of the Lord
> was over the tabernacle by day,
> and fire was in the cloud by night,
> in the sight of all the house of Israel
> during all their travels.
>
> —*Exodus 40:38*

After finally coming into the Promised Land, the Hebrews are called by God to replace the tabernacle with a grand Temple—the Temple of Jerusalem. Built by King Solomon, the Temple houses the Ark of the Covenant in a special chamber known as the "holy of holies." The *Shekinah* appears above the Ark, filling the chamber with Its radiance:

> For the cherubim
> spread their wings over the place of the ark...
> for the glory of the Lord
> filled his temple.
>
> —*1 Kings 8:7, 11*

Please note that up to now, every manifestation of the Light has been exterior to the people. Even the wondrous blessing of the Light from the Temple had been external. Now a new spiritual dispensation among the Jews is being readied, even in the face of inconstancy: an interiorization of the Light. The prophet Jeremiah is inspired to announce this "New Covenant" yet to come:

> I will put my law in their minds and
> write it on their hearts.
> I will be their God, and they will be my people.
>
> —*Jeremiah 31:33*

The Light of the World

Centuries later, the Light overshadows a young virgin of Nazareth, who later gives birth under a spectacular star—as if the *Shekinah* had taken to the zenith to signal the world that—

> The true light that gives light to every man
> was coming into the world.
>
> —*John 1:9*

When later the Fathers of the Church came to meditate on Christ's conception and birth, they were struck by its majestic and ingenious foreshadowings in the Hebrew scriptures, in the ways of the *Shekinah*. For just as the *Shekinah* overshadowed the Ark of the Covenant, so the Shekinah-Holy Spirit "overshadowed" Mary at Jesus' conception in her womb.

> The Holy Spirit will come upon you,
> and the power of the Most High will overshadow you.
> So the holy one to be born will be called
> the Son of God.
>
> —*Luke 1: 35*

And just as the Ark had contained the words of God, the tablets of the Ten Commandments, so Mary contained in her womb the eternal Word, the *Logos* of God, Christ. That is why the early Church called the Blessed Virgin the New Ark of the Covenant, ever canopied by the Light.[10]

During His public ministry, Christ said—without an iota of egoism:

---

[10] Scott Hahn, *Hail, Holy Queen: The Mother of God in the Word of God,* (New York, NY: Doubleday, 2002), pp. 49-67.

> I am the light of the world.
>
> —*John 8:12*

The Incarnation of the Light, Christ Jesus gave the apostles a glimpse of His inner glory mystically at Mt. Tabor.

> After six days Jesus took with him
> Peter, James and John the brother of James,
> and led them up a high mountain by themselves.
>
> There he was transfigured before them.
> His face shone like the sun,
> and his clothes became as white as
> the light.
>
> —*Matthew 17:1-2*

Ponder this: the Light which had appeared to Moses in the burning bush, defended the fleeing Hebrews in battle as a pillar of Fire, filled the tent-tabernacle, and blessed the Temple, now appears to the apostles perfectly united to Christ. It simply does not end there. Christ announces that His very mission is to share the Light, to make it *indwell* those who would welcome it:

> I have come to bring fire on the earth,
> and how I wish it were already kindled!
>
> —*Luke 12: 49*

(Years ago, on first hearing this verse, I thought the "fire" Christ was praying for was the "fire and brimstone" variety—a disturbing thought. After reading the Christian mystics, I found that the opposite was true: Christ was praying for the descent of the healing Spirit of God, the coming of his Holy Spirit, the transformer, the Enlightener.)

What Jesus is praying for, astonishingly, is that the Spirit by which the Son has ever been timelessly joined to the Father in the Trinity be sent into human beings to join us most inwardly to the Trinity! At his Last Supper he invokes again this mystic oneness, praying

> That all of them may be one,
> Father, just as you are in me and I am in you.

I have given them the glory that you gave me,
that they may be one
as we are one,
I in them and you in me, that they be brought to complete unity.

—John 17:20, 22

After His Ascension, Christ fulfills His promise by sending at Pentecost His Holy Spirit, the *Shekinah,* to indwell his disciples. The divine Fire has passed from the Great Temple into the human person, as the disciples become individual bodily temples.

They saw what seemed to be tongues of fire
that separated and came to rest
on each of them.

—Acts 2:2-3

Of this divine indwelling, St. Paul wrote:

Don't you know that
you yourselves are God's Temple,
and that God's spirit
lives in you?

—1 Corinthians 3:16

Soon, this Flame of love scatters from Jerusalem as flamelettes of love, like a wild scattering of red fall leaves. (In Italy, much later, it became the tradition to drop rose leaves from the ceiling of the churches to recall the fiery tongues; hence the Italian designation for Pentecost, *Pascha rosatum.*) Through Christ and in the Holy Spirit, a new Whole was aborning—the unsoundably vast Mystical Body of Christ, whose Soul is the Holy Spirit.

Jeremiah had prophesied a New Covenant—and Jesus Christ inaugurates it, filling women and men interiorly with His Shekinah-Light—emptying His pockets, offering His last coin to each who asks. It reminds us of St. Francis of Assisi's denuding himself and giving away all his possessions on the roads of the world. Christ retains nothing exclusively for Himself but shares the glory of the Father's heaven!

The Mystics Have Seen the Light

Since Pentecost, incorporation by the Light into the Mystical Body is effected in Baptism. The visible displays of the *Shekinah* as seen throughout salvation history since Pentecost are rare today, but not unknown. By certain mystical graces, some still see this fire-like expression of Spirit.

Twelfth-century Rhineland. It is spring, and the late afternoon sun has turned golden a smooth white birch, fresh with new leaves. Sitting beneath it, Hildegaarde von Bingen—artist, healer, and mystic—is writing in her journal:

> In the year 1141 of the Incarnation of Jesus Christ the Son of God...a fiery light, flashing intensely, came from the open vault of heaven and poured through my whole soul. Like a flame that is hot without burning it kindled all my heart and all my breast.... And suddenly I could understand what such books as the...Old and New Testament actually set forth.

Thirteenth-century Italy. One day Francis of Assisi visited his friend Clare (co-foundress of the Order of Poor Ladies) and her nuns, at the Church of St. Damien. At dinner, everyone at the table was so entranced by the beauty of Francis' spiritual conversation that they forgot to eat. As night fell, the convent was strangely illuminated. Seeing it from afar, the people in Assisi believed that St. Damien's was on fire, so they hastened to save the church. But there was no actual fire; instead, the fire was found to be that of divine love.[11]

Sixteenth-century Spain. John of the Cross writes of his experience of the indwelling *Shekinah* in *The Living Flame of Love.*

> The soul feels that this living flame of love
> is vividly communicating to it
> every good, since this divine love

[11] John Deedy, *A Book of Catholic Anecdotes,* (Allen, TX: Thomas More, 1997), p. 50.

> carries all things with it...
> And this is what happens, in an indescribable way,
> at the time this flame of love rises up within the soul.[12]

Seventeenth-century France. You may know him as a mathematical genius, but he was also the recipient of majestic mystical graces, though he kept them secret in his lifetime. A few days after his death, a manservant who was tending to Blaise Pascal's clothes discovered a curious bulge in his coat. He opened the lining and withdrew a folded parchment, written in Pascal's hand. It testified to a mystical illumination—two vivid hours in the divine presence.

> The years of grace 1654....
> From about half past ten in the evening until about half past twelve,
> ....FIRE..............................
> God of Abraham, God of Isaac, God of Jacob,
> not of the philosophers and scholars.
> Certitude, certitude, feeling, joy, peace.
> God of Jesus Christ.
> Thy God will be my God.
> Forgetfulness of the world and of everything, except GOD....
> Joy, joy, joy, tears of joy....[13]

The Mystical Body Unifies Planes of Existence

The Holy Spirit, the everlasting Light, connects all parts of the adorable Mystical Body. This Body, which is the Church, is not only on earth, but is transcosmic, beyond the physical universe. Sings St. Paul—

---

[12] *The Collected Works of St. John of the Cross,* trans. Kieran Kavanaugh and Otilio Rodriguez, (Washington, DC: ICS Publications, 1991), p. 647.

[13] Morris Bishop, *Pascal: The Life of Genius,* (Westport, CT: Greenwood Prager, 1964), p. 173.

> And God placed all things
> under his feet
> and appointed him
> to be head
> over everything for the church,
> which is his body,
> the fullness of him who fills everything
> in every way.
>
> —*Ephesians 1: 22-23*

St. Paul knew well the unwithering connection between Christ and His Body—finding this out first as "Saul," persecutor of the fledgling Christian community, and dedicated to its extermination. On the road to Damascus, to persecute anew, Saul is knocked off his horse by a blinding Light, and hears Christ's voice from everywhere and nowhere: "Saul, Saul, why do you persecute me?" (Acts 9:4).

"Me"? Saul had been persecuting not Jesus Christ, but Christians. There is no difference, Saul learned. "Christians are His members; they are mystically Christ"[14] (Emile Mersch).

This is the Body Vast, a seamless garment of three fibers—

- The "Church in Pilgrimage" on earth.
- The "Church Suffering" of purgatory.
- The "Church Triumphant" of Heaven.

> The members of the Kingdom of God on earth and in the other world sanctified by the redeeming grace of Christ are united in a common supernatural life with the Head of the Church and with one another.[15]
>
> —*Ludwig Ott*

---

[14] Emile Mersch, S.J., *The Theology of the Mystical Body,* trans. Cyril Vollert, S.J., (St. Louis, MO: B. Herder Book Co., 1952), p. 297.

[15] Ludwig Ott, *Fundamentals of Catholic Dogma,* James Canon Bastible, trans. Patrick Lynch, (Rockford, IL: Tan Books and Publishers, 1994), p. 314.

Imagine the earth from space, and see a baptismal Light indwelling every Christian now living, in every land. That is the Church in Pilgrimage—the Church wending its way through time. Now picture all Christians of the past, indwelled by the Spirit from Pentecost onward.

Now all Christians of the future, in this invisible flamelette procession—and all the surprising acts of beauty, truth, and love that our children and our children's children will do in the Savior's Name. But what of our non-Christian brothers and sisters? As they thirst for love and truth in God, they too belong to the Church spiritually. They belong to our visible Church, but by unseen mystic chords. And what of the men and women of prehistory?

> For the souls [in prehistoric times]
> who opened themselves
> to the promptings of his grace,
> Christian by anticipation,
> there was,
> even before Christ,
> a membership in Christ and his Mystical Body,
> Christ's Church.[16]
>
> —*Cardinal Charles Journet*

Having seen the Body Vast on earth, we rise to its second great dimension—the "Church Suffering," which is, generally speaking, the *post mortem* dimension of those who are journeying to fullness in God beyond residual resistance to the Light.[17] "The 'Church' is taken in the wider sense to designate all those redeemed and sanctified by the grace of Christ whether on earth, in Purgatory, or in Heaven. The Church in this wider sense is usually called the Communion of Saints"[18] (Charles Journet).

As noted, if we who do not love generously in this life and so have not been fully purified by love, and yet truly desire God, at death we pass through the balance of our purification, for it is impossible to know the fullness of Love without having been so purified. How long

---

[16] Charles Journet, *The Meaning of Grace,* trans. A.V. Littledale, (New York, NY: P.J. Kenedy & Sons, 1960), p. 83.

[17] For the relationship of purgatory to the dark night of the soul, see Chapter Nine.

[18] Ott, *op cit.*, p. 316.

does this purgation last? Time does not exist beyond death as we know it in this life. Suggesting the relativity of time, the poet Rabindranath Tagore wrote:

> The butterfly counts not months but moments,
> And has time enough.

We see the body of a loved one who has just passed on. In what may be a minute of time to us, she may have been transformed by Love beyond the grave and passed from the Church Suffering to the Church Triumphant. Her journey to heaven will have been aided by the prayers and works of love of Christ's faithful on earth, in an invisible but potent circulation of grace. "There can be no good and virtuous deed performed by individual members of the Mystical Body of Christ which does not through the Communion of Saints, redound also to the welfare of all"[19] (Pius XII).

The *Holism of the Mystical Body* is the intersolidarity of the Church in Pilgrimage, the Church Suffering, and the Church Triumphant in the Mystical Body of Christ, which Soul is the Holy Spirit. The prayers of earth rise to assist souls in purgatory, and to importune aid from the heavenly blessed for the needs of earth. Christ responds to these prayers by lavishing blessings and inspirations; for as the saints have testified to Him, He testifies to their faith by blessing in their name.

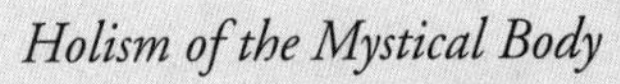

Holism of the Mystical Body *Holism of the Unitive State*

Affinity: The *Holism of the Unitive State* (Chapter Nine)

[19] Ott, *op cit.*, p. 314. The quotation is from Pius XII's encyclical, *Mystici Corporis.*

When a Christian comes into the unitive state, his or her very being becomes an ongoing prayer of petition, importuning God to bless the Church in Pilgrimage and Suffering.

What is heaven? What is the Church Triumphant? It is the Body of Christ in the bliss of the Father's glory, for we are fully transformed into Christ in heaven, as the Son alone knows the Father in the Spirit.

> The city does not need the sun or the moon to shine on it,
> for the glory of God gives it light,
> and the Lamb is its lamp.
>
> —*Revelation 21:23*

This Communion of Saints not only holistically unifies across national, racial, and ethnic boundaries, but also joins worlds, in a nesting of variegated dimensions of reality—earth and purgatory and heaven, the sentient and the material, the seen and the unseen.

> The union of two saints
> who do not know each other
> is far more real and intimate
> than the union of one branch with another
> from the same tree, fed from the same sap;
>
> incomparably more real and intimate
> than the union of people in the same city...
>
> It is from the union of the Mystical Body
> that all other union flows.[20]
>
> —*Jules Monchanin*

Behold the sacred circulation: the inspiration and respiration of the *Christus universus.* The Church is eminently real, true, healing, beautiful, poetic, sense-entrancing, sense-transcending, strong, majestic, sublime—above all, sublime.

---

[20] J.G. Weber, ed. and trans., *In Quest of the Absolute: The Life and Work of Jules Monchanin,* (Kalamazoo, MI: Cistercian Publications, 1977), pp. 113-144.

CHAPTER 15

The Bride of Christ: Cometh She Like a Dancer

"What does matter is that thanks to her, a certain Word has come down to us, not as a memory, not as something that can be called to mind, but as something active and living: 'Your sins are forgiven you.' 'This is my body given for you.'"[1]

—Francois Mauriac

"In the last analysis the effectiveness of the Church can't be measured at all. Its most essential forces—prayer, suffering, faithful obedience... escape all statistical analysis."[2]

—Hans Urs von Balthasar

There have been instances in your life when you turned the page of a book only to find, after a moment's reading, that the page had turned you. This happened to me about fifteen years ago now, soon after opening a library copy of Jacques Maritain's *On the Church of Christ: Her Person and Her Personnel.* I later found out that he had written it as he was approaching ninety, having retired to a life of prayer at a monastery of the Little Brothers of Jesus, after the death of his beloved wife, Raissa, poet and contemplative.

---

[1] Francois Mauriac, *What I Believe,* (New York, NY: Farrar, Straus, 1963), p. 5.

[2] Hans Urs von Balthasar, *Who Is A Christian?,* trans. John Cumming, (New York, NY: Newman Press, 1968), p. 118.

Paging through it as if in a dream, I found the sketch you will find on the next page. It is an icon that brings together two great images of the Church: as Christ's Mystical Body and as His Bride. The sketch produced on the following page was conceptualized by Maritain and drawn by his friend, the artist Jean Hugo. Our reflection on it and on Maritain's rich commentary will deepen our understanding of the metaphysical mystery of the Church.

As with the figure of the Mystical Body, the Bride of Christ is scriptural. The Apostle John writes in the closing lines of *Revelation:* "The Spirit and the bride say, 'Come!'" (Revelation 22:17). The Bride is the Church on earth, eager for her full unity with Christ. St. John also writes:

> I saw the Holy City,
> the new Jerusalem,
> coming down out of heaven from God
> prepared as a bride
> beautifully dressed for her husband.
>
> —*Revelation 21: 2*

Indeed, the original Greek title of *Revelation—Apokalypsis*—is a bridal reference. *Apokalypsis* literally means "unveiling," an allusion to the climactic moment in the wedding festivities of the Jews: the lifting of the bride's veil. *Revelation* is thus a visionary account of the mystic union of Christ and the Church. With John, St. Paul writes:

> Husbands, love your wives,
> just as Christ loved the church
> and gave himself up for her
> to make her holy, cleansing her
> by the washing with water through the word,
> and to present her to
> himself as a radiant church
> without stain or wrinkle
> or any other blemish, but holy and blameless.
>
> —*Ephesians 5:25-27*

An Iconic Representation

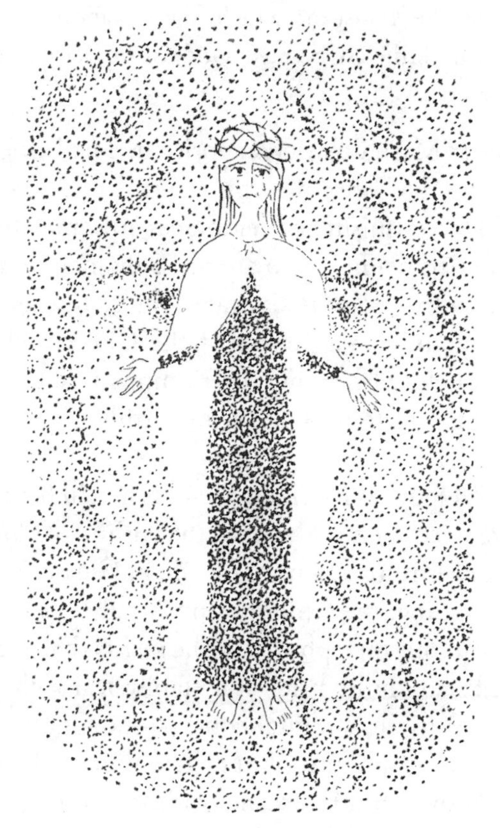

Disclosing its rich symbolism, Maritain says:

> And it is the Church here below, the Church in her state of earthly pilgrimage, which is thus represented. The woman who symbolizes her is crowned with thorns, in order to show that all through the ages and until the end of time she "completes…that which is lacking in the suffering of the Savior."[3]
>
> And her eyes shed tears—she is bathed in tears—which indicates that the immaculate Bride takes upon her, in imitation of Christ, the offenses of her innumerable members, and does penance for them….

---

[3] Colossians 1:24.

> Her feet are bare because she is poor, bloody because of the thorns in the midst of which she advances here on earth, vigorous nevertheless because God assists her and protects her on her way.[4]

Let us ponder Maritain's rich exposition. The Bride of Christ, this mysterious Figure, has been moving forward under our eyes century after century. Her exquisiteness embraces innumerable beings from every epoch, myriad beings "who are not only men, her members here on earth, but also the glorious separated souls, and the holy angels.... For it is a single and same person of the Church who finds herself under the state of glory [the Church Triumphant of heaven], where she sees, and under the state of 'way' or of earthly pilgrimage, where she believes."[5]

Imagine this Figure as Maritain presents her, in her munificent procession since Pentecost, embodying all the faithful of Christ, journeying through all the ages to the plenum of Life in Christ. Maritain has told us something startling: the Church is mystically one unitary "Person." He does not mean this metaphorically, he insists that the whole Church is actually one Person in its strictest metaphysical sense.

She embodies us all, simultaneously—the Church in Pilgrimage, the Church Suffering, and the Church Triumphant. Her personhood is analogous to our own, but transcends ordinary human personality as it involves "a multitude spread out through the whole world and through all ages...."[6]

"The witness of divine things among men, she already inhabits eternity."[7] Please meditate once more on the icon. Again: "her eyes shed tears—she is bathed in tears—which indicates that the immaculate

---

[4] Jacques Maritain, *On the Church of Christ: The Person of the Church and Her Personnel,* trans. Joseph W. Evans, (Notre Dame, IN: University of Notre Dame Press, 1973), pp. 35-36. The icon by Jean Hugo appears on p. 37.

[5] *Ibid.,* p. 33.

[6] *Ibid.,* p. 175.

[7] Henri de Lubac, *The Church: Paradox and Mystery,* (Staten Island, NY: Alba House, 1969), p. 53.

Bride takes upon her, in imitation of Christ, the offenses of her innumerable members, and does penance for them...."[8]

In other words, to the extent that Christians do evil in the world, they do not act from the Person of the Church, *but separate from her.* Her response is to do penance for the sins of her members, to restore them. That is to say, by various acts of love and self-sacrifice, we members of the Church do works of sacrifice and love for each other in the Church and beyond it, to draw healing grace upon the whole commonwealth of Christ.

The Frontiers of the Church Are in the Heart

The image of the Bride raises an important question. Paul calls the Church "without stain or wrinkle or any other blemish, but holy and blameless" (Ephesians 5:27). This affirmation ought to astonish us, for Paul is insisting that the Bride of Christ, the Church, is sinless in its inmost character. Obviously, he cannot be asserting that the members of the Church are sinless, nor that the institutional element of the Church is unflawed (as he and we know too well). What is Paul's meaning then?

Cardinal Charles Journet, a colleague and friend of Maritain, wrote with deep insight on Paul's saying. In Journet's view, though the Church of earth is not without sinners, she is without sin. The pied moral composition of the Church's members does not essentially define the Church; for its inmost soul, the Holy Spirit, is transcendent to our imperfections. Journet wrote:

> The sins of her members
> are not to be identified with the Church,
> or the imperfections of Christians with Christianity.
> It is not these that constitute her,
> or make her visible;
> but rather her true body,
> always illuminated by her soul—

[8] Maritain, *op cit.*, p. 35.

> though the intensity of the illumination
> may vary from one age to another.[9]

A certain phrase from Journet is particularly clarifying: *the true borders or frontiers of the Church.*

> Her true and precise borders circumscribe
> only that which is good and pure
> in her members, both the just and sinners,
> leaving out all that is impure, even in the just;
>
> it is in our own behavior, in our own lives,
> in our own hearts that the Church and the world,
> Christ and Belial, light and darkness,
> confront one another.[10]

This is Journet's stunning but compelling conclusion: "The Church divides in us the good from the evil. She keeps the good and rejects the evil. Her borderlines pass through our hearts."[11] Maritain found Journet's articulation especially helpful:

> To the extent that a man
> who has been baptized in the Church sins,
> to that extent he slips away from the life of the Church....
> To the extent that he lives by grace and by charity,
> he lives also by the life of the Whole
> of which he is a member...[12]

Whenever we act in goodness, you and I, we are acting as instruments of the Church, of Christ's Mystical Body, even unawares; and when we act hurtfully, we separate ourselves in that instant from her

---

[9] Charles Journet, *The Church of the Word Incarnate: An Essay in Speculative Theology,* vol. 1: *The Apostolic Hierarchy,* trans. A.H.C. Downes, (New York, NY: Sheed and Ward, 1955), p. xxviii.

[10] Maritain, *The Peasant of the Garrone, op cit.*, p. 188.

[11] Charles Journet, *Theologie de l'Eglise,* (Paris: Deslce'e De Brouwer, 1958), p. 236.

[12] Maritain, *On the Church of Christ, op cit.*, p. 14.

Soul, the Holy Spirit—the Church is not acting through us. This goes for all, lay and clergy.

In other words, in any good we may do, it is the Mystical Bride that is truly but invisibly acting through us. For her Spirit is Christ's Spirit, and Christ said, "Apart from me you can do nothing" (John 15:5). And anything we do apart from love and truth is done apart from the Church—even when done in Her name.

> But when men act without charity,
> even if the visible members of the Church,
> they withdraw from her life,
> they strip themselves of the life of the Church.
> And their actions are no stain on the Church,
> on the kingdom of God,
> because those actions are not hers.[13]
>
> —*Cardinal Charles Journet*

Our separations from Love do not corrupt Love—-they corrupt us.

Framed in this way, Paul's saying that the Church is "without stain or wrinkle" appeals to our intuition that the Church is a magnificent Mystery, as profound as the Incarnation, as Maritain put it earlier. It must be noted that Maritain and Journet were acutely aware of failures and errors of the institutional Church, and both worked for renewal. (Maritain presents an illuminating historical review of such scandals and errors in *On the Church of Christ.*)[14] Maritain and Journet insisted that a clear understanding of the Church's stainless essence should make us more zealous for the Church's institutional virtue, not less.

Francis of Assisi, kneeling in a deteriorating chapel, heard the voice of Christ come mystically from the crucifix: "Francis, go and repair my house which, as you see, is falling into ruin." At first he thought the command was to repair this dilapidated chapel, but later came to realize the deeper significance of it: to live and preach the gospel in imitation of the Lord, to renew the Church.

---

[13] Maritain, *The Peasant of the Garrone, op cit.*, p. 189.

[14] Maritain, *On the Church of Christ, op cit.* See in particular Chapters 11-14.

Zeal for the House of the Lord also inspired St. Catherine of Siena, a fourteenth-century mystic, to help free the Church of forces which sought to compromise its holy work. She was a decisive force to restore the papacy to Rome after political pressure had forced the pope to move the Holy See to Avignon, France. In a letter written to Pope Gregory XI, she urged:

> Answer the summons of God! Who is calling you to come, hold, and possess the place of the glorious shepherd St. Peter, whose vicar you are. Lift up the banner of the holy Cross. Come, that you may reform the Church with good shepherds.... But take heart, and come Father! Do not make the servants of God wait, who are afflicted with longing. I seem to die in pain, seeing God thus outraged![15]

And to Rome the papacy soon returned.

St. Hildegaarde von Bingen wrote: "The Church has yet to come to the...stature she will have, but with diligence and industry, she incessantly hastens toward her full beauty."

Grace and Truth

Christ foresaw that wheat and weeds would grow alongside one another in the Church (Matthew 13:24-30). The absurdity of the refusal to join a church because of the imperfections of its members was suggested by Fr. Andrew Greeley: "Search for the perfect church if you will; when you find it, join it, and realize that on that day it becomes something less than perfect."[16]

Maritain and Journet would add that imperfections in Church members and even scandals involving her clergy do not diminish the purity of gifts that Christ perennially and inexorably causes to flow through the Church. "I will build my church and the gates of Hades

---

[15] Evelyn Underhill, *Mystics of the Church,* (Harrisburg, PA: Morehouse Publishing, 1975), pp. 158-159.

[16] William F. Buckley, *Nearer My God to Thee,* (New York, NY: Harcourt Brace & Company, 1997), p. 254.

will not overcome it" (Matthew 16:18). Robert Hughes Benson states well the inviolability of Christ's gifts:

> Sins of omission and commission on the part of Catholics, stupidities, misunderstandings, apostasies, ignoble and unfashionable circumstances, countless failures, tragedies, comedies, even screaming farces—these simply do not touch the matter at all.[17]
>
> —*Robert Hughes Benson*

They do not—cannot—spoil the two high gifts Christ ever transmits through the Church: His revelation and transforming grace.

> For the law was given through Moses;
> grace and truth came through Jesus Christ.
>
> —*John 1:17*

The synergy of grace and truth remind us of the principle of companion planting—the sowing of two or more kinds of plants close together for a robust growth. Plants that do well in shade thrive in the company of taller plants; other plant-pairs share soil nutrients well. Native American lore says that sweet corn, climbing beans, and squash complement the growing-power of each. Without guiding truth, grace is a flowering vine without a trellis. Without transformative grace, truth is the roar of an ocean in a conch shell.

Truth is a participation in Christ's glance; grace is the Father-going footfalls of Christ's stride. The Church extends these gifts through time. Christ sings the Body electric with truth and grace, from age to age.

The Holism of the Seven Sacraments

Grace is God's life in us, which He communicates to transform the soul ever more into Christ. Grace is "the divinization flowing from Christ to the whole body of Christ"[18] (Emile Mersch).

---

[17] Robert Hughes Benson, *The Mystical Body and Its Head,* (New York, NY: Sheed and Ward, 1959), pp. 33-34 .

[18] Emile Mersch, S.J., *The Theology of the Mystical Body,* trans. Cyril Vollert, S.J., (St. Louis, MO: B. Herder Book Co., 1952), p. 595.

Though we cannot say where grace is not (as God communicates grace where and when He will), we can say where grace is: it is surely available through the seven Sacraments. "To relate to the Head, there must be single body. We are the Body of the Church through our acceptance of its form, that is, the sacraments which are its arteries"[19] (Paul Claudel). By these Sacraments, Christ recapitulates His Life in us.

Though two thousand years have passed since the historical Christ ministered in Judea, He miraculously continues as the true Minister of the Sacraments, every day in every land. Pope Pius XII wrote in his encyclical *Mystici Corporis* (1943): "And when the Church administers the Sacraments with external rite, it is He who produces their effect in the soul.... It is indeed He who baptizes through the Church, He who teaches, governs, absolves, binds, offers, and makes sacrifices."[20]

> If I remain in the Church, it is because she is a vital milieu. She is the paradise where the energies of the Holy Spirit are at work. This is where the great rivers of living waters wash me of my stains, where the tree of life nourishes me with its fruit.[21]
>
> —*Jean Danielou*

The Seven Sacraments are:

Baptism: Please recall that the Trinity was vividly revealed in Christ's own baptism (Matthew 3:16-17). In all baptisms since, the Trinity comes to indwell the soul of the believer, making the soul a heaven of the Trinity. At Baptism, Christ imbues His own winged Holy Spirit into the soul—like an eagle giving the power of its broad wings to a lady bug, to mount the highest peaks of prayer, of life in God.

---

[19] Paul Claudel, *I Believe in God,* Agnes du Sarment, ed., trans. Helen Weaver, (USA: Holt, Rinehart and Winston, 1963), p. 8.

[20] Ludwig Ott, *Fundamentals of Catholic Dogma,* James Canon Bastible, trans. Patrick Lynch, (Rockford, IL: Tan Books and Publishers, 1994), p. 341.

[21] http://www.praiseofglory.com/jdanielou.htm

Confirmation: At Pentecost, Christ sent His Spirit into the Apostles to strengthen and enlighten them. He does this still today, by the rite of Confirmation. "I can do everything through him who gives me strength" (Philippians 4:13).

Eucharist: Christ comes as the Blessed Sacrament to enact His most intimate and efficacious union with the soul. "God cannot love us more than by giving us His divine life"[22] (Roger Hasseveldt).

Reconciliation: Christ forgives all penitent hearts, granting a purely new start. "Let's have a feast and celebrate! For this son of mine was dead and is alive again; he was lost and now is found" (Luke 15:23-24).

Catholics confess their sins to priests because Christ authorized the Apostles, the first priests of His Church, to forgive sins in his Name. The Risen Christ said to them, "Peace be with you! As the Father has sent me, I am sending you.... Receive the Holy Spirit. If you forgive anyone his sins, they are forgiven; if you do not forgive them, they are not forgiven" (John 20:21-23). It is fitting that priests hear confessions as our sin is not only against God, but against each other, and it is good that we humble ourselves before another as a stand-in for all.

Marriage: A poet, visiting the house of a friend, was handed a special diamond-point pencil, and asked to inscribe a poem on a window pane. An apt metaphor for marriage: each partner writes her unique poem, his unique poem, indelibly on the glass of the other's heart. Christ's grace in this Sacrament enchants marriage with special graces of empathy, patience, joy, and love: "the two will become one flesh" (Matthew 19:5).

---

[22] Roger Hasseveldt, *The Church: A Divine Mystery,* trans. William Storey, (Notre Dame, IN: Fides Publishers, 1964), p. 55.

Ordination to the Priesthood:

Christ is the "High Priest" who sacrifices—Himself. Christ would recapitulate in us all the Mystery of His Priestly Sacrifice: the grace to go beyond self in Him.

Anointing of the Sick:

Christ "astonished fever with His snowlike touch and it retreated"[23] (Kahlil Gibran). Yet Christ's healing is sometimes subtler, touching the finest energies of the soul.

In summary, the Church's sacramental regime is eminently holistic. A sacrament for the newly born, and one for the dying; a Sacrament for union with God, another for the strength to persist in love, and yet another for healing from sin's alienation; a Sacrament for the consecrated single life, and one for marriage.

> The Christian
> is the result
> of the sacraments,
> and he carries their emanations with him....
>
> The water has given us birth,
> the oil has permeated and straightened us,
> the blood has purified us,
> the bread has sustained us,
> the wine has illuminated us,
> Holy Orders and Marriage have crept into our very bones.[24]
>
> —*Paul Claudel*

Francois Mauriac, a twentieth-century French novelist, was sometimes appalled by the institutional flaws of the Church, yet he also knew that the Bride of Christ has for twenty centuries irrepressibly communicated divine grace and truth. In spite of "everything which in

[23] Kahlil Gibran, *Jesus the Son of Man: His Words and His Deeds as Told and Recorded by Those Who Knew Him,* (New York, NY: Alfred A. Knopf, 1995), p. 22.

[24] Claudel, op cit., p. 183.

the visible Church shocks and irritates and scandalizes me...once again, I repeat what I believe: this organization safeguarded everything."[25]

The *Holism of the Sacraments* spiritually invigorates vital dimensions of human life, and ultimately transfigures us into Christ.

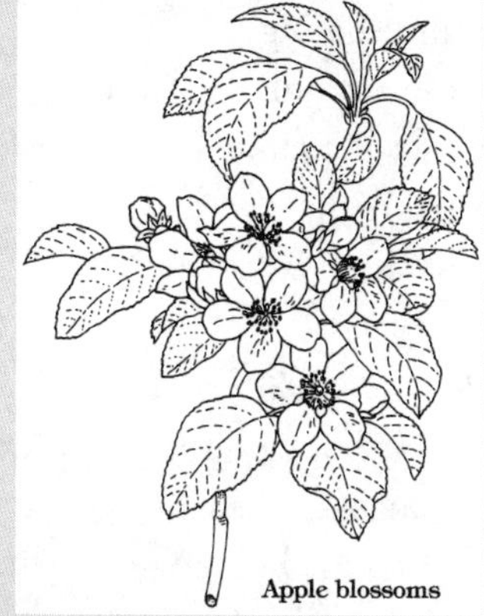

Holism of the Sacraments *Holism of the Mind-Body Partnership*

Affinity: The *Holism of the Mind-Body Partnership* (Chapter Eight)

Sacramental grace is active in us to the degree we cooperate with it. An artful knowledge of the interaction of mind, body, and spirit can help us be true to Love moment by moment, and so receptive to the transforming action of sacramental grace.

Another holism melds with the *Holism of the Sacraments*—that of the *Holism of Woman and Man.*

It is no accident that C.S. Lewis and G.K. Chesterton, who wrote with penetrating depth on Christianity, were fascinated by the distinctive character of the sexes, and wrote festively on love. How could it be otherwise, as love is the watchword of Christianity? Whatever celebrates delight and depth in love belongs to Christianity. Lewis and Chesterton join in the enmirthed song of Pablo Neruda in "Ode to a Couple":

> My queen, how beautiful
> to follow the path of

---

[25] Mauriac, *op cit.*, p. 10.

your small footprints,
how beautiful to see
your eyes
everywhere I look,
how beautiful your face
greeting each new day,
and sinking
every night
into the same
fragment
of shadow.[26]

The *Holism of Woman and Man,* especially in marriage, shows us in our spouse ways to be human that our limitations before prevented us from recognizing—and so brings us closer to God, who affirms the whole human person, woman and man.

Holism of Woman and Man

Holism of the Unitive State

Affinity: the *Holism of the Unitive State* (Chapter Ten)

As the finest cellos are a blend of three woods, so true marriage is a resonance of woman and man and God. "It is not surprising that in the New Testament the first miracle is set at a wedding, in Cana…All marriages take place at Cana, for in all marriages the necessary raw material of

[26] Pablo Neruda, *Selected Odes,* trans. and selected by Margaret Sayers Peden, (Berkeley, CA: University of California Press, 1990), p. 107. Used with permission.

life (water) is changed into a sparkling, tingling, inspiriting element of the soul (wine)"[27] (Thomas Moore).

Enamoured Circlings

Let us step back from our immediate study, to consider how a few of the "inter-animated and enamoured circlings" (C.S. Lewis) of our study to this point are woven together in a holoarchical unity flowing from the Trinity. (This is illustrated in terms of the Great Wreath of Being on the following page, though only certain of the Holisms are depicted to simplify the drawing.)

The Trinity, the *Holism of the Absolute,* exists as a timeless communication of Love before all things. The Father creates all things through the Son, the uncreated One in whom infinitely variegated creation exists *(Holism of the Christ-Logos).* By sufficiently complexifying matter, God creates humanity. Created in God's image, the human person innately aspires to light and love.

As God cares for all He has created, He sends His Spirit to awaken divine intuitions among peoples of diverse lands *(Holism of the World Religions).* In due season, the eternal Son incarnated as Jesus Christ to definitively reveal the Way to the Father *(Holism of the Incarnation).* At Pentecost, the Son and the Father send the Spirit into world to unite the faithful into the *Mystical Body of Christ,* to indwell them as Light and so recapitulate in them *Christ's Mysteries.* These Mysteries transform us to human maturity in this life and finally to the heaven of the Trinity.

Our journey is integrally supported by the *Holism of the Sacraments,* which imparts transforming graces. These graces are active in us according to our love of God. The *Holism of the Mind-Body* supplies us with an artful self-knowledge that supports that love.

---

[27] Thomas Moore, *Soul Mates: Honoring the Mysteries of Love and Relationship,* (New York, NY: HarperCollins Publisher, 1994), p. 68.

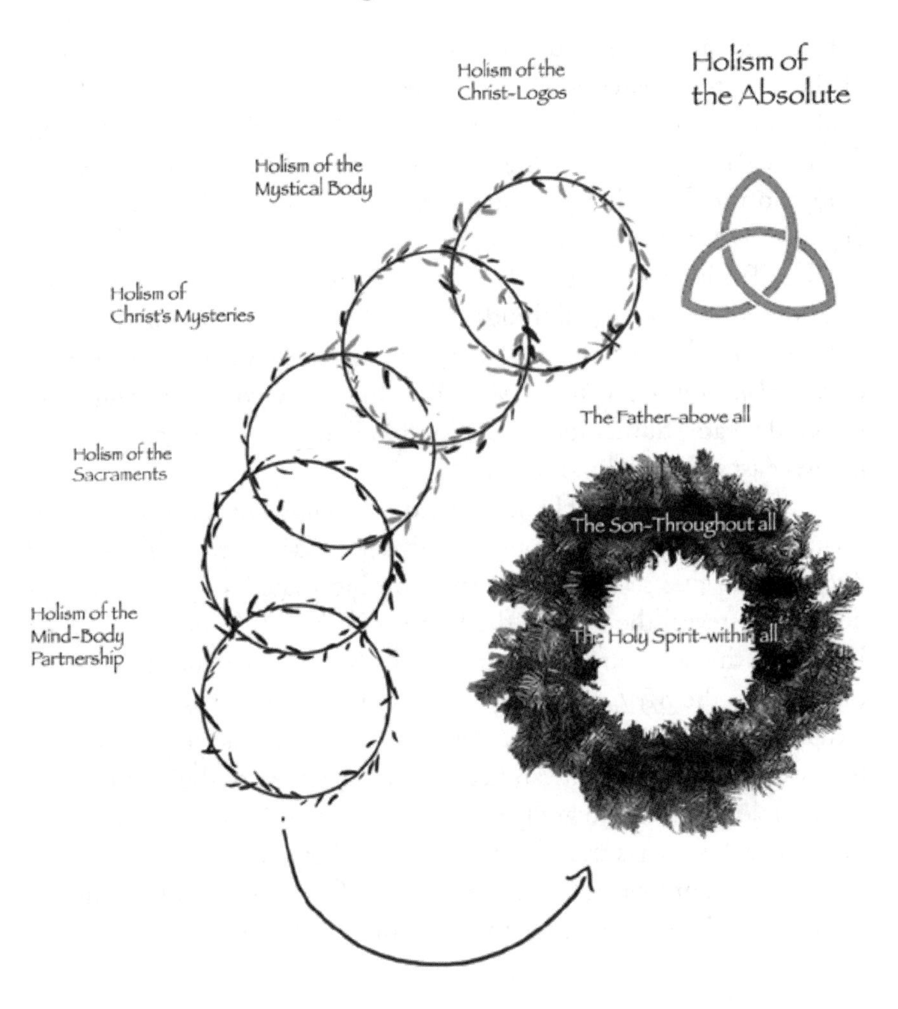
The Holoarchy of the Great Wreath of Being
Holism of the Christ-Logos
Holism of the Absolute
Holism of the Mystical Body
Holism of Christ's Mysteries
Holism of the Sacraments
Holism of the Mind-Body Partnership
The Father-above all
The Son-Throughout all
The Holy Spirit-within all

The Historical Lineage of the Church

To return to our reflections on the Mystical Body: It is spring and you have been waiting for the opening of the rose buds on a favorite bush in your back yard. It produces what are called "Old Garden" roses—some varieties of which, you find out, date back to the Roman Empire, when they were especially praised for their loveliness and perfume. You've had this bush in your yard for fifteen years, and every year it blossoms anew—as even today. For several of its buds have opened, and their tenderest yellow is breathing in the sun.

That bush grew from an organic cutting from another, and that from another, and that from another—back to one from which a Roman maiden plucked a blossom for her hair. Like that renewed ancient rose bush, the Catholic Church's lineage has an organic, unbroken history—for twenty centuries. By this Apostolic succession, Christ preserved the unity of His transmittable Life, grace, and truth.

> I [the Church] am the abiding Personage of the centuries.... I am never out of date, because the dateless; never out of time, because the timeless.... I am One, because I have the same Soul I had in the beginning: I am Holy, because the Soul is the Spirit of Holiness; I am Apostolic, because my origin is identical with Nazareth, Galilee, and Jerusalem.... I shall be crucified as I was on Calvary, but I shall rise again, and finally when time shall be no more, and I shall have grown to my full stature, then shall I be taken into heaven as the bride of my Head, Christ, where the celestial nuptials shall be celebrated, and God shall be all in all, because His Spirit is Love and Love is heaven.[28]

In the earliest letters of the Church (written at the time the New Testament was in formation), Christians called her the *Katholika*—the Catholic or "universal" Church. The earliest surviving record of this name is found in a letter of St. Ignatius of Antioch written in 95 A.D. He was of the first generation of Christian bishops after the Apostles,

---

[28] Leslie Rumble, M.S.C., *Radio Replies: 1588 Questions and Answers on Catholicism and Protestantism,* vol. 1, edited in collaboration with Charles Mortimer Carty, (Rockford, IL: Tan Books and Publishers, 1979), p. xi. Quote from F. Sheen.

a protégé of the Apostle John himself, and one of the first martyrs of the Church, dismembered by beasts in the Amphitheater during the public games.

Ignatius' designation of the Church as "catholic" occurs in his *Letter to the Smyrnaeans:* " Wherever the bishop shall appear, there let the multitude also be; even as wherever Jesus Christ is, there is the catholic church."[29] Soon the adjective "catholic" was regularly used to indicate the true, united Church that had been founded by the Apostles (rather than the pseudo-Christian gnostic groups that rejected the original deposit of faith to go their own way).[30]

Another first-century bishop of the *Katholika,* Clement of Rome, described how the bishops received their authority: "They [the Apostles] appointed such men, and made provision that, when these should die, other approved men would take up their ministry."[31]

After the Apostles, bishops succeeded bishops, in a lineage that has continued for twenty centuries. There are few analogues for such continuity in history. Consider the American presidency, which colonial beginnings appear primitive to us. It stretches back a little more than two hundred years. But the line of the Catholic bishops stretches back ten times that, in a collegial unity which preserves the oneness which Christ willed for the Church: "I pray that...all of them may be one, Father, just as you are in me and I am in you" (John 17:20-21).

The Church is One, for Christ is One. It is Visible, for He was historically Incarnate. It is universal teacher, for Christ is communicative Truth. It is giver of soul-quickening Sacraments, as His touch ever transforms. "The Church is the continuation of Christ"[32] (Emile Mersch).

---

[29] Mike Aquilina, *The Fathers of the Church: An Introduction to the First Christian Teachers,* (Huntington, IN: Our Sunday Visitor Publishing, 1999), p. 63.

[30] Philip Jenkins, *Hidden Gospels: How the Search for Jesus Lost Its Way,* (New York, NY: Oxford University Press, 2002), pp. 118-123.

[31] Donald W. Wuerl, *Fathers of the Church,* (Boston, MA: St. Paul Editions, 1982), p. 11.

[32] Mersch, *op cit.*, p. 22.

A Many-Colored Tunic

How could something as mysterious and evocative as the Church not excite poetic intuition? The Church Fathers turned ingenious figures to its beauty. They took delight, for example, in comparing it to the patriarch Joseph's coat of many colors—the *polymita tunica,* in their Latin. Christ, they held, stimulates each land and people to praise God according to its distinctive gifts. "A particular type of Christian spirituality has to evolve out of the particular genius of the people of each country"[33] (Jules Monchanin).

We have seen that, from the philosophical genius of Greece, the earliest Church drew the word *Logos,* adapting this Stoic principle—indeed, revolutionizing it—to express in John 1:1, the Cosmic Christ. On the level of custom, too, this holistic principle has been at work. When Northern European tribes converted to Christianity, they retained their pre-Christian practice of decorating evergreen trees with nuts, candles, and fruit to represent the moon, sun, and stars. The Church came to bless this custom, as a true intuition: just as the evergreen is ever-verdant, so God is eternal. Hence the Christmas tree.

Architecture also evinces Catholicism's coat-of-many-colors principle. In St. Peter's Basilica, the Blessed Sacrament Chapel is the principal place of prayer and devotion—its tabernacle is ornamented with bronze angels kneeling in adoration, the work of Renaissance master Bernini ("St. Teresa in Ecstasy"). An ocean away, at St. Joseph's Teepee Church in Alberta, Canada, located in the heart of the Little Red River Cree Nation, we find quite a different tabernacle: a miniature teepee.

"The Church spans the centuries somewhat as it spans the nations and continents"[34] (Cardinal Avery Dulles). The living genius of the saints is also an international *polymita tunica.* The merest sample:

---

[33] J.G. Weber, ed. and trans., *In Quest of the Absolute: The Life and Work of Jules Monchanin,* (Kalamazoo, MI: Cistercian Publications, 1977), p. 76.

[34] Avery Dulles, S.J., *The Catholicity of the Church,* (New York, NY: Oxford University Press, 1985), p. 88.

THE CHRISTUS UNIVERSUS
St. Paul, Israel
St. John Chrysostom, Syria
St. Francis, Italy
St. Francis Zhang Rong, China
St. Augustine, Africa
St. Teresa of Avila, Spain
St. Joan of Ark, France
St. Teresa of Calcutta, Bulgaria
St. Hildegaarde von Bingen, Germany
St. Juan Diego, Mexico
Blessed Julian of Norwich, England

But beyond these, the truly impressive diversity-in-unity of the Church is the diversity of gifts now available to the whole Body in the communion of saints:

> All creation, visible and invisible, all history,
> past, present, and future, all nature,
> all the wealth of the saints compounded by grace,
> all this is at our command, all this is our extended self
> and our wondrous equipment.
>
> All the saints, all the Angels, are ours.
> We can avail ourselves of the mind of St. Thomas,
> the arm of St. Michael, and the heart of St. Joan
> or St. Catherine of Siena,
> and of all the hidden resources
> which spring into effervescent life at our touch.
> Such is this mother by whom,
> through Baptism, we have received a second birth.[35]
>
> —*Paul Claudel*

The Universal Teacher

We have heard the spiritual truism, "Those who know do not speak, and those who speak do not know." There is indeed some truth in

---

[35] Claudel, *op cit.*, p. 181.

it—but it is thoroughly misleading if taken to mean that nothing can be truly said of God. If God is Love, and Love is communicative, why would Love stay silent?

God has not remained silent, but in Christ came to us to communicate in words and deeds illuminating and heartening tidings, including God's love for us, our destiny in Him, and our Way home. Even on the night of his birth, an angel sang to shepherds in lonely fields: "Do not be afraid. I bring you good news of great joy that will be for all the people" (Luke 2:10).

> How could anyone ever suppose that in coming to our earth He would forbear to impart knowledge, to reveal? He who gives Himself is the Word; how could we imagine that He would remain silent? Jesus is the Word of God made man and dwelling among men. Should we not say that, in His person, He is the Word of God addressed to the human race?[36]
>
> —*Emile Mersch*

Fragrant herbs can be tightly sealed in a jar, and the honeyed smoke of incense can be snuffed in sand. But the wind bearing the flowers of spring cannot be halted, nor Love's speech when it would speak.

"I have much more to say to you" (John 16:12). Truth did not get passed from generation to generation like a rock along workers in a quarry, but multiplied as do stars as the night deepens.

How was His Word passed on? His recorded word was the contraband of martyrs. Later on it was copied by monks, as the lake copies the sun, clouds, and birds which overfly it. His Word has always been an ocean for the mystics, who like waves carry bright ornaments from the deepest caverns of the sea, bringing them to shore for our wonder, the mystics themselves slipping beneath the sand.

The early Fathers wove the fine grasses of revelation into the Creed, a nest for the Church, hatchlings of the Absolute. Christ gave the Church His words and the way to unfold them. He promised the Apostles at the Last Supper to send a Spirit-Teacher, who would not

---

[36] Mersch, *op cit.*, p. 381.

leave the Church directionless—a Spirit to "guide you into all truth" (John 16:13). An event occurred before the Apostles' passing that put this promise to a test; it would establish the Church's pattern of enlightenment for twenty centuries to come.

Chapter Fifteen of *Acts* describes an assembly of the Apostles and elders who had come together to face the first doctrinal crisis in the Church. Some Jewish Christians were insisting that Greek Christians must also practice Jewish laws—hundreds of regulations, including male circumcision and kosher food laws.

The Greeks thought this ridiculous. They maintained that Jewish laws were non-binding on Christians. Freedom in Christ consisted essentially in loving God and neighbor—did not Jesus say as much? (Matthew 22:37-39).

Imagine a flute player piping his love for his beloved through precisely structured flute-holes on a strict four-beat rhythm—but then, overcome by the spirit of love, throws down his flute and sings his love full-throated and free. Similarly, these Greeks held that the rigid Torah law binding on Jews was no longer the instrument of the Spirit—and that their full-throated love for the Beloved sufficed to please Him.

To decide the matter, the Apostles and elders held a council in Jerusalem. (One wonders if their first questions to one another at the gathering were exasperated exclamations, "Did *you* ever ask Jesus about this?—because I didn't!").

They discussed, debated, meditated, and prayed. For they knew their prayer for guidance would be answered, as the Lord had said: "I will not leave you orphans.... When the Spirit comes He will guide you in all truth."

Finally, they had their answer. In sending word of it to the Church near and far, they said that their solution "seemed good to the Holy Spirit and to us" (Acts 15:28).

This decision is astonishing, especially in how it occurred. The Apostles were saying that, in Christ's absence, His voice would continue to be heard in the Councils. The Councils could speak in the Spirit's name ("it seemed good to the Holy Spirit") to perennially guide the Church. It was not only a charism of illumination but conciliation, an indispensable support of unity when theological division threatens the unity of the visible Church of Christ.

Certainly the Holy Spirit continually gives insight to individual Christians; but the Spirit has also guided the councils of the Church for twenty centuries (twenty-one ecumenical Councils to date). The Spirit has inspired these Councils to proclaim sublimities such as the Tri-Personal unity of God, the Blessed Virgin as *Theotokos* ("God-Bearer"), and the Real Presence of Christ as Eucharist. The Councils also established the official canon of the New Testament, elaborated seven Sacraments, discerned the reality of purgatory, proclaimed heaven to be a divinized participation in the Trinity, and revealed that non-Christians of goodwill are saved by Christ. All of these truths are lofty and related, like a sunlit conference of tree tops.

The Biblical Origins of the Papacy

The oneness of the Church suggested in the unity of the bishops is further expressed in the papacy—the pope is to be a sign of the unity of the Mystical Body. The papacy is thus a vivid holistic emblem.

The papal office is foreshadowed in Hebrew history, in the traditional relation of king to prime minister. The king of Israel was assisted by a prime minister in charge of the daily administration of the kingdom. A crisis during the reign of King Hezekiah involving his prime minister would have rich consequences beyond his time.

Hezekiah was to name a new prime minister—the trustworthy Eliakim.

> I will place the key of the House of David
> on his shoulder;
> when he opens, no one shall shut,
> when he shuts, no one shall open.
>
> —*Isaiah 22:20-22*

Notice the form of this announcement—the king gives "keys" to the prime minister. In the Hebrew idiom, "keys" signified the power to adjudicate the law of Israel. Notice the power to "open and shut" conferred on Eliakim—an allusion to the authority conferred on the prime minister, including his power to make laws (as Professor Scott Hahn has adeptly explained). Now compare the form and content of those words to the form and content of Jesus' speech to Peter, centuries later:

> I will give you the keys to the kingdom of heaven.
> Whatever you bind on earth
> shall be bound in heaven;
> and whatever you loose on earth
> will be loosed in heaven.
>
> —*Matthew 16:18-19*

Jesus' words are formulaic, drawing on idioms Hebrews of his time would know: the "keys" and the "binding and loosing" both signify the installation of a prime minister. Christ is the "King of Kings" (Revelation 19:16) selecting Peter as his prime minister. Since the office of the prime minister was dynastic in the House of David, a reasonable inference is that Christ is not only appointing one prime minister, but establishing a dynastic office that was to accompany the Church through all time. As Peter was the leader of the Church at Rome, the successors of Peter—the popes—are bishops of Rome. The primacy of the bishop of Rome is that of first among equals, his fellow bishops. Writes Cardinal Avery Dulles: "The collegiality mode of the papacy…requires the pope to be in vital relationship with the whole body of bishops and to be responsive to their pastoral concerns."[37]

"The primacy is given to Peter," said St. Basil, "that the unity of the Church may be proclaimed." This unity is not only symbolically profound, but has enormous practical consequences. If the Church lacked the office of the papacy, there would be no central figure to initiate the meeting of an ecumenical council of bishops. The Church has gathered many Councils on the summons of popes, to address new challenges of each age and to deepen the Church's penetration of the endless riches of Christ. Meeting in the grace of the Spirit, these Councils are informed by a *Holism of Knowledge.* They are enriched by the

---

[37] Avery Dulles, S.J., *The Catholicity of the Church,* (New York, NY: Oxford University Press, 1985), p. 143.

whole sacred deposit of the faith (including the mystical theology of the saints), are facilitated by the insight of their lay and religious contemporaries, and are enfolded in the prayers of the whole Church.

The Papal Office Is Inundated with Graces

A "servant of the servants of God"—that is how Gregory the Great regarded his office, articulating its ideal for the ages. Yes, there have been cardinals who have cagily schemed for election to the papacy; but most who have been elected did not hanker for it, but reluctantly assumed it, feeling unworthy. "I am made to tremble and I fear," said John XXIII, when he was told of his election to succeed Pius XII. (On a lighter note: "If someone had told me I would be pope one day, I would have studied harder," said Pope John I.)

In the sixth century, the monk Gregory was summoned to Rome, as he had been elevated to the papacy. But he grieved on leaving the contemplative precincts of the monastery to assume the elaborate responsibilities of his new position. He would write:

> I recall with sadness what I was not long ago in the monastery, how I grew in contemplation to rise over all that changes and decomposes, my only thoughts those of the enduring gifts of heaven...I heave a sigh, and am as a man who stares with longing at the shore he has departed.[38]

That is why at every Mass Catholics pray for the Pope, knowing the weight of responsibility he bears as the pastor of a billion Christians. The burdens of the papacy have been onerous from its start. Most of the earliest bishops of Rome were martyred, as they adamantly refused to deny Christ and burn a bit of incense to worship the Roman Emperor as a god.

Christ continues to assist the papacy with high graces that, if not resisted, supernaturally enlighten popes to guide the Church well. Yet these graces can be resisted, at least to a point. Rascally popes there

---

[38] Brandon Toropov, *The Popes and the Papacy,* (Indianapolis, IN: Alpha Books, 2002), p. 264.

have been and worse. But Christ has been true to His promise: "I am with you always, to the very end of the age " (Matthew 28:20). By His grace no pope has corrupted the doctrines of the Church, and many have enriched it, as witness in our time the theological contributions of John Paul the Great.[39]

Still, popes may err in private theological opinions (which do not enter the deposit of faith as essential doctrine.) John Henry Cardinal Newman, author of the influential *Essay on the Development of Christian Doctrine,* expressed this distinction well, in an offhand remark he made when asked to toast the Pope: "I shall drink to the Pope, if you please; still, to Conscience first, and to the Pope afterwards."[40]

The charism of the papacy partakes of mystery, but shouldn't it? Since the innermost character of the Bride is mystical, why should this office be exempt from mystical graces? We do not find a feather of a sparrow in the side of a swan. Scheeben summarizes this point in *The Mysteries of Christianity:*

> Why should He not bring the whole flock together in faith and love from that point [of the papacy], and through it impart unity and stability to the structure? Such union of the Holy Spirit with the head of the Church would be a tremendous wonder; but it ought to be precisely that.[41]

---

[39] George Weigel, *Witness to Hope: The Biography of Pope John Paul II,* (New York, NY: Harpercollins, 1999).

[40] John Deedy, *A Book of Catholic Anecdotes,* (Allen, TX: Thomas More, 1997), p. 183.

[41] Matthias Joseph Scheeben, *Mysteries of Christianity,* trans. Cyril Vollert, S. J., (St. Louis, MO: B. Herder Book Co., 1964), p. 555.

CHAPTER 16

How the Trinity Is the Secret Axis of All Religions

"Whether given by anticipation before Christ,
or by derivation after Christ,
whether transmitted by contact or at a distance,
after death grace will be fully developed,
beatifying, transfiguring.
All the differences, prevailing in the present world,
will be swept away."[1]
—Cardinal Charles Journet

At the opening of an art exhibit, a jeweler, an optometrist, and an art critic are having cocktails and chatting. The discussion touches on religion.

"Certainly, all religions are essentially the same," says the jeweler.

"Yes, Jesus, Buddha, Confucius, Socrates—they all taught the same doctrine," adds the optometrist.

"One can see an undergirding commonality in sacred symbolism which speaks of their identical realizations of God," says the art critic.

"Excuse me," says a guest, sidling up to the optometrist. "May I borrow your glasses? I wanted to read the label on the bottle of the great Chablis the gallery is serving tonight to honor our fine Impressionist."

"Sorry, these aren't reading glasses," says the optometrist.

---

[1] Charles Journet, *The Meaning of Grace,* trans. A.V. Littledale, (New York, NY: P.J. Kenedy & Sons, 1960), p. 126.

"And it's a Merlot, not a Chablis," says the gourmet.

"And she's a neo-Romantic, not an Impressionist," says the art critic.

When the man leaves, they continue discoursing on how differences in the religions are inconsequential, just surface details.

It is curious that in every walk of life, in every particular area of expertise, people know that differences are not idle, that they have consequences—except, it seems, in religion.

You cannot imagine taking a course in chemistry in which your professor insisted on showing only the similarities among the elements, and even banished the Periodic Chart as divisive; nevertheless, such is the tack of many popular and even academic presentations on comparative religion, which mute differences for fear of fomenting division.

But this is like stirring bright dollops of color on an artist's palette into a wretched brown—an amalgamation of religion produces a hue that no one in any of the religions will recognize as his own. As historian Henry Chadwick put it, such a concoction is simply an "unpalatable bouillabaisse of religions."

The idea that people of honesty and goodness can come to different conclusions regarding the truth of God, and so adhere in good conscience to different faiths, Catholicism readily appreciates—a mark of the Church's holistic vision of religious differences. Moreover, Catholicism affirms that non-Christians of goodwill and love of God invisibly belong to the visible Church, and are dear to her. They are graced by Him from afar, and are being saved by Christ even if they continue, this side of the grave, in not recognizing Christ as Savior.

Catholicism's Holistic View of Non-Christian Religions

A few years ago, the front page of the *Los Angeles Times* (September 6, 2000) featured the headline: "Vatican Declares Catholicism Sole Path to Salvation." The subject of the newspaper article was a document just published by the Vatican, *Dominus Jesus* (Latin for "Lord Jesus"). I read the article, then found a copy of *Dominus.* Comparing them, I could hardly believe that the *Times* journalist and I had read the same document. At no point in *Dominus Jesus* did I find any hint of a Vatican assertion that Catholicism is the "sole path to salvation." In fact, *Dominus Jesus* explicitly affirms the opposite: "the salvific action of Jesus Christ, with and through his Spirit, extends beyond the visible boundaries of the Church to all humanity."[2]

Unfortunately, partly due to misleading reporting, many non-Catholics have formed erroneous views regarding Catholic teaching—including the wrong view that non-Christians are doomed by non-belief in Christ as Savior. The truth is otherwise: Catholicism appreciates "all goodness and truth found in these religions," in the words of the *Catechism of the Catholic Church.*[3]

Christ said, "Not everyone who says to me, 'Lord, Lord,' will enter the kingdom of heaven, but only he who does the will of my Father who is in heaven" (Matthew 7:21). Surely, non-Christians do the will of the Father in many ways, and in doing so they adore Christ unawares, and receive His saving grace. Cardinal Charles Journet clarified this beautifully:

> Those who do not belong to the Church,
> even those who know nothing of Christ,
> if they are in good faith and have
> a real desire for God,
> loving him more than they love themselves,
> are justified;
> which means that they have received grace
> in a hidden manner, the same grace we have.[4]

And this grace connects non-Christians invisibly to the visible Church, which is Christ's Mystical Body. Continues Journet: "The

---

[2] Rome, from the Offices of the Congregation for the Doctrine of the Faith, June 16, 2000, the Feast of the Transfiguration of the Lord, *Dominus Jesus: On the Unicity and Salvific Universality of Jesus Christi and the Church,* ratified by Pope John Paul II.

[3] *Catechism of the Catholic Church,* (Mahwah, NJ: Paulist Press, 1994), p. 223.

[4] Journet, *op cit.,* p. 104.

person in question remains a Buddhist, a Jew, a Moslem...he still belongs corporally to the religious group...but he is already spiritually in the Church."[5]

The Catholic does not only believe non-Christians are saved, but is inspired by righteousness and piety in all who love God. She sees in the calm brow of Siddhartha Gautama, who sat for forty days under the Bo tree in patient receptivity to the Absolute, her own soul's thirst for the beyond. The Catholic sees in the chords of incense rising before a Confucian home-shrine of ancestors, the blessed ties that bind her own Communion of Saints. As a guest at a Friday night Sabbath-meal in a Jewish home, whose participants sing and talk for hours on end, the Catholic sees the brightness of Mary's gaze in the mother's eye, and Jesus' laughter in the men's delight.

A Hindu legend tells of the monkey Hanuman, utterly devoted to the divinities Rama and Sita. An icon depicts his consuming devotion: Hanuman's paws are sunk into his own chest, parting it in two, to actually bare his heart—upon which appear the very images of Rama and Sita! Upon seeing this, the Catholic feels his own heart uncovered before God.

Significant Doctrinal Differences

Catholicism approaches the non-Christian's experience of the divine in humility and wonder, and with an appreciation for the grace of God at work in these souls. However, that does not mean that Catholicism adheres to the absurdity of a radically pluralist view of religious diversity that holds that all religions are equally true, and that the truths of the religions are interchangeable.

The God of Martin Luther King, Jr. and the God of the Ku Klux Klan cannot be equally true. The former is the living God of Abraham, and the Father of Christ; the latter, the god of a febrile, racist imagination. The God of Mother Teresa of Calcutta who fed the starving and cared for the dying, is not the God of Islamist jihadists who in 2001 crashed two jets into the World Trade Center in Manhattan.

---

[5] *Ibid.*, p. 119.

Of course, much more subtle differences exist among the world religions. Judaism believes that God could never incarnate as a human being, as it would violate both the oneness of God and the complete immateriality of God; Christianity teaches that God did assume humanity, and remained One. Hinduism teaches that we live countless times, turning on a wheel of birth and death *(samsara)* until we reach liberation (*moksha*) by attaining Godhood; Christianity teaches that we live once, unto eternity.

Buddhism says there is no Creator, and that the whole matter of the existence of a God has no bearing on the quest for truth; Christianity teaches that the universe came into being from a Creator, who cares for all He has made, and lavishes transforming grace. Islam's Koran denies, as noted earlier, the doctrine of the Trinity as *shirk*—the sin of associating others with God, as the Trinity posits a Tri-Personal Godhead. But Christ revealed the Trinity—"the mystery of a divine life that superabounds in three Persons"[6] (Hans Urs von Balthasar).

Acknowledging Differences

Despite these obvious differences, some believe that downplaying differences among the religions is the only way to inter-religious harmony; differences, they hold, invariably cause friction. But ignoring differences can only produce an imaginary religious holism—a unity in appearance only, as it forces the religions into an unreal single mold. To unnaturally suppress differences is not only contrary to authentic holism, but to authentic mysticism. The mystic John Tauler wrote, "No one knows better the true meaning of distinction than they who have entered unity."[7]

Certainly inter-religious harmony is a great desideratum—but intentionally obscuring differences is hardly a workable approach to

---

[6] Hans Urs von Balthasar, *The Hans Urs von Balthasar Reader,* ed. Medard Kehl, S.J., and Werner Loser, S.J., trans. Robert J. Daly, S.J., and Fred Lawrence, (New York, NY: Crossroad, 1982), p. 115.

[7] Jacques Maritain, *The Degrees of Knowledge,* trans. Bernard Wall, (New York, NY: Charles Scribner's Sons, 1938), p. ix.

it. Yet a false equation of religions flourishes in universities today. R.C. Zaehner, longtime Chair of Eastern Religions and Ethics at the University of Oxford, saw this trend as early as 1953, and commented:

> Nor do I think that it can be a legitimate function of a university professor to attempt to induce harmony among elements as disparate as the great religions of mankind appear to be, if, as seems inevitable, the resultant harmony is only to be apparent, verbal, and therefore fictitious.[8]

Zaehner's remarks were prescient. The approach he protested is now routine. Because of it, the atmosphere of much interfaith dialogue has become surrealistically artificial. To make a distinctive truth-claim for one's religion is commonly denigrated as imperialistic; to question another's religious view is to be dismissed as intolerant; to suggest there is a difference between truth and error, narrow-minded; and to answer a misconception about one's faith, defensive and reactionary.

This atmosphere does not foster inter-religious understanding; instead it discourages real dialogue. Not wanting to appear offensive to any religious tradition, many participants engage in self-censorship and content themselves to recite please-all platitudes. We are reminded of Voltaire's complaint against the narrow-minded direction that the French Revolution ironically came to take. The Revolution had preached the overthrow of the old order as an intolerant one—but then enforced its own brand of intolerance, with flashing guillotines. Voltaire admonished them: "You talk of nothing but tolerance, and never was a sect more intolerant."[9]

---

[8] R.C. Zaehner, *Concordant Discord: The Interdependence of Faiths Being the Gifford Lectures on Natural Religion Delivered at St. Andrews in 1967-1969.* (Oxford: Clarendon Press, 1970), p. 6.

[9] H.W. Crocker III, *Triumph: The Power and Glory of the Catholic Church—A 2,000 Year History,* (Roseville, CA: Prima Publishing, 2001), p. 335.

The Real Basis of Inter-Religious Tolerance and Appreciation

If suppressing differences among the religions is not a true basis of inter-religious tolerance and appreciation, then what is? Ultimately, each religion must work this out for itself, according to its truth-principles. What follows is one Catholic approach.

Think of a guitarist who visits other lands—and sees a lute played in one, a mandolin in other, an Indian sitar in a third. The strings are familiar, but the sound is different, provocative, enlivening. The guitarist is inspired to new ways of approaching his own instrument. So it is when people of goodwill of different religions meet. They are touched to see persons of other faiths love the God they love, in ways other than their familiar ways, and are thankful for the inspiration.

This is one element of the Catholic vision of inter-religious harmony: appreciation that God is truly worshipped, and sublimely so, by people of other faiths. "It is somewhat similar to our discovery of strangers who know and love as we do a secret spot in the forest which was the goal of our lonely walks. We are surprised that they found it by other paths which we did not know existed"[10] (Francois Mauriac).

A second element is the recognition that we are children of a common Creator, who cares for all He has created, and "wants all men to be saved and to come to a knowledge of the truth" (1 Timothy 2:4). Theist, atheist, agnostic: all are beloved of the Father, and we please Him by caring for them too.

The third element involves finding an ultimate principle by which to establish an authentically holistic unity between non-Christian religions and Christianity. That principle, I am persuaded, is the Trinity. It is the secret Axis of the world's religions, and the primary and defining revelation of Christianity.

---

[10] Francois Mauriac, *What I Believe,* (New York, NY: Farrar, Straus, 1963), p. 68.

A Procession of Trinitarian Revelations

Think of the great Rocky Mountains—their misty vaults and trackless length. By these grand dimensions, the Rockies certainly affect weather over the vast territories which border them, east, west, north, and south. Likewise, the immeasurable Holy Trinity must have influenced the entire atmosphere of religious history, and continues to do so.

In other words, at all times in history and prehistory, and in every land, whenever truth-seekers have endeavored to scale the heights of the Absolute, they have found themselves, if unawares, on Trinitarian slopes. But as we saw earlier, the full truth of the Trinity was veiled until Christ's Incarnation. No religion prior to the Incarnation—including Hinduism, Buddhism, Judaism—had unfurled It in full. In these religions, elder to Christianity, God revealed one Trinitarian dimension or another. But the integral unveiling of the Trinity awaited the revelation of Jesus Christ.

Thus, the hidden basis of religious differences and the secret of their complementary unity is the Trinity. In the nature-oriented religions, God revealed the Trinitarian Son: the Eternal Manifest dimension of God, the divine mystery of Nature. In Judaism, God revealed the Trinitarian Father: the Unmanifest, the Transcendent dimension of God. In Hinduism, God revealed the inner Spirit: the Immanent dimension of God, God within, God as the divine Center of human beings.

Teilhard de Chardin describes a progressive revelation of the divine, culminating in Christ who integrally and explicitly revealed it:

> The fearful, anonymous labors of primitive man,
> the beauty fashioned through the age-long history
> by ancient Egypt,
> the anxious expectancies of Israel,
> the patient distilling of the attar of oriental mysticism,
> the endless refining of wisdom by the Greeks;
> all these were needed before the Flower
> could blossom on the rod of Jesse

and of all humanity.
All these preparatory processes
were cosmically and biologically necessary
that Christ might set foot on the human stage.[11]

The Logos-Son as the Wellspring of Nature Religions

Project your imagination back 6,000 years, when the world religions we know today—Hinduism, Buddhism, Judaism, Christianity, Islam—did not exist. What inspires your piety and awe? What moves your heart to worship? Is it not the mountains, the sky, the sun, the stars and moon, the earth itself? "The world is also a book that speaks to us of God"[12] (Jean Danielou).

The earliest religious strivings on earth were directed toward nature, kindled by its splendor and abysmal magnitude; St. Paul alludes to this in speaking to the Greeks—that God has "not left himself without testimony: He has shown kindness by giving you rain from heaven and crops in their seasons; he provides you with plenty of food and fills your hearts with joy"[13] (Acts 14:16-17).

Yet, what is it to love nature except to love the Cosmic Christ, the *Logos*—the creative Harmony of the universe? So it is that the Son-dimension of the Trinity is the sublime origin of the nature-oriented faiths. Ohiyesa was a reservation-born Native American who studied at American universities. With a foot in both worlds, Ohiyesa wrote his credo, *The Soul of an Indian:*

The elements and majestic forces in nature
—lightning, wind, water, fire, and frost—
are regarded with awe

---

[11] Teilhard de Chardin, *Hymn of the Universe,* trans. Simon Bartholomew, (New York, NY: Harper & Row, 1965), from *Pensees,* pp. 76-77.

[12] Jean Danielou, *God and the Ways of Knowing,* trans. Walter Roberts, (New York, NY: Meridian Books, 1957), p. 23.

[13] *Ibid.,* pp. 15-16.

as spiritual powers,
but always secondary and intermediate in character.

We believe that spirit pervades all creation
and that every creature possesses a soul in some degree, though
not necessarily a soul conscious of itself.
The tree, the waterfall, the grizzly bear,
each is an embodied Force,
and as such an object of reverence.[14]

That which Native faith reverenced in the "embodied Force" of each natural element is none other than the Christ-Logos, the holy pith of all things.

The *Logos* Principle as the Foundation of Greek Philosophy

The Son-dimension of the Trinity was obviously also the deep inspiration of Greek philosophy. As described earlier, the Greek Stoics intuited and reverenced the existence of God as divine Reason, *Logos.* Later, John the Apostle recognized by divine revelation that Christ was this very *Logos*—primordial divine Reason—become Man.

As Native American religion seems so different from Greek philosophy, how are they both *Logos*-oriented? Native American religion reverences a divine One pervading and harmonizing creation (in the Lakota faith, *Wakan Tanka,* "Great Mysterious" or "Great Spirit"), yet its daily focus is on the divine plurality in the natural world. Greek philosophers also found the *Logos* manifest through natural particularity (for example, as the basis of music and mathematics), but Greek sages also had a penchant for abstraction, and devoted much energy to elaborating a lofty metaphysics of the invisible *Logos,* the unknown of matter.

---

[14] Charles A. Eastman (Ohiyesa), *The Soul of An Indian: An Interpretation,* (Lincoln, NE: University of Nebraska Press, 1980), pp. 14-15.

Still, even among these abstraction-oriented Greeks, with their aptitude for philosophical systematizing, there existed a philosophical cult of beauty and its contemplation that is somewhat analogous to the Native Indian's reverencing of the *Logos* in nature. This element of Greek philosophy is wonderfully rendered in the last pages of Plato's *Symposium.*

Here Socrates relates how he was instructed as a youth by a mysterious figure, Diotima, who taught him how to ascend to divine Beauty: to start his meditation with earthly beauty, then rise to ponder exquisite moral principles, then to Beauty abstract—higher and higher, to the threshold of Beauty Absolute. Thus she instructed Socrates:

> "And the true order of going…
> is to begin from the beauties of earth
> and mount upwards
> for the sake of that other beauty
> ….from fair forms to fair practices,
> and from fair practices to fair notions,
> until from fair notions
> he arrives at the notion of absolute beauty,
> and at last knows what the essence of beauty is.
>
> "This, my dear Socrates,"
> said the stranger of Mantineia,
> "is that life above all others which man should live,
> in the contemplation of beauty absolute…
> and bringing forth and nourishing true virtue
> to become the friend of God and be immortal,
> if mortal man may." [15]

Thus the Son-dimension of the Trinity—the Principle of all nature and natural harmony, the Cosmic Christ—is the hidden ferment of both Greek philosophy and of nature-oriented religion.

---

[15] Plato, *The Symposium,* trans. Benjamin Jowett.

The Transcendent God of Judaism

To the Hebrews, another eternal Dimension of God was revealed: the Unmanifest God, the Father—the wholly Other, the transcendent Sovereign, apart from all phenomenal worlds. Writes Henri Frankfort in *The Intellectual Adventure of Ancient Man:*

> The Egyptians saw in the sun
> all that a man may know of the Creator;
> the Mesopotamians viewed the sun as the god Shamash,
> the guarantor of justice....
>
> The God of the psalmist and the prophets
> was not in nature.
> He transcended nature....[16]

God established His Father-transcendence among the Jews by beginning the Ten Commandments with a prohibition against image-making: "You shall not make for yourself an idol in the form of anything in heaven above or on the earth beneath..." (Exodus 20:4). No idol-making—lest we limit God by our human-size concepts. For the eye is presumptuous. But a thimble, it fancies itself a limitless bowl that contains the blue expanse of all space by day, and the dark lake of space at night. *How shall this eye be trusted with even a symbolic figure of God?* asked the Hebrew prophets.

"The heavens, even the highest heaven, cannot contain you" (1 Kings 8:27). This Father-transcendence was also revealed in God's answer to Job, who protests the calamities which have beset him, including illness and ostracism. God does not explain to Job the origin of his problems piece by piece, but shows him that the limited mind can grasp neither the ways of God nor the nature of divine goodness. God chides:

---

[16] Henri Frankfort, *The Intellectual Adventure of Ancient Man,* (Chicago, IL: University of Chicago Press, 1946), p. 363.

Where were you
when I laid the earth's foundation?
Tell me, if you understand.
Who marked off its dimensions?
Surely you know!
Who stretched a measuring line across it?
On what were its footings set,
or who laid its cornerstone—
while the morning stars sang together
and all the angels shouted for joy?

—*Job 38:4-7*

God's answer to Job is not mental or intellectual, but spiritual. God presses Job to see the complexity and grandeur of creation and to trust that He who made it all is in charge of the destiny of all, including Job's—that despite present appearances, the transcendent Father has an unfathomably good plan for Job's life.

The story is told of a Roman general who, upon taking Jerusalem, rushes to the Temple to see what the Jews are mysteriously and famously hiding behind the Temple curtain. He slashes the curtain before the Holy of Holies to take a look—nothing is there. At one time this room sheltered the Ark of the Covenant, above which God would manifest the Light, the glorious *Shekinah*. But later, when the Ark was lost in an enemy raid, the Holy of Holies was purposely left empty by the High Priest. Such is the God of the Jews—beyond all image: the Father, the Transcendent dimension of the Trinity.

The Hindu Discovery of God Within

Consider India five hundred years before the Incarnation of Christ. While God was raising prophets in Israel, and smoothing the dark hair of his daughter Zion, what was He doing in India? Did God leave India without His touch for centuries upon centuries? It is unthinkable. "My Father is always at his work" (John 5:17).

God's grace has ever been with the people of India, as they have thirsted for Him as much as any people ever has. He touched the hearts of her ancient sages, the *rishis.* India's holy books bear witness to this divine touch: the *Bhagavad-Gita,* the *Ramayana,* the *Upanishads.*

The *Upanishads* speak of God omnipresent (*brahman*) as the True Self (*atman*) of all. The traditional Hindu gesture of greeting, the *pronam*—the joining of the palms—signifies: "The divinity in me salutes the divinity in you." To reach this true center of being, the yogis endeavored to quiet their minds perfectly in meditation. So quiet did the yogis make their minds, they came to believe that peaceful pure consciousness, abstracted from conceptual thought, is God—a viewpoint they expressed in works of spiritual lore, including the *Yoga Vasistha:*

> I salute the self! Salutations to myself the undivided consciousness, the jewel of all the seen and unseen worlds! You have indeed been reached very soon! You have been touched, you have been gained, you have been realized...Salutations to you, my self, Siva, the Lord of Lords, the supreme self.[17]

The yogis were right in saluting God as the true center of being. As we have seen in our study of the Trinity, God at the center is the Holy Spirit. And yet the yogis' common interpretation of this experience—that God *is* Self—is not the truth of the matter. For although the Holy Spirit is God within, God immanent, *the self is not God*—consciousness, even the purest consciousness, is not God.

This analogy will help clarify how the Christian view of God within differs from the yogic one. Think of a rose, and of the lush aura of perfumed air which halos it. Imagine the rose as God within, at the center of being, and imagine the human consciousness which surrounds this center as permeated with the scent of that rose. So lovely was the air of consciousness suffused by the rose of God within, that the sages of Hinduism declared pure consciousness to be God in their philosophy of *advaita vedanta.* Yet the air is not the rose—it only carries the scent

---

[17] Swami Venkatesananda, *The Supreme Yoga: A New Translation of the Yoga Vasistha,* vol. I, (Elgin Cape Province, South Africa: The Chiltern Yoga Trust, 1976), section V, p. 34.

of the rose. So when the yogis declare pure consciousness to be God, they are mistaking the perfumed air that surrounds the rose for the rose itself.

In contrast, the Christian mystic recognizes God within, the Holy Spirit, but knows that consciousness or self mediates the presence of the Holy Spirit, but is not identical to the Holy Spirit. God is the true Center of consciousness, but consciousness is not God.

In terms of our analogy: while the Hindu yogis say that the rose-permeated air (consciousness) around the rose (God) is the rose, the Christian mystic says that the air (consciousness) only carries the scent of the rose (God), but is not the rose itself.

Earlier in our consideration of the last Mysteries of Christ, we discovered that Christ on the cross definitively demonstrated that God is not any manner of self or consciousness. Christ had lived His whole life in unitive consciousness, one with the Father. On the cross He died to even His most profound, God-centered consciousness and was resurrected beyond it to His original state of the divine *Logos:* the eternal Son, uncreated Absolute Knowing, which existed before any consciousness (which is a created energy) existed.

Thus, the *rishis'* realization of the divine at the center of being is relatively true: God is immanent in the human person, but the self is not God. As Christ recapitulates his Mysteries in us, we will come to the realization of God at the center (the Holy Spirit) in this life, but finally be transformed beyond consciousness in the Christic Mysteries of death, resurrection, and ascension to the Trinity, which is wholly beyond the reach of human consciousness. Finally, the soul is fully transubstantiated into Christ and knows the glory of the Father, heaven.

A Catholic holistic vision of world religions esteems the sages of India for their discovery of the immanent dimension of God—God within. It honors their tenacious love for the Absolute, and the classics of Hindu spiritual literature which celebrate God at the center, a Spirit that radiates existence, truth, and bliss.

Christ exclaimed on the cross, "It is finished" (John 19:30). Historian of religion Zaehner found in these words an affirmation that the revelation of Christ integrally completed the Trinitarian revelation that God had begun in the elder faiths.

How the Christian Journey Recapitulates the World's Religions

Christianity holds that by the grace of Baptism, the whole Trinity comes to indwell the soul most intimately. Since each of the world religions magnifies a distinctive dimension of the Trinity, we may draw this further conclusion: that the Christian journey to God recapitulates the successive revelations of the world's religions, as the soul receives the inundation of each Trinitarian dimension along the Way.

In the course of a lifetime, Christians are lured by the omnipresent Christ-Logos to love God in nature: the Over-Soul of the Nature-oriented religions. Christians are inspired to worship the Father, the Transcendent, wholly beyond this world: the God of the Jews, of Abraham, Isaac, and Jacob. Christians are drawn within to tranquility at the soul's center by the Holy Spirit: the indwelling God intuited by Hindu sages. As Christ recapitulates the final Mysteries of His Death and Resurrection in the Christian, his soul is transubstantiated beyond self, a condition hailed perhaps by the Buddha as *anatma, no-self.*

Perhaps it were better, then, to just syncretistically practice all the world's religions, taking up each in turn, until one has come to the essential truths of them all. But this is not the integral Way which Christ revealed, and enacts in us through the Spirit: "Remain in me, and I will remain in you" (John 15:4). Nor does any religion other than Christianity express our final condition in Christ in Trinitarian glory. We remain in Christ through the sacramental life of the Church, by which He recapitulates His Life in us, finally to the disclosure of all Trinitarian truth.

The central revelation of each the world's religions is rooted in a distinct dimension of the Trinity. In the *Holism of the World's Religions,* the complementarity of these revelations is recognized as arising from the Tri-Personal God, which was finally revealed in an integral way by Christ. Studying the literature of the world's religions intuitively and with a welcoming and humble spirit, the Christian can find Trinitarian riches, and be prompted to questions and insights that can deepen his own faith. At the same time, this holism prompts us to seek clarity regarding the differences among the faiths, charity in speaking of these differences, and thoughtfulness in interfaith dialogue.

Holism of the World's Religions

Holism of Christ's Mysteries

Affinity: The *Holism of Christ's Mysteries* (Chapters Five and Eleven)

As Christ recapitulates His Mysteries in us, He leads us through all the major revelations of the world's religions, as these are revelations of distinct dimensions of the Trinity.

CHAPTER 17

The Happy Trinity Is Her Home: The Beatific Vision

"The Happy Trinity is her home: nothing can trouble her joy."[1]
—C.S. Lewis

As the liquidlike chirpings of a sparrow draw one's gaze to a branch, God draws our inner eye to Himself in a moment of grace and conversion. To know God becomes our focused pursuit.

As a child you reached out to touch a rainbow but it ever eluded your grasp. Adults laughed, assuring you, as your heart secretly broke, that the rainbow could never be caught; it was merely the play of the sun and the mist. So it seems sometimes with our pursuit of God.

But God is the rainbow that lets us catch it—and then colors the ceiling of our soul. This is the unitive state. This is our knowing of God as He is in ourselves, the divine Center of the soul.

But we want more: to know God in Himself. In our study of ecstasy, we found that the unitive self's knowing of God is not the full revelation of God. For God cannot be known through self, even the God-united self. The soul in the unitive state is like a chick in an egg that enjoys her mother's warmth, but does not yet see her.

---

[1] C.S. Lewis, *The Great Divorce: A Dream,* (San Francisco, CA: HarperSanFrancisco, 2001), p. 134.

Imagine a prince cursed to only see the face of his beloved in a mirror—to never behold her face directly, or embrace her. Yes, he has the consolation of her near presence in the glass, but not her embraceable presence. When he turns to see, she is not there. Frustratingly, she is only in the looking glass.

In the unitive state, God is present to us in the soul, but as a face in a looking glass. Just as earth's boldest north wind cannot pierce the heavens and traverse the stars, and its purest river cannot run upon the sun, even the loftiest self cannot know the transcendent goodness, truth, and beauty of heaven.

But God has promised us this full vision: "Now we see but a poor reflection as in a mirror; then we shall see face to face. Now I know in part; then I shall know fully…" (1 Corinthians 13:12).

What is the way to fully know God? Meister Eckhart summarizes: "As long as we are just human beings…we do not see God. We have to be raised up, established in pure tranquility, and thus see God."[2] This is the beatific vision!—the consummate Unity to which all partial unities have pointed.

What Is the "Beatific Vision"?

Christ reveals the essence of heaven in his Sermon on the Mount:

> Blessed are the pure of heart, for they will see God.
>
> —*Matthew 5:8*

Because this saying is one of a number of blessings pronounced by Christ known as the *beatitudes,* Christianity calls the divine experience of heaven the *beatific vision:* the direct and limpid vision of the divine Essence, a participation in the light and love of the Trinity, for "if the Three Divine Persons give themselves to us it is so that we may possess them, that they be ours"[3] (Jacques Maritain). The beatific vision knows a Tri-Personal

---

[2] Bernard McGuinn, ed., *Meister Eckhart, Teacher and Preacher,* with the collaboration of Frank Tobin and Elivira Borgstadt, (New York, NY: Paulist Press, 1986), p. 318.

[3] Jacques Maritain, *The Degrees of Knowledge,* trans. Bernard Wall, (New York, NY: Charles Scribner's Sons, 1938), p. 318.

Wholeness that exceeds every created wholeness seen or dreamed, the most exquisite of these being mere sketches of shadows of the One.

> Transformed in God,
> these blessed souls will live the life of God
> and not their own—
> although it will be their own life because
> God's life will be theirs.
>
> Then they will truly proclaim:
> We live, not now we, but God lives in us.[4]
>
> —*John of the Cross*

The destiny of the soul is to be transformed into Christ, to know the Father through Christ. Heaven is the glorious condition of the Father in which the glorified Son forever dwells. Meister Eckhart truly observed: "The scripture says, 'No one knows the Father but the Son' (Matthew 11:27); and so, if you want to know God, you should not just be *like* the Son. Rather, you should be the Son himself."[5]

Clement of Alexandria wrote in the second century:

> I say, the *Logos* of God
> became man
> so that you may learn from man
> how man may become God.[6]

God has ever poured this heavenly draught, for the universe is awash with God, but the ocean of it has rushed over the sides of our little sea-shell. In the beatific vision, God the Father is the draught and God the Son is the chalice—and the flow thereof is heaven.

---

[4] *The Collected Works of St. John of the Cross,* trans. Kieran Kavanaugh O.C.D., and Otilio Rodriguez, O.C.D., (Washington, DC: ICS Publications, 1991), p. 518.

[5] Bernard McGuinn, ed., *Meister Eckhart, Teacher and Preacher,* with the collaboration of Frank Tobin and Elivira Borgstadt, (New York, NY: Paulist Press, 1986), p. 278.

[6] Bernard McGuin, *The Foundations of Mysticism: Origins to the Fifth Century,* vol. I, *The Presence of God: A History of Western Christian Mysticism,* (New York, NY: Crossroad, 1994), p. 107.

Our understanding of heaven as the beatific vision of God gives us new insight into Christ's prayer to the Father:

> All I have is yours, and all you have is mine.
>
> —*John 17:10*

Christ's All is the Father in the Spirit, a heaven which He miraculously and fully shares with us by transforming us into Himself.

When the soul has been wholly transubstantiated into Christ by His recapitulating His Ascension in it, and thus has come to perfect Trinitarian rapport with the Father through the Spirit, there arises the ultimate Whole: The *Holism of the Beatific Vision*—the Trinity being the beginning and end of Wholeness.

Holism of the Beatific Vision

Holism of the Absolute

Affinity: The *Holism of the Absolute* (Chapter Three)

The heaven we will know is no different from the heaven the glorified Christ knows in the Trinity.

Father, by Your unfathomable grace, everything of Yours shall be ours! Your Vision will consume our separateness from You, like deer consuming sweet grasses.

Beyond Caricatures of Heaven

Unfortunately, the Church's magnificent view of heaven has been overshadowed by misconceptions. Just the other day I heard a fundamentalist Protestant pastor say on the radio, "In heaven you can ski all day, and never fall! As you fly down the slopes, you take every hill perfectly, and never fall as on earthly skiing vacations. In all heavenly fun activities, you're a winner!"

In the same vein, a friend told me about a conversation he had with a Christian friend in her twenties who told him: "In heaven, people do different fun things. Some serve God. Some sit around on clouds reading magazines all day." (We wondered, as you are, what was in the magazines!)

Such views of heaven are sadly abetted by literalistic reading of *The Book of Revelation,* the New Testament scripture that symbolically depicts the paradisiacal condition. "The wall was made of jasper, and the city of pure gold, as pure as glass" (Revelation 21:18). Some Bible literalists take this to be a city-plan that specifies the materials of a heavenly city. But that is not the way the great Church tradition has read these verses. Early in Christian history, theologians developed a four-fold typology of biblical interpretation—a typology that discerns symbolism in scripture, and not only literal significance.

From a symbolic perspective, the "walls" of heaven may represent its transcendence of all that is below the Absolute. That heaven is made of "pure gold" does not mean that its substance is the metal designated AU on the Periodic Chart, but may signify that heaven is a participation in the uncontainable beauty of God's inner Life.

> There is no reason to be worried about facetious people who try to make the Christian hope of "Heaven" ridiculous by saying that they do not want 'to spend eternity playing harps.' The answer to such people is that if they cannot understand books written for grown-ups, they should not talk about them. All the scriptural imagery (harps, crowns, gold, etc.) is, of course, a merely symbolic attempt to express the inexpressible.[7]
>
> —*C.S. Lewis*

[7] C.S. Lewis, *Mere Christianity,* (New York, NY: Macmillan, 1952), pp. 120-121.

Ecstasy Points to Our Soul's Destiny

As noted in Chapter Eleven, the ecstasy of the saints clarifies enormously the nature of our final estate in God, heaven. Though ecstasy is not, strictly speaking, identical to the heavenly condition, ecstasy's state beyond all self in God suggests the character of the transformation which finally reveals heaven: the heavenly condition is a divine Knowing beyond all self, all consciousness. So ecstasy offers a unique clue to our destiny.

We earlier noted that the nature of consciousness allows us to really sense God's presence from a standpoint of self, but prevents our fully knowing God as God knows God. Ecstasy is a special grace by which God temporarily suspends all self-consciousness, resulting in divine knowing beyond self. Here are a few more lines from Teresa of Avila's description of ecstasy, in addition to her earlier remarks:

> What God communicates here to the soul in an instant is a secret so great and a favor so sublime—and the delight the soul experiences is so sublime—that I don't know what to compare it to. I can only say that the Lord wishes to reveal for that moment, in a more sublime manner than through any spiritual vision or taste, the glory of heaven.[8]

Certainly if God can temporarily suspend self in some of his saints to reveal His own Knowing, He can do it permanently in all of us! Thus ecstasy reveals that the human journey, ultimately, is a journey beyond self, beyond consciousness, into the everlasting splendor of the Trinity's innermost Life and Knowing.

That divine Life is so transcendent in beauty, light, and love to anything we know through self, that normally a glimpse of it is incompatible with continued mortal life.[9] We might say that people die because of the divine beauty their inner gaze comes to behold as they lie on

---

[8] Tessa Bielecki, *Teresa of Avila—Ecstasy and Common Sense Tessa Bielecki,* (Boston, MA: Shambhala Press, 1996), p. 103.

[9] The saints in ecstasy do not experience the fullness of glory; that is why they do not instantly die of ecstasy.

their deathbed. This is the mystic meaning of words God spoke to Moses, who asked to see God. "I will cause all my goodness to pass in front of you.... But you cannot see my face, for no one can see me and live" (Exodus 33:19-20). Not idly did John of the Cross say:

> Reveal your presence,
> and may the vision of your beauty be my death.[10]

Father, everything of Yours will be ours! You hide Your Face from the world, behind thickets upon thickets, for a universal glimpse of You would faint the world in an unrecoverable swoon of love.

The Mysteries Are Fulfilled in the Beatific Vision

God transforms us beyond self-knowing to divine knowing through the Way of Christ's Mysteries. "I am the way and the truth and the life. No one comes to the Father except through me" (John 14:6). By Christ's recapitulating in us the Mysteries of His death, resurrection, and ascension to the glory of the Father, He transforms our souls into Himself, the one Trinitarian Son who knows the Father. Just as He changed bread and wine into Himself, He transforms us into Himself, whose Body dwells in the everlasting *doxa* or glory of the Father. At every Catholic Mass this truth is symbolized, as the priest dissolves a little water—our humanity—into the chalice of wine, His divinity.

> [A]s a little drop of water, mixed with much wine,
> seems to vanish completely
> as it takes on the taste and color of the wine...
> as air flooded with sunlight is transformed
> into the same brilliant light, so that it seems
> *to be no longer lighted but rather light itself.*[11]
>
> —*St. Bernard of Clairvaux*

---

[10] Kavanaugh and Rodriguez, *op cit.*, p. 510.

[11] Bernard of Clairvaux, *The Steps of Humility,* trans. George Bosworth Burch (Cambridge, MA: Harvard University Press, 1950), p. 89.

Dante called the blessed of heaven in Christ, *splendori,* after the Latin, *splendere,* Light.[12] Transformed into Christ, the soul becomes

> in some manner the Whole,
> the very infinity of God's life
> which erupts in it
> as if the whole sea
> were to flow into a river,
>
> I mean a sea of love
> surging with vital operations
> and able from its very source
> to become one single spirit with the sea.
>
> —*Jacques Maritain*

Father, everything of Yours will be ours! Your Vision devours our concepts of heaven as sparrows consume a scattering of seeds.

The Mysticism of Purgatory

At death, all immediately see God. But whether we are drawn instantly into the beatific Vision or pull back from it depends on all the moments of our life that precede that one.

What if our love has been faint, mediocre, capricious? What if we have significantly resisted purifying love? What if we have shirked great lessons of Love, even to the end?

> The body is gone, has done its work.
> The soul is naked.
> The veil which separated it from God is vanished…
> Vainly would she strive to say "Give me a little time."
> *Time is no more.*
> Before the Face of God she enters

[12] Jeffrey Burton Russell, *A History of Heaven: The Singing Silence,* (Princeton, NJ: Princeton University Press, 1997), p. 79.

> on a state of things in which time
> as we know it here below is no more an element.[13]
>
> —*Paul Claudel*

If we have been ungenerous in love, we will find this clear hard Light of Love shocking, daunting, seemingly unendurable, and will shrink back from it to a point that is tolerable to our gaze. Now begins our purgatory: our withstanding the trial of Love, and by grace gravitating closer to it, until Love paves the soul with mirth and becomes its All-in-all.

> And now it came. It was fiery, sharp, bright and ruthless, ready to kill, ready to die, outspeeding light: it was Charity, not as mortals imagine it…fallen upon them from the Third Heaven, unmitigated. They were blinded, scorched, deafened. They thought it would burn their bones. They could not bear that it should continue. They could not bear that it should cease.[14]
>
> —*C.S. Lewis*

A rose of fire—Dante's phrase for heaven. A Fire-rose ever-blossoming, ever-renewed, in a timeless moment. "Nothing impure will ever enter it" (Revelation 21:27). To the degree the soul bears the Vision, it goes forward into it, transformed into Christ, who alone dwells in the glory of the Father.

Father, everything of Yours is mine!

Like lightning that falls upon the earth with bright talons as if to bear her away, You bear the soul beyond itself to Your nest.

The Hidden Nature of Faith

Some time ago on our spinning mote, a man went in quest of God, accompanied by his companion named Faith. Faith was an unobtrusive

---

[13] Paul Claudel, *Ways and Crossways,* trans. Fr. John O'Connor, (Freeport, NY: Books for Libraries, 1967), p. 51.

[14] C.S. Lewis, *That Hideous Strength: A Modern Day Fairy-Tale for Grown Ups*, (New York, NY: Simon & Schuster, 1996), p. 323.

and gentle friend, and sometimes he found curious comfort in a phrase she would whisper to him, "All is well. God is here." Other times he hardly heard these words, so absorbed was he in his quest for exciting experiences of God.

As the years continued, he indeed had a number of supernatural experiences. When he would tell Faith about them, she would smile and gently say, "All is well. God is here." Even as long spells passed without such experiences, and he began to despair, Faith would say, "All is well—"

"Yes, yes, I know—God is here," he would sigh.

Finally, he passes beyond death—his companion by his side. As he nears heaven, he hears Faith saying once again, "All is well. God is here"—but now in a strangely new voice, beyond that of a whisper, a voice exquisite, roiling with majesty.

He turns to her, puzzled. And as his glance falls on her, Faith flings off the veil that veiled her from him. It is God! Faith has been God with him, all along!

"God is here. All is well!"

Yes, faith is a grace, and grace is God's Life in us!

Faith is the Beatific Vision with us, even now—gently pressing against consciousness! But since self-consciousness cannot *see* God, we tend to downplay the importance of this inner Voice, this mysterious knowing—regarding it as non-mystical. But in truth, faith—God in us—is the mysticism of the Most High because it is beyond all human experience…as God is! "All of this darkness signifies the obscurity of faith with which the divinity is clothed while communicating itself to the soul"[15] (John of the Cross).

Faith is clothed divinity! Faith is not an intellectual capacity, or a "conditioned belief," or an emotional response: faith is a supernatural instrument, a divine channel, given to us directly by God; most truly conceived faith is none other than Almighty God in us!

Father, everything of Yours is mine! Your Vision rises in us as faith even now, like the rearing of white stallions on a moonless night.

---

[15] Kavanaugh and Rodriguez, *op cit.,* p. 177.

The Other Side

At the very beginning of our exploration of Christianity holistically conceived, we reflected on the wistful pang that the beauty of the earth evokes in us. Now, in meditating on the beatific Vision, we have come to the final cause of this nostalgia, and That to which it beckons. C.S. Lewis stated this most piquantly:

> God has given us the Morning Star already; you can go and enjoy the gift on many fine mornings if you get up early enough. What more, you may ask, do we want? Ah, but we want so much more—something the books on aesthetics take little notice of. But the poets and the mythologies know all about it. We do not want merely to *see* beauty, though, God knows, even that is bounty enough. We want something else which can hardly be put into words—to be united with the beauty we see, to pass into it, to receive it into ourselves, to bathe in it, to become part of it.
>
> ...For we believe that God will one day *give* us the Morning Star and cause us to *put on* the splendour of the sun, then we may surmise that both the ancient myths and the modern poetry, so false as history, may be very near the truth as prophecy. At present we are on the outside of the world, the wrong side of the door. We discern the freshness and purity of the morning, but they do not make us fresh and pure.
>
> We cannot mingle with the splendours we see. But all the leaves of the New Testament are rustling with the rumour that will not always be so. Some day, God willing, we shall get *in.*[16]

And we get in only by being transformed into Christ, our Life.

Father, Everything of Yours is Mine! Creation is Your laughter, but the Beatific Vision is Your inmost smile.

---

[16] C.S. Lewis, *The Weight of Glory and Other Addresses,* (New York, NY: Macmillan, 1980), pp. 16-17.

EPILOGUE

"The Trinity created the world only in order to render it divine in Christ."[1]

—Roger Hasseveldt

In an exhalation of beauty, God creates the universe: the Many issue from the One. But as the Many have an affinity for the One—as each created nature bears the imprint of its Creator, and bears a nostalgia for the One—the Many seek a return.

> Thus there is a great double "movement"
> in the universe of actual being
> from the Source
> outward toward creation and from creation back
> towards its Source.
>
> St. Thomas calls this
> the great circle of being *(circulatio entium),*
> the exodus of the Many from the One,
> and the return home again of the Many to the One.[2]
>
> *—W. Norris Clarke*

We return by way of this Great Circle of Being to the One, having been transformed into Christ, our Savior.

---

[1] Roger Hasseveldt, *The Church: A Divine Mystery,* trans. William Storey, (Notre Dame, IN: Fides Publishers, 1964), p. 39.

[2] W. Norris Clarke, S.J., *Person and Being,* (Milwaukee, WI: Marquette University Press, 1998), p. 101.

Think of the shore of an ocean—waves breaking on rocks and sliding up the sandy coast. Some distance inward from the shore, the waves begin their rolling, coherent movement forward.

Just as these sapphire waves plunge together shoreward, so myriad divine-human holisms ramify communally to forward the soul to union with God, and finally to bear it upon the divine shore, the unwithering *Gloria* of the beatific Vision. "Christianity is the taking up of the universe of mankind into the unity of God through the unity of Christ"[3] (Emile Mersch).

Thus does Christ bind the end of our journey to the beginning of all things, and all holisms as one, as if binding fronds of evergreen into a wreath exuberant.

[3] Emile Mersch, S.J., *The Theology of the Mystical Body,* trans. Cyril Vollert, S.J., (St. Louis, MO: B. Herder Book Co., 1952), p. 37.

RECOMMENDED READING

Bernadette Roberts has made a significant contribution to the literature of Christianity in the following books:

- *The Experience of No-Self: A Contemplative Journey.* Albany, NY: State University of New York Press, 1993.
- *The Path to No-Self: Life at the Center.* Albany, NY: State University of New York Press, 1991.
- *What is Self? A Study of the Spiritual Journey In Terms of Consciousness.* Boulder, CO: Sentient Publications, 2005.
- *Contemplative: Autobiography of the Early Years* (self-published, available)
- *A Passage Through Self: An Overview of the Journey* (DVD, self-published, available)

Elizabeth of the Trinity's writings continue to inspire Christian contemplatives. The best introduction to her works:

M.M. Philipon, O.P., *The Spiritual Doctrine of Sister Elizabeth of the Trinity.* Westminster, MD: Newman Press, 1948.

Ruth Burrows' works on prayer will speak deeply to your spirit:

- *Guidelines for Mystical Prayer.* Denville, NJ: Dimension Books, 1981.
- *Ascent to Love: The Spiritual Teaching of St. John of the Cross.* London: Darton, Longman, and Todd, 1987.
- *Fire Upon the Earth.* Denville, NJ: Dimension Books, 1980.

BIBLIOGRAPHY

Ackerman, Diane. *A Natural History of the Senses.* New York, NY: Random House, 1990.

Adels, Jill Haak. *The Wisdom of the Saints: An Anthology.* New York, NY: Oxford University Press, 1987.

Alighieri, Dante. *The Divine Comedy, Paradiso,* trans. by Charles S. Singleton. Princeton, NJ: Princeton University Press, 1975.

Anderson, James F. *Introduction to the Metaphysics of St. Thomas Aquinas.* Chicago, IL: Henry Regnery Company, 1953.

Aquilina, Mike. *The Fathers of the Church: An Introduction to the First Christian Teachers.* Huntington, IN: Our Sunday Visitor Publishing, 1999.

Athanasius. *On the Incarnation,* trans. and ed. by Sister Penelope Lawson. New York, NY: Macmillan Publishing, 1981.

Balthasar, Hans Urs von. *Who Is a Christian?,* trans. by John Cumming. New York, NY: Newman Press, 1968.

———. *The Von Balthasar Reader,* ed. Medard Kehl and Werner Loser, trans. Robert J. Daly and Fred Lawrence. New York, NY: Crossroad, 1982.

Benson, Herbert with Miriam Z. Klipper. *The Relaxation Response* . New York, NY: Avon, 1975.

Benson, Herbert. *Beyond the Relaxation Response: How to Harness the Healing Power of Your Personal Beliefs.* New York, NY: Berkley Publishing Group, 1994.

Benson, Robert Hughes. *The Mystical Body and Its Head.* New York, NY: Sheed and Ward, 1959.

Bernard of Clairvaux. *Saint Bernard on the Love of God,* trans. Terrence L. Connolly. Techny, IL: Mission Press, 1943.

Bernard of Clairvaux. *The Steps of Humility,* trans. George Bosworth Burch. Notre Dame, IN. 1963.

Bielecki, Tessa. *Teresa of Avila—Ecstasy and Common Sense.* Boston, MA: Shambhala Press, 1996.

Bishop, Morris. *Pascal: The Life of Genius.* Westport, CT: Greenwood Prager, 1964.

Brown, Dan, *The Da Vinci Code.* New York, NY: Doubleday, 2003.

Burrows, Ruth. *Ascent to Love: The Spiritual Teaching of St. John of the Cross.* London: Darton, Longman, and Todd, 1987.

———. *Fire Upon the Earth.* Denville, NJ: Dimension Books, 1980.

———. *Guidelines for Mystical Prayer.* Denville, NJ: Dimension Books, 1981.

Butler, Dom Cuthbert. *Western Mysticism: The Teaching of Augustine, Gregory and Bernard on Contemplation and the Contemplative Life,* third edition. New York, NY: Barnes & Noble, Inc., 1967.

Carroll, Warren H. *The Founding of Christendom, A History of Christendom,* vol.1. Front Royal VA: Christendom Publications, 1985.

Carroll, Vincent and David Shiflett. *Christianity on Trial: Arguments Against Anti-Religious Bigotry.* San Francisco, CA: Encounter Books, 2002.

Catechism of the Catholic Church. Paulist Press, Mahwah, NJ, 1994.

Chardin, Teilhard de. *Hymn of the Universe,* trans. Simon Bartholomew. New York, NY: Harper & Row, 1965.

———. *The Prayer of the Universe,* trans. by Rene Hague. New York, NY: Harper & Row, 1973.

Chervin, Ronda De Sola. *Prayers of the Women Mystics.* Ann Arbor, MI: Servant Publications, 1992.

Chesterton, G.K. *Saint Thomas Aquinas, "The Dumb Ox."* Garden City, NY: Image Books, 1956.

———. *The Everlasting Man.* London: Hodder and Stoughton, 1925.

Childre, Doc and Deborah Rozman, *Overcoming Emotional Chaos.* San Diego, CA: Jodere Group, 2002.

Clarke, W. Norris. *Person and Being.* Milwaukee, WI: Marquette University Press, 1998.

Claudel, Paul. *I Believe in God,* Agnes du Sarment, ed., trans. Helen Weaver. USA: Holt, Rinehart and Winston, 1963.

————. *Ways and Crossways,* trans. Fr. John O'Connor. Freeport, NY: Books for Libraries, 1967.

Clement, Olivier. *The Roots of Christian Mysticism.* New York, NY: New City Press, 1995.

Congar, Yves M.J. *The Word and the Spirit,* trans. David Smith. San Francisco, CA: Harper & Row Publishers, 1986.

Convert, H., ed. *Eucharistic Meditations: Extracts from the Writings and Instructions of Saint John Vianney,* trans. Sr. Mary Benvenuta. Trabuco Canyon, CA: Source Books & Anthony Clarke, 1993.

Crocker III, H.W. *Triumph: The Power and Glory of the Catholic Church—A 2,000 Year History.* Roseville, CA: Prima Publishing, 2001.

Danielou, Jean. *God and the Ways of Knowing,* trans. Walter Roberts. New York, NY: Meridian Books, 1957.

Darcy, Martin C. *Of God and Man: Thoughts on Faith and Morals.* Notre Dame, Indiana: University of Notre Dame Press, 1964.

Deedy, John. *A Book of Catholic Anecdotes.* Allen, TX: Thomas More, 1997.

De Mello, Anthony. *The Heart of the Enlightened: A Book of Story Meditations.* New York, NY: Doubleday Books, 1991.

Dillard, Annie. *Pilgrim at Tinker Creek.* New York, NY: HarperCollins, 1974.

Doering, Bernard E. *Jacques Maritain and the French Catholic Intellectuals.* Notre Dame, IN: University of Notre Dame, 1983.

Dubay, Thomas. *Fire Within: St. Teresa of Avila, St. John of the Cross, and the Gospel—on Prayer.* San Francisco, CA: Ignatius Press, 1989.

Dulles, Avery. *The Catholicity of the Church.* New York, NY: Oxford University Press, 1985.

Eastman, Charles A. (Ohiyesa). *The Soul of an Indian: An Interpretation.* Lincoln, NE: University of Nebraska Press, 1980.

Ellwood, Robert S. and Barbara A. McGraw. *Many Peoples, Many Faiths: Women and Men in the World Religions,* seventh edition. Upper Saddleriver, NJ: Prentice Hall, 2002.

Fenelon, Francois, *Let Go.* New Kensington, PA: Whitaker House, 1973.

Fox, Matthew. *Breakthrough: Meister Eckhart's Creation Spirituality in New Translation.* New York, NY: Doubleday Books, 1980.

Frankfort, Henri. *The Intellectual Adventure of Ancient Man.* Chicago, IL: University of Chicago Press, 1946.

Franklin, Benjamin. *The Autobiography of Benjamin Franklin,* Kenneth Silverman, ed. New York, NY: Penguin Books, 1986.

Garrigou-Lagrange, Reginald. *Life Everlasting And the Immensity of the Soul,* trans. Rev. Patrick Cummings. Rockford, IL: Tan Books and Publishers, 1991.

————. *Our Savior and His Love for Us,* trans. A. Bouchard. Rockford, Illinois: Tan Books and Publishers, 1998.

————. *Reality: A Synthesis of Thomistic Thought,* trans. Rev. Patrick Cummings. St. Louis, MO: B. Herder Book Co., 1958.

Gasnick, Roy M., ed., *The Francis Book—800 Years with the Saint from Assisi.* New York, NY: Macmillan Publishing, 1980.

Gaudoin-Parker, Michael L., ed. *The Real Presence Through the Ages.* Staten Island, NY: Alba House, 1993.

Gibran, Kahlil. *Jesus the Son of Man: His Words and His Deeds as Told and Recorded by Those Who Knew Him.* New York, NY: Alfred A. Knopf, 1995.

————. *The Prophet.* New York, NY: Alfred A. Knopf, 1998.

Gibran, Jean and Kahlil Gibran. *Kahlil Gibran: His Life and World.* Boston, MA: New York Graphic Society, 1974.

Gilson, Etienne. *The Spirit of Medieval Philosophy,* Gifford Lectures 1931-1932, trans. A.H.C. Downes. Notre Dame, IN: University of Notre Dame Press, 1936.

Goldberg, Bernard, *Bias: A CBS Insider Exposes How the Media Distort the News.* Washington: Regnery Publishing, 2002.

Gordon, James S. *Manifesto for a New Medicine.* New York, NY: Perseus, 1997.

Guyon, Jeanne, *Union with God.* USA: Christian Books, 1981.

Hahn, Scott. *First Comes Love: Finding Your Family in the Church and the Trinity.* New York, NY: Doubleday, 2002.

———. *Hail, Holy Queen: The Mother of God in the Word of God.* New York, NY: Doubleday, 2002.

———. *The Lamb's Supper: The Mass as Heaven on Earth.* New York, NY: Doubleday, 1999.

———. *The Real Jesus: Christ in the Creeds and Councils,* audiotape series. West Covina, CA: Saint Joseph Communications, 1998.

Hardy, Sir Alister. *The Spiritual Nature of Man: A Study of Contemporary Religious Experience.* Oxford: Clarendon Press, 1979.

Hasseveldt, Roger. *The Church: A Divine Mystery,* trans. William Storey. Notre Dame, IN: Fides Publishers, 1964.

Hoffman, Bengt, trans. *The Theologia Germanica of Martin Luther.* New York, NY: Paulist Press, 1980.

Howard, Thomas. *On Being Catholic.* San Francisco, CA: Ignatius Press, 1997.

Huxley, Aldous. *Adonis and the Alphabet and Other Essays.* London, England: Chatto & Windus, 1956.

Huxley, Aldous. *Ape and Essence.* Chicago, IL: Ivan R. Dee, Publisher, 1948.

Irenaeus. *The Scandal of the Incarnation: Irenaeus Against the Heresies.* ed. Hans Urs von Balthasar, trans. John Saward. San Francisco, CA: Ignatius Press, 1990.

Jenkins, Philip. *Hidden Gospels: How the Search for Jesus Lost Its Way.* New York, NY: Oxford University Press, 2001.

John Paul II. *Crossing the Threshold of Hope,* Vittorio Messori, ed. New York, NY: Alfred A. Knopf, 1994.

Johnson, Robert A. *She, Understanding Feminine Psychology.* New York, NY: Harper & Row, 1986.

Johnston, William. *The Mystical Way.* New York, NY: HarperCollins, 1993.

Johnston, William. *The Mysticism of the Cloud of Unknowing.* New York, NY: Fordham University Press, 2000.

Journet, Charles. *The Church of the Word Incarnate: An Essay in Speculative Theology,* vol. 1: *The Apostolic Hierarchy,* trans. A.H.C. Downes. New York, NY: Sheed and Ward, 1955.

———. *The Dark Knowledge of God,* trans. James F. Anderson. London, England: Sheed & Ward, 1948.

———. *The Meaning of Evil,* trans. Michael Barry. New York, NY: P.J. Kenedy & Sons, 1961.

———. *The Meaning of Grace,* trans. A.V. Littledale. New York, NY: P.J. Kenedy & Sons, 1960.

———. *Theologie de l'Eglise.* Paris, France: Deslce'e De Brouwer, 1958.

———. *The Wisdom of Faith: An Introduction to Theology,* trans. R. F. Smith. Westminister, MD: The Newman Press, 1952.

Kavanaugh, Kieran and Otilio Rodriguez, trans. *The Collected Works of St. John of the Cross.* Washington, DC: ICS Publications, 1991.

Keating, Thomas. *Open Mind, Open Heart: The Contemplative Dimension of the Gospel.* Amity, NY: Amity House, 1986.

Kelly, J.N.D. *Early Christian Doctrines,* rev. ed. San Francisco: Harper & Row, 1978.

Klauder, Francis. *A Philosophy Rooted in Love: The Dominant Themes in the Perennial Philosophy of St. Thomas Aquinas.* Lanham, MD: University Press of America, 1994.

———————. *Aspects of the Thought of Teilhard de Chardin.* North Quincy, MA: The Christopher Publishing House, 1971.

———————. *The Wonder of Intelligence: A Study of Human Knowledge.* North Quincy, MA: The Christopher Publishing House, 1973.

———————. *The Wonder of the Real: A Sketch in Basic Philosophy.* North Quincy, MA: The Christopher Publishing House, 1979.

Knasas, John F.X., ed. *Jacques Maritain: The Man and His Metaphysics.* USA: American Maritain Association, 1988.

Knille, Robert, ed. *As I Was Saying: A Chesterton Reader.* Grand Rapids, MI: William B. Eerdmans Publishing Company, 1985.

Kreeft, Peter. *A Summa of the Summa: The Essential Philosophical Passages of St. Thomas Aquinas'* Summa Theologia *Edited and Explained for Beginners.* San Francisco, CA: Ignatius Press, 1990.

Lewis, C.S. *A Grief Observed.* New York, NY: Bantam, 1976.

———————. *Mere Christianity.* New York, NY: Macmillan, 1952.

———————. *Miracles.* New York, NY: Macmillan, 1960.

———————. *Perelandra.* New, York, NY: Scribner Paperback Fiction, 1996.

———————. *That Hideous Strength: A Modern Day Fairy-Tale for Grown Ups.* New York, NY: Simon & Schuster, 1996.

———————. *The Lion, the Witch, and the Wardrobe.* New York, NY: HarperCollins, 1978.

———————. *The Weight of Glory and Other Addresses.* New York, NY: Macmillan, 1980.

Louth, Andrew, ed. *Early Christian Writings, The Apostolic Fathers,* trans. Maxwell Stanforth. London, England: Penguin Books, 1987.

Louth, Andrew. *The Origin of the Christian Mystical Tradition, From Plato to Denys.* Oxford, England: Clarendon Press, 1983.

Lubac, Henri de. *The Church: Paradox and Mystery.* Staten Island, NY: Alba House, 1969.

Main, John. *Moment of Christ.* New York: Crossroad, 1985.

Malik, Charles N. *The Wonder of Being.* Waco, Texas: Word Books, 1974.

Maloney, George A. *Mysticism and the New Age: Christic Consciousness in the New Creation.* Staten Island, NY: Alba House, 1990.

————. *The Cosmic Christ; from Paul to Teilhard.* New York, NY: Sheed and Ward, 1968.

Margerie, Bertrand de, S.J. *The Christian Trinity in History,* trans. Edmund J. Foreman, S.J. Still River, MA: St. Bede's Publications, 1982.

Maritain, Jacques. *Creative Intuition in Art and Poetry.* New York, NY: Pantheon Books, 1953.

————. *Moral Philosophy: An Historical and Critical Survey of the Great Systems.* New York, NY: Charles Scribner's Sons, 1964.

————. *Notebooks,* trans. Joseph W. Evans. Albany, NY: Magi Books, 1984.

————. *On the Church of Christ: The Person of the Church and Her Personnel,* trans. Joseph W. Evans. Notre Dame, IN: University of Notre Dame Press, 1973.

————. *The Degrees of Knowledge,* trans. Bernard Wall. New York, NY: Charles Scribner's Sons, 1938.

————. *The Peasant of the Garrone: An Old Layman Questions Himself about the Present Time,* trans. Michael Cuddihy and Elizabeth Hughes. New York, NY: Holt, Rinehart and Winston, 1968.

Maritain, Jacques, ed. *Raissa's Journal.* Albany, NY: Magi Books, 1974.

Mauriac, Francois. *What I Believe.* New York, NY: Farrar, Straus, 1963.

McBrien, Richard P. *Catholicism.* Minneapolis, MN: Winston, 1980.

McBride, Alfred. *Celebrating the Mass, A Guide for Understanding and Loving the Mass More Deeply.* Huntington, IN: Our Sunday Visitor Publishing Division, 1999.

McBrien, Richard P. *Catholicism.* New York, NY: HarperSanFrancisco, 1994.

McGrath, Alister E. *Intellectuals Don't Need God and Other Modern Myths.* Grand Rapids, MI: Zondervan Publishing House, 1993.

McGuinn, Bernard. *The Foundations of Mysticism: Origins to the Fifth Century,* vol. I, *The Presence of God: A History of Western Christian Mysticism.* New York, NY: Crossroad, 1994.

McGuinn, Bernard, ed. with Frank Tobin and Elivira Borgstadt. *Meister Eckhart, Teacher and Preacher.* New York, NY: Paulist Press, 1986.

Mersch, Emile. *The Theology of the Mystical Body,* trans. Cyril Vollert. St. Louis, MO: B. Herder Book Co., 1952.

Merton, Thomas. *Contemplative Prayer.* Garden City, NY: Image Books, 1971.

————. *New Seeds of Contemplation.* New York, NY: New Directions Book, 1972.

————. *Soul Mates: Honoring the Mysteries of Love and Relationship.* New York, NY: HarperCollins Publishers, 1994.

————. *The Living Bread.* London, England: Burns & Oats, 1956.

Neruda, Pablo. *Selected Odes,* trans. and selected by Margaret Sayers Peden. Berkeley, CA: University of California Press, 1990.

Novak, Philip. *The World's Wisdom.* New York, NY: HarperSanFrancisco, 1995.

Ott, Ludwig. *Fundamentals of Catholic Dogma,* trans. James Canon Bastible and Patrick Lynch. Rockford, Ill: Tan Books and Publishers, 1994.

Pearsall, Paul P. *The Heart's Code.* New York, NY: RandomHouse, 1999.

Peck, M. Scott. *Denial of the Soul: Spiritual and Medical Perspectives on Euthanasia and Mortality.* CA: Three Rivers Press, 1998.

Pelikan, Jaroslav. *Jesus Through the Centuries: His Place in the History of Culture.* New Haven, CT: Yale University Press, 1985.

Pelletier, Kenneth R. *Mind as Healer, Mind as Slayer: A Holistic Approach to Preventing Stress Disorders.* New York, NY: Delta Books, 1992.

Philipon, M.M., ed. *Sister Elizabeth of the Trinity: Spiritual Writings, Letters, Retreats, and Unpublished Notes.* New York, NY: P.J. Kenedy & Sons, 1962.

Pinker, Steven. *The Blank Slate, The Modern Denial of Human Nature.* New York, NY: Viking Penguin, 2002.

Prabhavananda Swami and Christopher Isherwood, trans. *The Bhagavad-Gita.* New York, NY: Penguin Books, 1972.

Prabhavananda Swami and Frederick Manchester, trans. *The Upanishads.* New York, NY: New American Library, 1975.

Rahner, Karl. *Mary, Mother of the Lord: Theological Meditations.* New York, NY: Herder and Herder, 1963.

Rodwell, J. M., trans. *The Koran.* North Clarendon, VT: Tuttle Publishing, 1994.

Rosten, Leo, ed. *Religions of America: Ferment and Faith in an Age of Crisis.* New York, NY: Simon and Schuster, 1975.

Rumble, Leslie with Charles Mortimer Carty. *Radio Replies: 1588 Questions and Answers on Catholicism and Protestantism,* vol. 1. Rockford, IL: Tan Books and Publishers, 1979.

Russell, Jeffrey Burton. *A History of Heaven: The Singing Silence.* Princeton, NJ: Princeton University Press, 1997.

Scheeben, Matthias Joseph. *The Mysteries of Christianity,* trans. Cyril Vollert. St. Louis, MO: B. Herder Book Co., 1964.

Schillebeeckx, Edward. *God is New Each Moment: In Conversation with Huub Oosterhis and Piet Hoogeveen.* trans. David Smith. New York, NY: Seabury Press, 1983.

Schreck, Alan. *Catholic and Christian: An Explanation of Commonly Misunderstood Catholic Beliefs.* Ann Arbor, MI: Servant Books, 1984.

Schurmann, Riner, trans. and commentary. *Wandering Joy: Meister Eckhart's Mystical Philosophy.* Great Barrington, MA: Lindisfarne Books, 2001.

Sheed, F.J. *Theology for Beginners.* Ann Arbor, Michigan: Servant Books, 1981.

Shrady, Maria, trans. *Johannes Tauler: Sermons.* New York, NY: Paulist Press, 1985.

Simon, David. *The Wisdom of Healing: A Natural Mind Body Program for Optimal Wellness.* New York, NY: Random House Inc, 1997.

Smith, Huston. *The World's Religions, Our Great Wisdom Traditions.* New York, NY: HarperSanFrancisco, 1991.

Squire, Aelred. *Asking the Fathers.* Westminister, MD: Christian Classics, 1993.

Tauler, John. *Spiritual Conferences,* trans. and ed. by Eric Colledge and Sister M. Jane. Rockford, IL: Tan Books and Publishers, 1978.

Teresa of Avila. *The Interior Castle,* trans. Kieran Kavanaugh and Otilio Rodriguez. New York, NY: Paulist Press, 1979.

Toropov, Brandon. *The Popes and the Papacy.* Indianapolis, IN: Alpha Books, 2002.

Underhill, Evelyn. *Mystics of the Church.* Harrisburg, PA: Morehouse Publishing, 1975.

Venkatesananda, Swami, trans. *The Supreme Yoga: A New Translation of the Yoga Vasistha,* vol. I. Elgin Cape Province, South Africa: The Chiltern Yoga Trust, 1976.

Way, Robert, ed. *The Cloud of Unknowing and The Letter of Private Direction.* Wheathampstead, England: Anthony Clarke, 1986.

Weber, J.G., ed. and trans. *In Quest of the Absolute: The Life and Work of Jules Monchanin.* Kalamazoo, MI: Cistercian Publications, 1977.

Weigel, George. *Witness to Hope: The Biography of Pope John Paul II.* New York, NY: HarperCollins, 1999.

Weil, Simone. *First and Last Notebooks,* trans. Richard Rees. New York, NY: Oxford University Press, 1970.

————. *Gravity and Grace,* trans. Emma Craufurd. London, England: Routledge and Kegan Paul, 1963.

————. *Waiting for God,* trans. Emma Craufurd. New York, NY: Harper & Row Publishers, 1973.

Willard, Dallas. *The Divine Conspiracy, Rediscovering Our Hidden Life in God.* New York, NY: HarperSanFrancisco, 1998.

Williams, Paul. *The Unexpected Way: On Conversion from Buddhism to Catholicism.* New York, NY: T & T Clark, 2002.

Wiseman, James A., trans. *John Ruusbroec: The Spiritual Espousals and Other Works.* New York, NY: Paulist Press, 1986.

Woods, Richard. *Eckhart's Way.* Wilmington, DE: Michael Glazier, 1986.

Wuerl, Donald W. *Fathers of the Church.* Boston, MA: St. Paul Editions, 1982.

Zaehner, R.C. *Concordant Discord: The Interdependence of Faiths Being the Gifford Lectures on Natural Religion Delivered at St. Andrews in 1967-1969.* Oxford, England: Clarendon Press, 1970.

INDEX